Concepts of Indian Philosophy

CONCEPTS OF INDIAN PHILOSOPHY

SARASVATI CHENNAKESAVAN
Professor and Head of the Post-Graduate Department of Philosophy
Sri Venkateswara University, Tirupati
Fellow of the Royal Asiatic Society

South Asia Books
P.O. Box 502, Columbia, Mo. 65201

Concepts of Indian Philosophy

First Published 1976

ISBN 0 88386 734 6

Orient Longman Ltd.

Registered Office:

3/5 Asaf Ali Road, New Delhi 110 002

Other Offices:

Kamani Marg, Ballard Estate, Bombay 400 038

17 Chittaranjan Avenue, Calcutta 700 013

36A Anna Salai, Mount Road, Madras 600 002

1/24 Asaf Ali Road, New Delhi 110 002

80/1 Mahatma Gandhi Road, Bangalore 560 001

3-5-820 Hyderguda, Hyderabad 500 001

S. P. Verma Road, Patna 800 001

Published by V. Abdulla, Orient Longman Ltd., Madras 600 002 and printed at Kalakshetra Publications Press, Madras 600 041

To

Dr. William Henry Harris

who was a genial friend, a profound scholar and a devoted teacher

"Who knows for certain? Who shall here declare it?
Whence was it born, and whence came this creation?
The Gods were born after this world's creation:
Then who can know from whence it has arisen?

None knoweth whence creation has arisen;
And whether he has or has not produced it:
He who surveys it in the highest heaven,
He only knows, or haply he may know not."

ṚG VEDA, X, 129.
(Macdonell's Translation)

"...None so blind as they that will not see."

—Jonathan Swift

FOREWORD

Is there a "history" of Indian philosophy? No, not exactly; as there is no strict chronology, Indian philosophy is not strictly a "history". But Indian philosophy is a "development". Its development is like that of a tree with innumerable spreading branches. Diversity of thought and doctrine is a fundamental quality of the development of Indian philosophy. Therefore this development must be looked at from many points and not only as a succession and opposition of "schools". The proper study of Indian philosophy should be a comparative study of its fundamental concepts. This is a more intelligent and intelligible study as it enables the student to compare it with Greek and modern Western philosophy, and compare one phase of the development of Indian philosophy itself with another.

This is what Dr. Sarasvati Chennakesavan has done in this book. Dr. Chennakesavan's book is a substantial essay, learned, authentic and readable. It is an impressive book. In only six chapters, she has covered the entire ground and marked out the important phases of the evolution of Indian thought. This book should serve therefore as a good introduction to the study of Indian philosophy.

Dr. Sarasvati Chennakesavan is a well-known writer on Indian philosophy and has published several books and she is a Professor of Philosophy in the Sri Venkateswara University at Tirupati. Therefore her book does not need a Foreword and does not require to be introduced. It can shine in its own right.

Plato said that Philosophy should not be studied in the intervals of money-making and house-keeping. But he had not met Dr. Sarasvati Chennakesavan. For, she has done what Plato thought should never be done. She has studied Philosophy and also brought up a family. If it can be done, why should it not be done? Therefore Dr. Chennakesavan has excelled ancient Greek women and done what they could never do. Is it because of this that we never hear about any Greek woman-philosopher like Gargi in the Upaniṣads or Sarasvati Chennakesavan in our times?

August 1974 N. A. NIKAM
Bangalore.

PREFACE

I started planning for this book in the years 1958-60 when I was a visiting Professor at Southern Illinois University, Carbondale. Dr. W. H. Harris, a dear friend and colleague initiated the process when he drew my attention to the hardship which both the students and teachers of Indian Philosophy have been facing for want of a good book which the American with his empirical background and sceptical mentality could read and understand. Dr. Harris and I started to work together to chalk out a sort of working programme for the writing of this book. Then he undertook to write on metaphysics and I started my part of the work by writing on epistemology. It is indeed true that what man proposes, God disposes. I had to return to my University after my assignment. We were carrying on our individual tasks hoping that some day in the near future we would meet to work together again. Alas! fate willed it otherwise. Dr. Harris succumbed to the after-effects of an accident to his already delicate health. With his demise, the manuscript with him was also lost. I had neither the heart nor the mind to resume the work for some time afterwards. But then I could not simply put it off. So I have now incorporated the material on which we had worked together and produced a book which I hope will serve the purpose for which it was intended.

My task has been a difficult one. So far Indian philosophy has been presented by many eminent Indian philosophers as a history of philosophy. This method of approach proved to be inadequate for one who was not trained in the Indian tradition. So I had to sift much material and ignoring the irrelevant, present the relevant ideas as a conceptual development. My purpose has been to impress upon the reader that all metaphysical and epistemological arguments usually accepted and argued upon in Western philosophy are also to be found in Indian philosophy. As a philosophy, Indian thought is not only rich in tradition, but also in content.

However, in this book, I have not only attempted to make Indian philosophy easy for a student who has been trained only in Western philosophy, but also to examine logically the various concepts of Indian philosophy with a view to determine how far the opinion that Indian philosophy is "spiritual" is a viable one. I have also tried to eliminate the pseudo-historical bias usually given to Indian philosophy. In what sense can we describe Indian philosophy as a historical development? In those ancient days, there was no sense of history. Indian thinkers prided themselves, not on their personal achievements in terms of time and date but by the acumen and veracity of ideas passed on to them by their masters. Sages and savants were not known by their given names, but either by their family names or by the names of the teachers whose ideas they were propagating. We know of the systematisers only in this manner. Even after the systematisation of Indian philosophy had taken place in later eras, it was not a systematisation of some conceptual ideology of one man or a group of persons. The ideas had already been there floating around in a nebulous manner which were given a systematic clothing by later thinkers. Thus except for known historical developments within the Christian era, it is very difficult to maintain a historicity for classical Indian philosophy. Even such historicity is sometimes doubtful because of the habit of these philosophers to be known either by the name of their gurus or by their family name. Under such difficult conditions, while we may, from one point of view, look at Indian philosophy as a historical development, it is not, according to me the most appropriate view. Internal evidences from the writings of the various systematisers show that the development of Indian philosophical concepts has always been a dialectic process rather than a historic process. It has been my purpose, in this book, to look at concepts pertinent to strict philosophy in the light of such a dialectic development and present them in their proper perspectives.

While all that has been said so far is, no doubt true, still, for purposes of expounding, we have to start somewhere. If history is an account of man's activity on this earth, then the earliest activity should have historical priority. The first chapter is called "a historical background". Here I have used the word "history" not in its chronological meaning, but in its wider meaning as the activity of man. My concern in the first chapter is to express the basic ideas which are said to belong to all levels of philosophy starting with Vedic thought followed by Upaniṣadic and Purāṇic thought. Conceptually these three lines of thought form a unit. Vedic thought represents man in his most innocent and pious stage while Upaniṣadic thought represents the heights of intellectual development which man had reached even in those early days, purely by the strength of his capacity for conceptualisation. In the third phase we find how such highly intellectual conceptualisation of philosophic ideas cannot be the accepted ideology of the common man. So we have the popularisation and symbolisation of the Upaniṣadic truths during Purāṇic times. Again, I view these three developments more as a dialectic process of each step involving the other and growing out of it rather than as a historical and chronological development of one following upon the other in a causal sequence. My idea of such a development seems to be strengthened by the later systematisation known as *darśanas*, for we find all the systems claiming to have their foundations in the Upaniṣadic thought, some of them supporting the ideas in the Upaniṣads and some negating them.

The impact of the three *nāstika darśanas* of Cārvāka, Bauddha and Jaina on the development of the *āstika darśanas* is tremendous. In terms of development, indications are that all these developed simultaneously, for each is criticised by the other and such critical evaluations had led to many a modification of the theory as first formulated by its originators. More than all this, what should be of importance here is the sweeping boldness and intellectual honesty of these ancient seers who formulated their rebellions against traditionalism in no moderate terms. In those early days of human civilisation, when, on a perusal of the history of the peoples of the world, it could be expected that spiritual authority and divine revelations held complete sway over the thinking processes of human beings, it is like the blowing of a life-giving and refreshing fresh breeze when "rebels" theorised against accepted authority. While their postulated theories are of immense value, the spirit of rebellion that they had manifested speaks much for the wealth and breadth of thinking and the rationality of those early people. They were not as prepared to bow down to "public opinion" in important issues as we are today!

All the six *āstika darśanas* also manifest this rational approach. When challenges were put forth by opponents, it became imperative to call on reason to support one's views. The development of polemics encouraged more and more dependence on rational and valid arguments. This aspect of the development became so very important that systems of philosophy which drew all their sustenance from scriptural sources had of necessity to adopt a polemical method to sustain their position. This becomes strongly evident in the three Vedāntic systems.

This aspect of Indian philosophy can be explicitly presented and emphasised if it is studied as a development of concepts. So in this book I have made an attempt to trace the different metaphysical and epistemological concepts as a continuous and rational development, though the concepts were, as a matter of fact, developed by the different systems. For example, the concept of substance is subsumed under "Reality" and presented with its different connotations such as pluralism, dualism and finally monism or idealism. The task of presenting the ideas of substance given by various *nāstika* and *āstika* schools purely under these headings is a difficult one, for we find that there is an overlapping of metaphysical and epistemological ideas everywhere. Yet, as far as possible, I have tried to weed out the metaphysical from the epistemological and present each separately. This might have led to certain repetitions which it is almost impossible to avoid. Metaphysical concepts like the nature of Self, (which includes the nature of God), the theory of causality, have been discussed as a cross-sectional development.

The chapter on the Theory of Knowledge (Chapter III) has been a comparatively easy one to tackle. For most of the systems except in certain aspects, accept the general theory of *pramāṇas* developed by the Nyāya. The differences with regard to the nature and validity of knowledge have been discussed in detail. The importance of an epistemology for a theory of metaphysics is well established in Indian philosophy. No metaphysical truth can be accepted unless it passes the tests laid down by epistemology. For example, the Nyāya maintains that not only correspondence established through identity of content but also a pragmatic validity is essential for anything, including metaphysical truths, to be acceptable. The Advaita goes a step further than this and maintains that a pragmatic validity can be established even for illusory objects. Hence they maintain that non-contradiction and non-sublatability should be the tests for any truth. Thus we find that from an epistemological point of view, no experience, whether it be a transcendental or an empirical one, can be considered true unless it passes the epistemological tests. However much the system may swear by its loyalty to the scriptures, when it comes to maintaining its position, it is always these tests that are called upon to establish their metaphysical theories. Thus we find a close relationship between the metaphysical position and the epistemological tenets.

A very important deviation by Indian epistemology from Western epistemology is the lack of an absorbing preoccupation with language for its own sake, which is exhibited by the latter. At the same time *śabda* or testimony of language, recognised as a valid means of knowledge, leads to an analysis of the nature of words, sentences, their meanings and implications. But the pure and formal linguistic analysis that is attempted by logicians based purely on the structure of sentences is not present in Indian thought as such. Of course in recent years, led by that erudite Indologist from the U.S.A., Professor Ingalls, many philosophers both in the West and in India have attempted to reduce Indian epistemology to a sort of Indian logic involving an analysis—Western style—of Saṁskrit sentences. This procedure is bound to be rather involved, for the Saṁskrit language is not verb-oriented. It is again a most important fact that in Indian philosophy the purpose of epistemological arguments is to establish truth conveyed by language statements and to have a trans-language reference. Such a position, as far as I understand formal logic, is not acceptable to these logicians.

The chapter on the Principles of Morality (Chapter IV) involves a problem that is entirely different. The question of judging a man's action as good or evil is done from two reference-points. One is the larger social good, *lokasaṁgraha,* and the other is the personal perfection and freedom, *mokśa.* These two are not disparate nor can they be dichotomous. So the development of Indian ethics has taken a special and individualised turn which emphasises not only the purity and goodness of one's behaviour, but makes an assessment of this from the above two points of view. Unless a man is good in his social relations, his aspirations for freedom or *mokśa* cannot be achieved. The nature of the social good arises from the idea of a perfect society where all causes for friction and contrariness are non-existent. Indian Ethics is not purely self-regarding as sought to be established by Western thinkers, but also other-regarding and emphasises social welfare.

The chapter on the Philosophies of Religion (Chapter V) is self-explanatory. A more elaborate account of the various aspects of the systems could have been attempted. But lack of competency and fear of biased interpretation have held me back from doing this. This does not mean that religious philosophy is of no account to me. The vast literature on the subject requires a patient and objective study and assessment which is not possible as yet for me.

In the final chapter I have set out some of the problems which I think have to be tackled by lovers of Indian philosophy. The long and interesting tradition of Indian philosophy has posed some problems when read in the context of modern developments in science and philosophy elsewhere in the world. While Indian philosophy is, metaphysically speaking, centred round some postulates regarding consciousness, modern developments have come to threaten the very existence of such consciousness. Can we as part of and as participants in the world of today, enjoying its technological and scientific civilization, ignore the threat that such a civilization poses to our philosophical concepts? What is the answer that Indian philosophy can give? Mere assertions and footnotes will not help. A reassessment of our basic philosophical concepts is perhaps needed.

My thanks are due to my many friends who have encouraged me in this effort, specially Dr. Willis Moore, retired Professor of Philosophy at Southern Illinois University. My husband has been a source of great encouragement, giving me a fillip whenever my enthusiasm flagged. I could not have finished this book but for his understanding and affection. My students Sai Babu and Ravindranath Seshan have rendered great help by going through the manuscript carefully providing the diacritical marks and correcting typographical errors. My thanks are due to them. Sri K. Vasudeva Reddy, my Research Assistant, has devoted much of his time and patience, to preparing the glossary for the Saṁskrit terms used in the book. I am deeply grateful to him. I am appreciative of D. Venugopal Reddy's clerical assistance. I am indeed very grateful to Professor N. A. Nikam, retired Vice-Chancellor of Mysore University and a well-known philosopher of deep and unostentatious scholarship, for his very understanding and appreciative Foreword to this book. Very often I wonder how I could have achieved anything but for friends and well-wishers like him.

I would be failing in my duty if I do not acknowledge the inspiration I have derived from my teachers Dr. T.M.P. Mahadevan and Dr. V.A. Devasenapathy, both professors at Madras University. Their devotion to Indian philosophy and their firm conviction that Indian philosophy has a "spiritual" connotation has been instrumental for my desire to examine Indian philosophical concepts more thoroughly and critically. I am deeply appreciative of their silent guidance and implicit encouragement.

Tirupati
December 1976

SARASVATI CHENNAKESAVAN

CONTENTS

	Page
Foreword	vii
Preface	ix
Guide to Pronunciation of Saṁskrit Words ..	xix
Key to Abbreviations of Saṁskrit Texts	xx
Chapter I Historical Background	1
Chapter II Metaphysics	50
Chapter III Theory of Knowledge	132
Chapter IV Principles of Morality	195
Chapter V Philosophies of Religion	226
Chapter VI Some Stray Thoughts	233
Bibliography	243
Glossary of Saṁskrit Terms	245
Index	252

GUIDE TO THE PRONUNCIATION OF SAṀSKRIT WORDS

letter		*key-word*
ā	as in	g*a*rden
ī	as in	w*ee*k
ū	as in	l*oo*se
ai	as in	n*i*ne
ṛ	as in	*r*eturn
k	as in	*k*ing
g	as in	*g*o
c	as in	tou*ch* (light)
ch	as in	*ch*ur*ch* (sharp)
ṭ	as in	*t*ime (light)
ḍ	as in	*d*ate (light)
ñ	as in	si*n*ew
ṇ		a palatal "*n*" sound
ṁ	as in	si*ng* (semi-nasal)
s	as in	*s*ong
ś	as in	*Sch*ubert (light)
ṣ	as in	*sh*ut (sharp)

Names of Saṁskrit texts have been abbreviated in the footnotes as below:

Text	*Abbreviation*
Atharva Veda	Ath. V.
Bhāṣapariccheda	Bh-par.
Brahma Sūtra	B. Su.
Brahma Sūtra Bhāṣya	B. Su. Bh.
Bṛhadāraṇyaka Upaniṣad	Br. Up.
Chāndogya Upaniṣad	Ch. Up.
Kēna Upaniṣad	Ke. Up.
Mādhyamika Sūtra	Ma. Su.
Maitri Upaniṣad	Mai. Up.
Manu Dharma Śāstra	M. Dh. Sa.
Mundāka Upaniṣad	Mu. Up.
Nyāya Bhāṣya	Ny. Bh.
Nyāya Sūtra	Ny. Su.
Nyāyavartika	Ny-var.
Ṛg. Veda	R. V.
Sāṁkya-Kārika	Sam-kar.
Sāṁkhya Pravacaṅa Bhaṣya	Sam. Pr. Bh.
Sarvadarśana Saṁgraha	Sar. Sam.
Śāstradīpika	Sa-di.
Svetāśvatara Upaniṣad	Sv. Up.
Sūtra Bhāṣya	Su. Bh.
Taittiriya Upaniṣad	Tai. Up.
Tarkasaṁgraha	Tar-sam.
Tattvakaumudi	Tatt-kau.
Tattvārthādhigama Sūtra	Tatt. Su.
Vaiśeṣika Sūtras	Vai. Su.
Vedanta Paribhāsa	Ved. Par.
Vedānta Sāra	Ved. Sar.
Yoga Bhāṣya	Y. Bh.
Yoga Sūtra	Y. Su.

CHAPTER I

HISTORICAL BACKGROUND

It is a trite saying that Indian philosophy is one of the most ancient philosophies of the world. In the very early dawn of human history a separation between the different human disciplines could not have taken place. Religion, philosophy, magic, mathematics, astrology and astronomy were all interwoven into one texture which was the daily life of those people. Man had no need to struggle for his existence, for nature was bountiful and the seasons kind. He had leisure on his hands and thus started speculations of various kinds. Such speculations were directed towards finding answers to the interminable questions which were plaguing the ancient Indian mind. But how could he arrive at concrete answers? His instruments were his conceptual capacities and his guides were the variegated processes of nature. He saw wonders all around him and withdrew into himself to cogitate upon them and find answers. Thus we have in India an enquiry into the meaning of experience, both external and internal. Thus was born the forerunner of philosophical speculation, a religious speculation. Actually, these two were so intertwined that it is impossible to be sure where one ends and where the other begins. In fact, such an investigation into the limitations of the nature of enquiry is irrelevant as far as the ancient Indian was concerned. At that stage, his religion was his philosophy. If religion is a way of life and philosophy is a view of life, in India both these coalesced and philosophy became not only a view of life but also a way of life. The beginnings of philosophy in India were indistinguishable from her religion and this identification dogs the footsteps of philosophy in India even today. Many have been the comments which have characterised Indian philosophy either as mysticism or magic, either as spiritism or as occultism. It is equated, very often, with "some notions about *māyā* or the delusiveness of the world, *karma* a belief in fate and reincarnation and *sanyāsa*, renunciation". Even an educated and enlightened Indian is not free from such misconceptions, not to speak of non-Indians. Many of these ideas have different connotations, though considered innate to Indian philosophy, as we shall explain in the course of this book.

Indian philosophy consists of an extraordinary diversity of philosophical thinking, starting from rank empiricist materialism to the most transcendental absolute idealism, covering all the intermediate shades of thinking. Before we come to the actual philosophical concepts, it is necessary to trace the history of the various shades of philosophical thinking. But there should be no anticipation of actual chronology. To the ancient Indian mind concepts were more interesting and important than personalities limited by time and space. We can only gather a sort of historicity from a study of various conceptual concurrences and literary evidences. It would pay to start with an analysis of that which was common ground for religious and philosophical thinking, namely the Vedas.

It is an accepted fact that the sources of all later philosophising are two-fold: *śruti* and *smṛti*. *Śruti* is the basic testimony, heard and passed down the generations by the ancient seers. It is primarily the outcome of mystical experiences. *Smṛti* is the remembered word. The Vedas and the Upaniṣads belong to the first category, while all the rest are clubbed together under the second. However, as we progress, we shall find that the weight of testimony is shifted mainly to the Upaniṣads. Later systems acknowledge the Vedas and Upaniṣads as their sources, either because it is the custom to do so, or because it would be difficult to propagate their theories if the Vedas and Upaniṣads were unacknowledged.

There are various versions about the origins of the Vedas in the Vedas themselves. It is commonly believed that the Vedas are preserved in the mind of Brahmā, the creator and that, at the commencement of each *kalpa* or cycle of time, Brahmā reveals them to the various seers whose names are associated with the Vedas. The inherent contradiction involved in such a theory becomes apparent when we find that Brahmā himself is one of the Vedic gods, created by the Indian to explain natural phenomena. In the *Śatapatha Brāhmaṇa* there is a verse which says that the Vedas were dug out of the mind-ocean with the shovel of speech by the gods (iii: 39,1). This is a very poetic way of saying that the Vedas were the product of the human mind. Another evidence that the Vedas originated in the human mind is the fact that the names of the authors of the hymns are preserved in the *anukramaṇī* or explanatory contents. For example, in the *Ṛg Veda* there are statements such as: "I have created this hymn for thee, O powerful, as a skilful workman fashions a car".[1]; "Vṛhadukta, the maker of hymns has thus uttered this acceptable hymn to Indra"[2]; "Nodhas, descendant of Gotama fashioned this new hymn to Indra"[3]. On the face of such internal evidence it is not proper to hold that the Vedas are not of human origin.

In spite of such and various other evidences cited by scholars, it is, more often than not, held that the Vedas are revealed scriptures. Such compulsion to attribute revelation to scriptures, perhaps, arises from two facts. First, since human knowledge suffers from all kinds of limitations, it cannot be the source of truths which are ultimately real. At the same time, the source of any religion must also be such that it should not be subject to challenge by any limited human knowledge. Hence, the argument continues, scriptures must have a non-human agency. Therefore, it is maintained that God reveals His purposes to man through the spoken word. Secondly, perhaps the compulsion arises out of a real need to establish authority for the scriptures. A mere man's word could not be ultimately authoritative. Hence it is maintained, that the word of God, as revealed by the scriptures must possess such an authority. Thus the Vedas are maintained to be revelatory.

The above-mentioned arguments are not sufficient to establish the divine origin of the Vedas in the light of stronger counter arguments. One such argument that the Vedas are the products of the ineffable experiences of the saints and seers is already mentioned. Perhaps this is another argument which may indirectly lead to the postulation of divine origin. It may be said that the mystical experiences of the saints are the result of a devotion to God, hence indirectly, their utterances might be said to be utterances of God. But we should not also forget that these saints searched long and wide for the truth and are said to have realised it ultimately. They sang of such awareness in song and poetry which, when recorded through the ages, became the Vedas. In a way it might be called revelation. Yet it is not the revelation

[1] V: 2, 11.
[2] X: 54, 6.
[3] I: 62, 13.

of any single person. The beginnings of the Vedas are shrouded in darkness and stretch far back into almost the limbo of oblivion. So it is impossible to fix any authorship for them. Since no known agency can be prescribed for the Vedas, they are said to be *apauruṣeya*—non-personal. A negative interpretation of this word to mean the agency of God is not warranted. The word *Puruṣa* is the word of reference to God in the Vedas as well as at present. So, *apauruṣeya* would not only mean impersonal, but also that which is not to be traced to God. If this interpretation is not accepted then the connotation of the word *Puruṣa* would suffer. Again, the truths embodied in the Vedas are *nitya*, eternal.

The very word Veda is derived from the root *"Vid"* which means knowledge. Hence the Vedas are compendiums of knowledge. This is literally true, as there is no branch of knowledge that is not discussed in the Vedas. I would contend that this is another reason to maintain that the Vedas are not revelations in the traditional meaning of the term. A revelation need not concern itself with how to drive away devils or even how to prepare love potions.[1] These are instructions for a method of action and hence do not deserve the title of revelatory truths. The Vedas contain all these and much more. To maintain that only such portions of the Vedas as deal with the ultimate nature of reality are revelatory while the rest owe their existence to a human agency is to forego the right to name the Vedas as one whole compendium of knowledge.

There are at least two or three versions of the origin of the Vedas in the Vedas themselves, all of which conflict with each other as we have already noticed. It is evident that the ancient saints were conscious of higher influences. This, however, is very different from saying that the Vedas are revelatory inspirations of the ancient seers.

It has already been stated that the Vedas date so far back into the history of mankind, that it is impossible to fix a date for them. Those who have made a study of world scriptures maintain that the Vedas are the earliest extant religious material. Hence to fix a date for them is a difficult task. Even the codification

[1] *Ath. V.*, I, Quoted by Bloomfield, p. 43.

and compilation of the thoughts of these ancient seers must have taken place long after such thoughts had been in usage and circulation. The tradition of handing down such thoughts from father to son and from teacher to disciple extends the possible date of such compilation further back into the past. However, considering both internal and external evidences, several scholars suggest differing dates. Max Müller, the doyen of Indology, puts the date of the Vedas at 1200 B.C. Usually the long period between 2500 and 600 B.C. during which wave after wave of Aryan invaders entered India and consolidated their position, is referred to, by historians, as the Vedic period. It is, technically speaking, not a period when there was a conscious development of either religious or philosophical ideas amongst the common people. It was a period of wondering, groping for an anchor, a struggle to find an answer to the upsurging wonderment about the unpredictable activities of nature. Hence we find a reflection of these traits in the hymns of the Vedas. In the course of transmission down the ages from father to son, from teacher to disciple, much must have been lost, and much must have been discarded as well as added. In my opinion, this is another reason for not claiming divine revelation as the origin of the Vedas. It is usual to say that there are four Vedas: the *Ṛg, Sāma, Yajur and Atharva Vedas.* Of these the first three are supposed to be the older ones and the last one a later compilation. Scholars maintain that although they are named differently, these Vedas cannot be put into watertight compartments. The three Vedas describe the functions of the different priests during the performance of sacrifices. The *Ṛg Veda* is a collection of Ṛks or hymns compiled for the use of the Hotṛ priest whose function was to invoke the gods. The priest known as Udgātṛ used a collection of chantings known as the Sāman. This later became the *Sāma Veda.* A third priest, Advaryu, was in charge of the actual rites during a sacrifice. The procedural instructions for the Advaryu priest are known as the *Yajur Veda* which literally means "sacrifice Veda". The common suffix Veda used for all these three types of hymns comes from the root *"vid"* which means "to know". So, a Veda is a book of knowledge. Each of these Vedas is again subdivided into four sections, each section serving a definite purpose. The *mantras* are the liturgical portions praising the several gods and we have a very cogent and vivid description of gods in this section. These are also prayers addressed to these various gods in order to gain their goodwill and thus earn prosperity in this world. The second division of the Vedas is known as *brāhmaṇas*. Here we find a detailed instruction as to not only the nature of the procedure for offering sacrifices, but also advice as to what sacrifices are to be performed for different purposes. The *āraṇyakas*, which is the next section, deals with the philosophical speculations about the purpose and meaning of many activities involved in life. The last section is the *Upaniṣad* which contain the quintessence of all philosophical thinking and the basic philosophic presuppositions of Hindu religious thought of the highest form.

There is another way in which these divisions of the Vedas might be understood. The *mantras* indicate the simple, trusting nature of the early Vedic Indian. Lost in the wonder that is nature, man poured out his soul in the worship of the beautiful and the awe-inspiring. His tendencies towards anthropomorphism made him speculate about the possibilities of contractual relations with these nature-gods. As man became slowly sophisticated, his heartfelt naive outpourings became calculated rites. He planned sacrifices and entered, as it were, into a definite give-and-take relationship with the deities.[1] The *brāhmaṇas* are detailed instructions to the priest on the conduct of such sacrifices. It became necessary to delegate the duties of conducting sacrifices to one or more priests, since, more often than not, such sacrifices were long-drawn out affairs, involving a great deal of time. The *āraṇyakas*, as their name suggests, are the forest books. These are the musings of the men retired from the stresses and strains of this world on the relation between man and this universe. These ideas slowly merged into the philosophical speculations of the Upaniṣads. Although it is possible to divide the Vedas into these four sections, the thought of each merges into the other almost imperceptibly.

Indian thinkers like to interpret the meaning of these four sections of the Vedas in another manner also. Man's life consists of four stages. The first stage is that of a student seeking knowledge through study and prayers. This is the stage when the *mantras* are useful to him. The second stage is that of the family-man whose duties include the performance of sacrifices and keeping

[1] Sometimes the saints were severe with the gods for not responding to their devotee's worship. See *R.V.*, viii. 19; 25 and 44:3. This characteristic becomes markedly evident in later Hinduism.

the sacred fires burning where the *brāhmaṇas* are of extensive use. When he retires, his thoughts centre round higher problems where *āraṇyakas* and the Upaniṣads are useful.

Like all ancient people, the Vedic Indian was also extremely extroverted in his interest in nature. Nature provided a never-ending puzzle to his powers of understanding. There were the unpredictable deluges and the appalling droughts. There were days of plenty and peace as well as days of turbulence and destruction. These vagaries of nature were attributed to human-like agencies by the Vedic Indian. Man is able to do so many things at his own will. It must be similar, he argued, with these natural phenomena. The touch of anthropomorphism that is seen here is the result of an effort to establish a correlation between man's activities and the activities of nature. The ancient Indian was no doubt naive as he did not possess tools of explanation. But he had a very intensely inquisitive mind. Hence he tried to read natural phenomena in terms of his own behaviour. Thus when there were floods, he thought the rivers were angry and in spring-time when there was peace and plenty, he thought that the gods were pleased. The Vedic gods were not merely nature gods. They were also functional gods. Thus there were gods like Agni or the fire god who was not only a nature god but also a functional god inasmuch as he acted as a mediator between the gods and man.[1] He was the priest for both gods and men.

It is most inappropriate to use the word "god" for these extraordinary creatures of the early Vedas. The word "god" is usually made out to be an equivalent to the Sanskrit word '*Iśvara*" which is suggestive of a personalised concept. This word *Īśvara* is not used in the Vedas. On the other hand these nature-spirits are referred to as "*Deva*" meaning the "shining one". This is understandable. Whatever was so dazzling that one could not look upon it and understand became a "*Deva*", a shining one, to the Vedic Indian. One important characteristic of these Vedic deities is that they are not fully personalised entities, unlike as in Greek mythology where we have definite personalities developing out of the deification of nature. In the latter the natural basis of

[1] 1 : 123 of the *Rg. Veda* clearly shows this characteristic of the god Agni. Refer to Oldenberg's translation. Similarly X. 125 claims that *Vāk* is a functional deity.

the deities becomes lost in the progressive attribution of human passions and vagaries to them. But in the Vedic mythology the language used is transparent enough to indicate the relation of both the deity and its name to its physical basis. In many instances, the anthropomorphism is very lukewarm and undefined. But this is manifestly so only when the names of the deities are also the names of the natural phenomena such as Agni, Ushas etc. Somehow the imagination is held in check and personification is arrested. But this is not so in the case of the gods who are slightly removed both in name and concept from their physical basis. Thus the gods Viśvakarma, Aditi etc., are attributed qualities which are more anthropomorphic than those of the other gods. However, at all stages, personification has not become completely anthropomorphic as in other ancient religions.[1]

To classify and enumerate the Vedic gods according to their importance is not possible. There is no dependable measuring rod to determine their relative importance or greatness. It is only possible to say which god was the favourite at any given particular time and occasion. This is not and cannot serve as a measuring rod. A more satisfactory method of dividing and classifying these gods would be to do so on the basis of their physical origin. Of course, even this is not a very satisfactory method as sometimes the physical origins of these deities become obscured and doubtful because of the confusing similarity of descriptions. Vedic scholars have classified all the deities into those who occupy the celestial regions, those who occupy the atmosphere and those who belong to the terrestrial regions.

The Vedic Indian apparently was not a naïve person notwithstanding appearances. For we see that he very quickly developed a questioning attitude with reference to these deities who, after all, were his own brain-children. The very tendency to raise the importance of the sacrificial ritual above the presiding deity, caused the Vedic Indian to pause and assess his gods. Thus we find this agonised refrain in the Hymn to Prajāpati: "What God with our oblations shall we worship"[2] and "They call him Indra, Mitra, Varuṇa, Agni and he is heavenly nobly-winged Garutman. To what is one, sages give many titles, they call it Agni, Yama, Matarisvan."[3]

[1] Such as the Egyptian, Greek and Roman religions.
[2] R.V., 10.121.
[3] *Ibid.*, 1. 164, Griffith's translation.

These statements clearly indicate that the early Vedic pantheon did not satisfy the enquiring mind of the ancient Indian. Hence we find that they slowly drifted towards a monotheistic conception of the god-head. Various methods were used in their search for such a monotheistic answer. One process was to lump all the previous gods together and by drawing upon the common elements produce a conceptualised god. Another was to create new gods on a functional basis. Thus we have Viśvakarma, the maker of all things, Prajāpatī, the Lord of all creatures, Brāhmaṇaspati, the Lord of sacred power, and lastly the cosmic man *Puruṣa.* Each of these divinities are interesting because each of them symbolises the answer to one type of question. Viśvakarma is the causal agency of creation, Prajāpatī is the king-father notion, Brāhmaṇaspati is the esoteric idea. The most important of all is the concept of *Puruṣa,* the cosmic man, who may be considered not only as equivalent to the material cause of this universe but also as the equation sought between the universe and God. It is evident that the people of this time were overobsessed with the cause of the universe. Yet at the same time, the act of creation was always thought of as an act of sacrifice. It is necessary to stress here that although these abstract gods were conceived separately yet their separateness was never emphasised, but always in the background. It is, somehow, the idea of one creator that attracted these Vedic Indians rather than a plurality of causes as indicated by these various conceptions.

There are three hymns dealing with creation in the *Ṛg Veda.* One hymn pertains to Prajāpatī seen as *Hiraṇyagarbha.* It is here that the Vedic Indian postulates an answer to his questions about the origin of this universe. He sees Prajāpatī as the supreme Lord who, by becoming one with unconscious matter, vitalises it and creates from out of it, the sky, the earth and all the creatures of this earth. He not only creates the world and its creatures, but also by entering into them becomes the Lord of all his created things. The next hymn of creation is one that is associated with *Puruṣa* and is usually referred to as "*Puruṣasūkta*". The emphasis here is on sacrifice. *Puruṣa* is the sacrificial offering and the sacrifice is performed by the gods. As a result of this sacrifice all things come into being, the idea being that creation itself is an act of sacrifice. It is not only the beasts and the birds that came into existence as a result of such a sacrifice but also the Vedas were brought into existence by him. It is also said that human beings belonging to the fourfold castes emerged from the various parts of the body of *Puruṣa.* The idea is still maintained that God is both the material as well as the efficient cause of this universe. God is both immanent and transcendent.

Another important fact that arises from the *Puruṣasūkta* is the tendency to identify the physical and the sacrificial object with cosmic phenomena. It is this process of identification that reaches its culmination in the Upaniṣads, where the spiritual element in man and the sustaining principle of this universe are identified as one and the same. The *Brāhmaṇas* devote much time in establishing such identities. Every aspect of the sacrifice such as the altar, the fires, the sacrificial animal, the Sāman hymns that are chanted, are all in some sense or other, identified with cosmic nature.[1]

The third hymn which speculates on the process of creation is what is generally known as the Hymn of Creation. This hymn is an expression of the deep agitation fermenting the Vedic Indian's mind about the origin of creation. In this hymn there is a note of scepticism regarding any agency in creation[2] for they were very much aware that the gods of their times were their own brain-children. The important contribution of this hymn is the postulation of one indefinable principle—not a personality—as the cause of this universe. This principle is referred to by the impersonal pronoun as "That One". This was produced by heat and from that arose the first characteristic of mind, desire, and later others. This desire was seen as the bond between the original non-existence of everything and the later existence of the universe. But the Vedic Indian could not proceed after this, for he was overcome by doubts. Hence his cry "Who knows for certain?"[2]

This hymn of creation is the forerunner of the monism of the Upaniṣads. The naïve pantheism of the early Vedic Indian has

[1] *Ath. V.*, 9.7. In this hymn the various parts of the sacrificial animal *ox* are identified with the gods and the natural forces.

[2] *R.V.*, 10-129. The last verse of the hymn reads: "Who knows for certain? Who shall here declare it? Whence was it born after this world's creation? Then who can know from whence it has arisen?".

given place to a profound monism. No doubt the gods played their part, but these were of lesser importance than the fundamental questions of the origins of this universe troubling the minds of these men. The enquiry was objective. Man was intrigued by nature and when he found that he could not explain nature either by the postulation of divinities or by rational thinking he was lost in bewilderment. It is this that leads smoothly on into the speculative thinking of the Upaniṣads.

The Upaniṣads are also known as the "*Vedānta*" (*Veda+anta*), meaning the end portions of the Vedas. We have already stated that Vedas mean books of knowledge. The word "*anta*" has two meanings in the same manner in which the word "end" has two meanings. It means the final place which is reached as a result of effort and it means the ideas, the goal, towards which all effort is to be oriented. It is more in the latter meaning that the Upaniṣads have become famous. The word Upaniṣad, etymologically, means the teaching imparted to a pupil who is devotedly sitting near the teacher. Hence it was considered to be an esoteric teaching. But the teaching was open to anyone who qualified for it. The qualifications were many and severe. Not the least of them were *śraddhā*, a desire to learn, and *brahmacarya*, the capacity to walk in the ways of *Brahman* or truth.

The Upaniṣads are earlier in terms of chronology than the Purāṇas and the Epics. Amongst these, some are older than the others. Dr. S. Radhakrishnan says, "We cannot assign any exact date to them. The earliest of them are certainly pre-Buddhistic, a few of them are after Buddha."[1] Whatever may be their number or the date of their origin, it is a fact that the Upaniṣads arose as a protest against the over emphasis given to rituals and sacrifices in the earlier portions of the Vedas. The religion of the Vedic Indian was one of sacrifices, in which the predominant note was that of give and take between the gods and men. For instance, during the *Brahman* period the actual rite of the sacrifice became more important than the gods for whom it was intended. Then the sacrifices, being propitiations to the gods, became themselves acts of cosmic importance in which the gods were compelled to

[1] *Philosophy of the Upaniṣads*, p. 17.

take part by the very power of the sacrifice. It was an age of exaggerated formalism and ritualism. This jarred on the spiritual susceptibilities of the Upaniṣadic seers. However, they did not and could not completely do away with all sacrifices. Hence, they diverted their emphasis from mere external formalism to one of internal symbolism. Thus all sacrifices were treated as allegories. It is rather intriguing to note that the attitude of the Upaniṣadic seers to the Vedas is ambivalent. In some Upaniṣads the Vedas are attributed divine origin:

> "....Verily, from this great Being (*bhūta*) has been breathed forth that which is *Ṛg Veda, Yajur Veda, Sāma Veda,* of the Atharvaṇas and Angīrasa, legend (*ithihāsa*), ancient lore (*purāṇas*)...."[1]

In another place, the sacredness and the importance of the Vedic knowledge is treated as of secondary grade. Nārada says "I know the *Ṛg Veda,* Sir, the *Yajur,* the *Sāma Veda,* with all these I know only the *mantras* and the sacred books, I do **not** know the self."[2] In spite of the fact that they were conscious that they had to uphold the traditional idea that the Vedas were sacred, still they could not accept that it contained the highest form of knowledge. In their non-acceptance of the sacrificial religion of the *Brāhmaṇas* the Upaniṣadic seers went to the extent of ridiculing them. In the *Chāndogya Upanisad* there is a passage which compares the procession of the priests to a procession of dogs, each holding the tail of the other and saying "Om! let us eat, Om! let us drink, etc."![3]

Scholars accept thirteen Upaniṣads as older than others although the total number of Upaniṣads is 108. Amongst the older Upaniṣads are the famous Chāndogya, Bṛhadāraṇyaka, Taittirīya, Aitareya, Īśa, Kena, Kaṭha etc. These Upaniṣads used a most interesting method of instruction. The naive people of the Upaniṣadic times had to be cajoled into a type of thinking that was almost alien to them, namely non-ritual thinking. Hence the method they used was one of dialogue, parables, stories, and allegories. In spite of the danger that the allegorical import of such teaching might become lost in the course of time and that

[1] *Br. Up.*, 2, 4, 10. Hume's Translation.
[2] *Ch. Up.*, 2. See also *Br.* 3, 5, 1, Kauśītakī 1, Muṇḍaka, 1.
[3] *Ch. Up.*, I:12:4 & 5 (quoted by Dr. S. Radhakrishnan, ***Philosophy of the Upaniṣads,*** p. 25.

the allegory itself might be accepted as true yet it was considered the best form of conveying profound thought to not-so-profound minds.

There is another characteristic of the Upaniṣadic teaching which must be mentioned here. Hitherto, man's interest was directed towards the external world. This was superseded by an interest in the physical body of man and he began to draw parallels between his body and the external world. In the first instance sacrificial procedures and the bodily parts were identified. Secondly, sacrifices and the world processes were also in some sense established to be identical. This process of identification was going on from early *Brāhmanas.* For example, in the *Puruṣasukta* we have the idea that the universe is a macrocosmic man corresponding in every way, part by part, to the microcosmic man. When this idea, that a sacrifice and the universe are in some form or other identical, took root in the minds of the Upaniṣadic seers their enquiry turned from an examination of the external world to an analysis of the internal world. Many ideas were taught by the Upaniṣadic seers. The wealth and diversity of such ideas is so great that it becomes difficult to pinpoint any one idea as the central teaching of the Upaniṣads. To claim that only one particular teaching is the teaching of the Upaniṣads is not to do justice to Upaniṣadic thought. Some ideas are no doubt more emphatic than others, but the diversity of ideas still remains.

In many parables in the Upaniṣads, the successive identification between the *Brahman*, the cosmic principle and *Ātman*, the personal principle is described. First of all, let us define the words. Etymologically the word "*Brahman*" means "prayer," being derived from a root *"bṛh"* meaning "to grow" or "burst forth". *Brahman* as prayer, is what manifests itself in audible speech. From this should have been derived later, the philosophical significance which it bears in the Upaniṣads viz., the primary cause of the universe—"what bursts forth spontaneously in the form of nature as a whole and not as mere speech only".[1] It is evident from this that the notion of *Brahman* in the Upaniṣads was used to refer to the world-ground. Incidentally we find that the word is also used to mean sacred knowledge.[2] There

[1] M. Hiriyanna, *Outlines of Indian Philosophy*, p. 54.
[2] *Tai. Up.*, 3, 5.

are many attempts made in the Upaniṣads to expressly define *Brahman*. Three of the most important definitions will be considered here. The Upaniṣadic thinkers adopted two methods of definition, the regressive method and the progressive method. In the regressive method, an analysis of several answers was made and rejected till the final answer was reached. In the progressive method each answer was examined and a more all-inclusive final answer was sought. Gārgī, one of the two women philosophers of the Upaniṣads, questioned Yājñavalkya as follows. The Vedic cosmology, as was already indicated, started with postulating water as the primary basis of the world. Gārgī starts with this and asks "since all this world is woven, warp and woof"[1] Step by step Yājñavalkya explains that the final world ground is the wind, the atmosphere, the worlds of the *gandharvas* (celestial beings), the worlds of the sun, the worlds of moon, the worlds of the stars, the worlds of gods and so on till finally he reprimands Gārgī and tells her not to raise questions which are not answerable: "In truth, you are questioning too much about a divinity about which further questions cannot be asked. Gārgī, do not over-question."[2] Thus *Brahman* is something that cannot be grasped by the ordinary intellectual reaches of man. There is another story in the same Upaniṣad where a definition of *Brahman* is attempted.[3] A renowned *Brahman* saint, Gārgya Bālākī, approached King Ajātaśatru and offered to teach him *Brah nan*. The presumptuous philosopher's definitions were all rejected by the king who in his turn gave either a wider definition which included the philosopher's definition or a definition which supplemented the one given by Bālākī or opposed it. Thus while Bālākī defined *Brahman* as the person occupying all the quarters of Heaven, Ajātaśatru says that such a person can be only the inseparable companion of all things that exist and not the final answer. When Bālākī was not able to furnish any further answers to the questions, then Ajātaśatru himself started instructing the philosopher in the nature of *Brahman* and told him that *Brahman* is to be conceived as that in which everything else exists. Using the

[1] *Br. Up.*, 3.6, Hume's Translation.

[2] *Ibid.*, 3.6, Hume's Translation.

[3] *Ibid.*, 2.1.

well known analogy of the man in deep sleep, he said that sleep is the fundamental stage of a soul's existence from which everything else comes. This he called "The Real of the Real" (*Satyasya satyam*) a phrase which occurs again as a description of *Brahman* in the *Maitri Upaniṣad*[1].

In the *Bṛhadāranyaka Upaniṣad* we get another definition of *Brahman*, this time a progressive definition. Various definitions are examined one after another and a more inclusive one is developed out of them. For example, it was maintained that *Brahman* was breath without doubt; but it was inadequate since it also must have a seat and a support which is the "dear" (*priya*). Slowly the instruction proceeds from speech, through the mind and the heart, till it ends in the cosmic *Ātman*, which cannot be described. A correlation between the various parts of the microcosmic human body and the cosmos viewed as a macrocosmic person is established first and then it is stated that such a soul can never be defined, because it is not this, it is not that (*neti-neti*). The most important thing to be noticed here is that the idea of *Brahman* comes to be equated to the psychical activities of man starting with the sense organs. This is an indication of the later developments.

The last definition of *Brahman* which we shall deal with is that given by Sanatkumāra to Nārada.[2] It is here propounded that there is greater truth than even Vedas, for when Nārada tells Sanatkumāra that he is the master of seventeen disciplines including the Vedas, the latter tells him that these are only "names", and that there is one which is greater than "name" which is speech. A knowledge of "name" as constituted by the Vedas etc., is not deemed useless. But on the other hand, it is not enough since there is something "more" than "name" which is speech which makes all things manifest. Successively a "more" is seen in mind, in will, in thought, in meditation, till the idea of a spirit for which everything else exists is arrived at. This is *Brahman*.

[1] *Mai. Up.*, 6. 32, Hume's Translation. "From Him, indeed (who is) in the soul (*Ātman*) come forth all breathing creatures, all worlds, all the Vedas all Gods, all beings. The mystic meaning (Upaniṣad) thereof is The Real of Real."

[2] *Ch. Up.*, 7.1 onwards to almost the end of the section.

In these definitions of *Brahman*, it is possible to distinguish two developments. Firstly it was felt necessary to postulate a universal principle which would embrace the whole of this universe in every aspect. Secondly, it was also felt that such a principle must necessarily be a correlate with the spirit of the individual person. But the Upaniṣadic philosopher did not stop here. The idea of universal ground for all existence must include the individual self which is not material. Hence an enquiry into the subjective nature of the person starts.

An enquiry into the nature of the soul or self is evident in the Vedas. But such an enquiry is not explicit. The Upaniṣads take up the idea, pursue it and present a logical build-up about the nature of the self thus paving the way for the identification of the innermost level of the subjective "I" with the ground of the objective universe.

The nature of the *Ātman* is not discussed anywhere in the Upaniṣads fully so as to present a detailed picture. We obtain material from various dialogues and have to piece them together so as to get a coherent picture of the whole. In the *Chāndogya Upanisad*,[1] there is a dialogue between Prajāpatī and Indra about the nature of the soul. The first answer to the question "What am I?" is that the Self is the body. So Prajāpatī asks Indra to adorn himself in the best of clothes and all his jewellery and look into a pool of water which then reflected his adorned image. The sage then says that the reflected person is his Self. But Indra is shrewd and asks the question, "As this Self in the shadow is well-adorned when the body is well-adorned, well-dressed when the body is well-dressed, well-cleaned when the body is well-cleaned, that Self will also be blind if the body is blind, lame if the body is lame, crippled if the body is crippled, and perish in fact, as soon as the body perishes. I see no good in this"[2]. Thus Indra realises that the body cannot be that which is eternal and that the soul cannot

[1] *Ch. Up*, viii, 3-12.
[2] *Ch. Up.*, viii, 9, 1.

be identical with the body. Next Prajāpatī equates the dream states to the Self thus indicating that the mind which can roam abroad independent of the body might be considered to be the Self. But this is not satisfactory to Indra. The Self must be sustained as the ground of all experience, that based on which the waking as well as dream experiences must become explicable. These states cannot be self-existent. Thus Prajāpatī next postulates the one continuous consciousness which is the basis of both the dreaming and waking experiences as the Self. The Self that merely exists, without any experience of the objective, is the real Self. But Indra does not accept this since such a contentless existence is a mere myth of the imagination. But the purpose of Prajāpatī was to emphasise the identity and continuity of Self which is not affected by changing experiences. Such a Self is not the individual subjective experience, which is also vitiated by differences in the form of the subject's experiencing the object. Hence, the Upaniṣadic seer emphasises the idea that the true Self is truly universal in nature, since the Self persisting as a continuous consciousness is the common experience of all people.

The same idea is presented with little variation in the *Mān kya Upaniṣad.* It is seen that man's experience comprises of three states, the waking state, the dreaming state and the deep sleep state. In the first condition of wakefulness, the Self is opposed to the world of objects and there is the experience of a subjective Self which knows the objective world. In the second condition, although the experience of a subjective Self and the objective world are still present, the objectivity of the experienced world becomes a free objectivity without the bondages of time and space. In the third state, objectivity is lost and the Self alone is present. Since pure identity cannot be known by the discursive mind, the knowledge of the existence of the Self during deep sleep becomes evident only after awakening, when we say that we slept so well that awareness of all other things was excluded from such an experience. But the Upaniṣadic seer is on his guard, for he well anticipates the possibility of equating the experience of deep sleep with one of unconsciousness which in its turn could lead to a form of nihilism. So, he maintains that there is a fourth state, the *Turīya* state, which includes all the above-mentioned three states and goes beyond them. The Self of the deep-sleep experience is defined as that which is not a Self limited by the waking and dream experience. That is, it is at best a negative idea and perhaps as we have stated before, could be only a figment of the imagination. So the Upaniṣadic seer says that the positive aspect of such a negative idea is the *Turīya* state. It is the witness-self and is the same as that which is to be found in all states of experience and which, at the same time, transcends them. These four states are known as *Viśva* (the bodily self), *Taijasa* (the vital self), the *Prajña* (the intellectual self) and lastly the *Turīya* (the pure self).[1] This analysis can only mean that the physical, the psychological and the vital functions of man cannot be self-explanatory, but can be known only as grounded in something which is more permanent and which is known through them. The search for such a principle is the background of the whole teaching of the Upaniṣads. For example, in the *Kena Upaniṣad*, we find the question, "By whom willed and directed does mind light on its objects? By whom commanded does life the first, I have? At whose will do people utter speech? And what God is it that prompts the eye and ear?"[2]

These two principles of reality, *Brahman* and *Ātman*, the objective and the subjective are established to be one and the same. *Brahman* is *Ātman*.[3] The tendency of identifying the personal with the cosmic which has been noted, now achieves its height in the identification of *Brahman* with *Ātman*. The objective reality *Brahman* can have meaning and purpose only when viewed in the context of a knowing person. Hence the identity of these two in the last resort becomes imperative.

The objective not-self becomes merged with Self. This truth is expressed in the famous statements of the Upaniṣads: '*Tat tvam asi*' (that thou art) and '*Aham Brahmāsmi*' (I am *Brahman*). This is not an egocentric predicament. On the other hand it stresses the fact that both the objective and the subjective are nothing other than manifestations of the same reality. However much the reality and certainty of the objective world may be stressed, it cannot be as real or as certain as the knowledge of the existence of one's own self. For the reality of the external world to

[1] The translations of these words are adopted from Dr. S. Radhakrishnan's *Philosophy of the Upaniṣads*.

[2] *Ke. Up.*, 9-10, Hume's Translation.

[3] *Tai. Up.*, 1.5, *Ibid*.

be indubitable, and not to be a dogma or a hypothesis, it must be fundamentally one with *Ātman* because we can never hypothesize our own existence nor can we have doubts about it.[1] Such an ultimate reality is characterised by the seer as *Satyam* (certainty), *Jñānam* (of the nature of thought) and *Anantam* (all-inclusive and eternal). It is the same reality that is known as Self sometimes and the world at other times, but is so neither exclusively nor collectively. This idea is ably taught by the story of the father and son in the *Chāndōgya Upaniṣad.*[2] The son Svetaketu had become learned in the Vedas and was proud of his knowledge. The father Uddālaka asked him if he had learnt that knowledge by a mastery of which, everything else becomes known. The son professed ignorance of any such knowledge, and the father instructed him. He taught him that that which is ultimate is the Being or *Sat* of which the whole universe is a manifestation.

> That which is the finest essence, this whole world has That as its Soul. That is Reality (*Satya*). That is *Ātman*. That art thou, Svetaketu.

Thus the father identified the essence of all Reality with the *Ātman* which is the Self of Svetaketu. That is, whatever may be the reality of the external world, it cannot be as certain and immediately real as our own self. Hence, the dramatic identification of the Self with the *Brahman*. Uddālaka gives two analogies to establish this truth. The bees collect honey from various sources and reduce all these different source-materials into honey which is one in essence. In this honey the source-materials cannot be distinguished. Similarly the waters of every river are distinct from one another, though they may flow in the same direction. But the individuality of such waters becomes lost when they become merged in the waters of the ocean. It becomes impossible to say which is the ocean's water and which is the river's water. Thus, Uddālaka says to this son Svetaketu, the differences of this world become one in the Soul which is the only Reality. It is not the individual Soul of Svetaketu that is thought to be of the highest essence here, but the universal Self, the *Ātman*, which is also the Being, *Brahman*.

[1] This is exactly what the western philosopher Descartes said: "Cogito ergo sum". But as shown later, the criticisms levelled against the Cartesian starting point are not applicable to the Upaniṣadic position.

[2] VI.

Such a *Brahman* is said to be indescribable by the Upaniṣadic seer. They said that any positive description of this tends to limit the ultimate reality to that which is so described, leaving out the rest. Thus, for example, if *Brahman* the complete and total reality is described as "good" then evil stands apart from it thus limiting the concept. This is why *Brahman* is described in negative terminology in the Upaniṣads.

> That, O Gārgi, Brahmins call the Imperishable (*akśara*). It is not coarse, not fine, not short, not long, not glowing (like fire), not adhesive (like water), without shadow and without darkness, without air and without space, without stickiness, odourless, tasteless, without eye, without ear, without voice, without wind, without energy, without breath, without mouth, (without personal or family name, unaging, undying, without fear, immortal, stainless, not uncovered, not covered), without measure, without inside and without outside. Verily, O Gārgi, that Imperishable is the unseen seer, the unheard Hearer, the unthought Thinker, the ununderstood Understander. Other than it there is naught that sees . . hears . . thinks . . understands . . ."[1]

In spite of such an elaborate description, it is conceded that such a *Brahman* cannot be a religious ideal. No doubt that which is ultimate cannot be defined by any definitions, but yet for purposes of worship and prayer it was found necessary to have a more limited conception. Hence following the Ṛg Vedic tradition, parallels between a human personality and that which is the ultimate reality, as personified, were drawn.

Subject (*Ātman*)[2]	*Object* (*Brahman*)
1. The bodily self—*Viśva*	1. Cosmos—*Virāt* or *Vaiśvānara*
2. The vital self—*Taijasa*	2. World soul—*Hiraṇyagarbha*
3. The intellectual self—*Prajña*	3. Self-consciousness—*Īśvara*
4. The intuitive self—*Turīya*	4. *Ānanda—Brahman.*

The *Ātman-Brahman* identity becomes a concrete fact only at the fourth level. But in the other levels of existence, empirical differences persist. Thus it is possible to conceive the ultimate

[1] *Br. Up.*, 3, 8 and 11.

[2] This scheme is taken from S. Radhakrishnan's *Indian Philosophy*, Vol. I, p. 172.

Brahman as *Īśvara* from a limited standpoint. The word *Īśvara* means etymologically the "Supreme Controller". Thus, that which is the organised world owes its existence to, or is to be understood as part and parcel of *Īśvara* its controller. The body of man can have no meaning or value if the intellect is dumb. So also, the world's existence centres round this concept of *Brahman* known as *Īśvara.* This *Brahman* is shown to be not necessarily an abstract ideal but that it could also be thought of as a living dynamic spirit. Such a reality is indicated by the mystic symbol *Aum.* This is said to stand for the three aspects of all existence namely, creation, preservation and destruction. The term *Puruṣa* which we have already referred to in the first chapter is applicable to both man and God. It is because just as man is one who is imprisoned in the citadel of the body, so also *Īśvara* is one who is imprisoned, in a manner of speaking, by the universe. This does not mean that the world is the body and *Īśvara* is the soul. Such a conception would lead to pantheism or naturalism. It does not also mean that *Īśvara* is different from this universe, because then the whole effort of the Upaniṣads to find that one ultimate principle, becomes useless. Still *Brahman* as *Īśvara* is the ultimate and yet not the limited. Yet, that these two conceptions, positive and negative, are not separate is indicated by that celebrated passage in the *Muṇḍaka Upaniṣad.*[1]

> That which is invisible, ungraspable, without family, without caste
> Without sight or hearing of it, without hand or foot,
> Eternal, all-pervading, omnipresent, exceedingly subtle,
> That is the imperishable, which the wise perceive as the source of Being.

Thus the monism sought after from the beginning of the Ṛg Vedic times finds fruition in the Upaniṣads.

> As all the spokes are held together in the hub and pulley of a wheel, just so in this. So all things, all gods, all worlds, all breathing things, all selves are held together.[2]

The *Svetāśvatara Upaniṣad,* though one of the classical ten, is of later date and signifies a later development in the Upaniṣadic

[1] 1, i, 6.
[2] *Br. Up.,* 2. 5, 15.

religion. The idea of a personal God is not non-existent in the Upaniṣads. But such a God is not the same as the one found in the Vedas. In the latter, Gods were objective conceptions. But in the Upaniṣads, this objectivity is not solely emphasised. For example, we find the *Bṛhadāraṇyaka Upaniṣad* saying

> Whoever worships a deity thinking that one and himself another—he does not know.[1]

Hence we have here a conception of God that is fundamentally different from the Vedic conception. Here God is described as "immortal inner ruler" and as the thread that runs through all things and binds them together. This theistic doctrine is to be found full-fledged in the *Svetāśvatara Upaniṣad.* Here we find all the requirements of theism such as belief in God, devotion to such a God being considered as the true means of salvation. Another indication of the development of theistic tendency here is the use, again, of the word *Deva*, God. Here *Deva* is not merely the shining one as in the *Ṛg Veda*, but the omnipresent, omnipotent ruler of the universe. Such a God is identified in the *Svetāśvatara Upaniṣad* with the Ṛg Vedic God, Rudra-Śiva. Here the conception of this God is different from the Vedic one. He is no more the terrible God, but the supreme Lord of all creation and the Auspicious. He is also called the Great Controller, Maheśvara. He is the "person of the measure of a thumb, the innermost soul (*antarātman*) ever seated in the heart of the creatures."[2] Such a God is both immanent and transcendent. As the internal immanent principle, He is the *antarātman*: as the transcendent God, He is the creator and destroyer of this universe and thus, is the object of worship. We find thus, that the beliefs of the Vedic seers, their speculations, and conclusion had much to do in colouring the vision of the Upaniṣadic seers.

An account of Upaniṣadic thought would be incomplete if theories of creation of this universe are not considered. The two views of *Brahman*, the cosmic and acosmic, the positive and the negative, make the very question of creation a matter of doubt. However, one thing is certain. According to both the views, "the emergence of the world from *Brahman* is conceived as the differentiation of names and forms".[3] The acosmic view considers that

[1] *Br. Up.*, 1.4.10 and also *Ke. Up.*, 1, 4-8.

[2] *Sv. Up.*, 3-13

[3] S. Radhakrishnan, *Philosophy of the Upanisads*, p. 142.

such emergence is only apparent since there can be no other than *Brahman* that is real. But the cosmic view maintains that unless the world of experience of man is endowed with some reality all human effort becomes meaningless. Hence it considers the emergence of the world of *nāma* and *rūpa*, name and form, from *Brahman* as the actual process of creation. However, the universe is not created out of something other than *Brahman*. *Brahman* itself is both the efficient and the material cause of this universe. We have stated elsewhere that *Brahman* is viewed as *Prajñavān*, the self-conscious principle, *Īśvara*. To postulate a matter different from God, would be marring the monism of the Upaniṣads. Hence in the Upaniṣads, both form and matter, the cause and the effect, the conscious principle and the unconscious matter are all one single reality. That is why one finds that matter itself is said to be God. "*Brahman* is food", says the *Taittiriya Upaniṣad*.[1] Intelligent life and discursive intellect are dependent on food which is matter. Matter and spirit are intricately woven together and *Brahman* is both. To find that one is not only the eater of food[2] but also the food that is eaten, is to say that one is not only the individual self but also is the transcendent reality. This truth is expressed very succinctly in the same Upaniṣad when it is said

> He who is here in a person and He who is yonder in the sun—He is one.[3]

Thus each man also partakes in the immortality of the whole. But such a creation does not affect *Brahman*. The light coming from the sun does not affect the sun. Once this general nature of creation or evolution is accepted, the Upaniṣadic seers proceed to give the details of the things derived from *Brahman*.

In the *Bṛhadāranyaka Upaniṣad*, there is an account of creation where it is said to be the outcome of the will of *Brahman* which is referred to here as "I". It is, in a way, anthropomorphic and speaks of the creation of this world, in the first instance, as the result of the union of the two sexes which themselves were first separated out by *Brahman* from out of itself.

1 *Tai. Up.*, 3, 1, 2.
2 *Ibid.*, 3, 10, 6 "I, who am food, eat the eater of food."
3 *Ibid.*, 3, 10, 4.

The *Svetāśvatara Upaniṣad* considers the various theories of creation and the sources of creation and rejects them. By this process it tries to establish its theistic approach to the problem. "Neither Time, nor inherent nature, nor necessity or chance, nor the elements, nor a womb (female), nor a (male) person are to be considered (as the cause); nor a combination of these, because of the Self (*Ātman*)."[1]

Here all things are criticised and shown to be incapable of being the source of creation, for one reason or another, and finally it says Rudra is established as the creator.

"He by whom this whole world is constantly enveloped
Is intelligent, the author of time, possessor of qualities, omniscient,
Ruled over by Him (his) work revolves."[2]

At the same time, the two views that God is both the transcendent creator and the immanent Lord is also emphasised.[3] Such is the theory of creation in the *Svetāśvatara Upaniṣad.*

The above account examines the question of the first cause. But once this is determined to the satisfaction of the seer, then, accounts of secondary creation of the objects of this universe, are usually discussed. As already mentioned the process of life appearing from life is an accepted theory. First of all a distinction is made between organic and inorganic matter. Of the latter, the Upaniṣads recognise five fundamental elements (*bhūtas*). These are earth, water, fire, air and ether. All were not known simultaneously in the beginning. First there was water, then fire and earth were added. In the final sections in the *Taittirīya Upaniṣad*[4] we find all the five were recognised. As for the organic creatures, they were divided into those born out of eggs (*aṇḍaja*), out of germs (*jīvaja*), out of soil (*udbīja*) and out of sweat (*svedaja*). Thus we have a crude attempt at explaining the things of this world. However crude, the attempt is significant since it was the result of conceptual thinking without the aid of any external instruments.

The Upaniṣadic thinkers also raised a fundamental question about the nature and proofs for the existence of the soul (*jīva*)

1 *Sv. Up.*, 1. 2.
2 *Ibid.*, 6.2.
3 *Ibid.*, 4.1, 9-10 and 19-20.
4 *Tai. Up.*, 2.1

as an empirical reality. Apart from the importance of such a question from the philosophic point of view, it is also important from the religious point of view because *mōkṣa* or freedom is for the soul. So one must know what it is and where it is. That the *jīva* is fundamentally identical with *Brahman* is the basic philosophy. But actually a *jīva* is one which has forgotten its essential identity and considers itself as a separate individual. Still sometimes the soul rises above its limitations and gets glimpses of its own true nature when man, becoming unaware of individual predilections, becomes identified with the object of attention or adoration. Such moments of self-transcendence are suggestive of the universal nature of the *jīva.* However, in its limited aspects the nature of *jīva* is discussed in the *Taittirīya Upaniṣad.*[1] It is *Purīśaya,* meaning that which lies imprisoned in the body. Without the body and its constituents, a *jīva* cannot have individuality. Hence the *Kaṭhā Upaniṣad* says that the *jīva* is one apart from which the mechanism of the body would become meaningless. Such a *jīva* is first identified with matter or food and is known as *annamaya kōśa* (sheath of matter). Secondly, it is that which resides in *prāṇa* and occupies the *prāṇamaya kōśa* (sheath of life). Similarly the *manōmaya kōśa* (conscious or intellectual sheath), and *vijñanamaya kōśa* (or self-conscious sheath) are enumerated as the places where the Self resides. Lastly, it is identified with *ānandamaya kōśa* whose characteristics are pure peace and pure bliss. This is where the Self is aware of itself as a pure being without any conflicts and utterly at peace with itself. The word *jīva* itself means "to continue to breathe". In addition to this the Upaniṣads characterise the Self as *bhōkta,* one who experiences, and *kartā,* one who is the agent of all actions. Breathing is an unconscious activity indicated by *prāṇa* and the other two are sentient activities indicated by mind or *manas.* The *jīva* or Self is one that is limited by these two principles in its empirical existence. The way to achieve its freedom from these two is first of all to control the mind and then the unconscious impulses. An elaborate development of these processes of control form the substance of a later philosophy known as *Yoga.*

The vast amorphous period which begins at the close of the Upaniṣadic age and ends with the systematisation of the philosophic trends into what are known as *Darśanas,* is the period

[1] *Tai. Up.,* 2.1-5.

known as the epic age. Dr. S. Radhakrishnan is of the opinion that although the thoughts and events recorded in the epics have been in existence for quite a long period, they were actually codified and recorded somewhere about the sixth century before Christ.[1] Between the Upaniṣadic period and the rise of the epics, much historical water seems to have flowed under the bridge. There were invaders after invaders swarming the country with their own religious beliefs and ideals. It became absolutely necessary for the original inhabitants either to "āryanise" the newcomers or to give in to the pressure of these new ideals. The original Āryans realised early that the only way to exercise any secular control over a people was to control the religious belief of the people. Hence the process of assimilation occurred mostly at the spiritual levels.

This spiritual atmosphere was a stormy one. The highly intellectual theories of God, soul and the world put forth by the Upaniṣads were not appreciated by the common man as he could neither understand them since they were too abstract, nor, consequently, could he practise them. Therefore he either went back to the barren ritualism of the Vedic religion or fell an easy prey to rebellious doctrines promulgated by the *Svabhāva vādins* or naturalists. These latter rebelled against the ritualism and the polytheism of the Vedic religion. Politically, this must have been a most unsettling time. This is evident from the fact that both the great epics, the Mahābhārata and the Rāmāyaṇa, are war stories. The historicity of both is doubtful. However there must have been some sort of a fratricidal war ballad which must have constituted the nucleus for these epics. In such unsettling times, it became necessary to bring the people together under one banner and explain to them the fundamental beliefs of the Vedic and the Upaniṣadic religion and moral codes. This had to be done in such a manner that it would appeal to the metaphysically child-like minds of the people and provide enough motivation for implementing them in their lives. What more suitable medium for such instruction than the readily available ballads of national heroes? Thus we have, developing round these stories, the epics of the Mahābhārata and Rāmāyaṇa.

[1] S. Radhakrishnan and C. A. Moore, *Source Book of Indian Philosophy*, p. 99. Also refer to S. Radhakrishnan's *Indian Philosophy*, the footnote on p. 481.

The process of clothing the abstract *Brahman* of the Upaniṣads with flesh and blood and making it into a personality which is the Supreme Being thought of in religion, had already begun in the *Svetāśvatara Upaniṣad.* This process gains momentum in the epic age and becomes almost a solid theory of personalism. In spite of such personality-cults developing we find, more often than not, passages in the epics and in most of the Purānas which echo the Absolutism of the Upaniṣads. There seems to have been a nagging doubt, as a background, in the minds of these people, about the propriety of a God who is to be worshipped being described as *Ātman* and also about the possibility of reconciling a transcendental reality with an immanent personalistic deity. This is revealed in the fact, that this God is described in terms which echo both his immanent and transcendental qualities.

Both the epics Mahābhārata and the Rāmāyaṇa are codes of morals given in the form of stories of national heroes. We have ethical codes prescribed for all walks of life from governing a country to sexual habits, all given in the context of the stories. There is no aspect of life which is not covered here. What started as a heroic ballad, became in the course of time, not only a code of morals, but also a theistic manual. The gods of the Vedas such as Viṣṇu and Śiva became, in turn, identified with the supreme reality, *Brahman* of the Upaniṣads. In addition the idea of *Brahman* became reduced, from being a neutral reality, to one of the creator God. Thus the concept of the three gods, *Trimūrti* each representing one aspect of the universe such as creation, sustenance and destruction became popular. This triple personification grew as the ages passed, sometimes overlapping, and sometimes becoming rivals. Today it is impossible to distinguish between them as their characteristics overlap and each god is described in identical terms.

One important development which followed from such personalisation is the doctrine of *avatāra* or descent of God into the world. As this is a religious concept, we need not spend muce time on it except to quote the definition given by Dr. Radhakrishnan: an *avatāra* is "God who limits Himself for some purpose on earth, and possesses even in His limited form the fullness of knowledge."[1]

[1] *Indian Philosophy,* Vol. I, p. 545.

In addition to this idea, there is also the idea that man can raise himself to Godhead by leading a life of righteousness. The Bhagavad-Gītā belongs to this period and its doctrines, inasmuch as they are relevant for our purposes, will be discussed in another chapter.

The age of the epics is also known for some other factors. The caste system became well established by this time. The reason for this was that it was more convenient to delegate duties and responsibilities to groups of people rather than for all people to do all things. It was not very rigid in the social and religious context as it was in the occupational and administrative contexts. A perusal of the two great epics shows many intermixtures between the castes and many a man changed his caste because of a change in profession.

The doctrine of *karma* developed into a rigid belief in rebirth and reincarnation according to merit and work. The meaning of the word *karma* is twofold. It means the rituals prescribed in the Vedas and it also means any action calling forth a reaction. When these two are combined we get the idea of *karma* as rebirth. It is maintained that those who do good actions reap the benefits of their goodness either in this life or in another life. Unfulfilled righteousness or its opposite, becomes accumulated and influences the manner in which man is to attain his fulfilment in future lives. This also we shall discuss in detail in a later chapter.

The bhakti cult or the method of devotion gained precedence over the method of knowledge for the attainment of *mōkṣa* during this age. This is to be expected. The personalisation of reality must necessarily replace knowledge by devotion, for a God is to be worshipped and adored. The twin idea of God's grace being necessary to attain *mōkṣa* follows immediately. The gods Viṣṇu and Śiva, are described as being moved to pity by their devotees to save them (*bhaktānukampin*).

This was also the period of the great Buddha who gave his eight-fold path to realisation. The characteristics of early Buddhism were the *Kṣaṇikavāda* the doctrine of momentariness and *Nairātmya vada*, the doctrine of no-soul. By the former, Buddha destroyed substance as Being and by the latter he removed Soul as the substratum of all reality. For the Buddhists, like Heraclitus of old, only change was real. The unchanging, eternal reality was only a myth. One can easily trace the rebellious spirit here. While the Upaniṣads stressed upon *Brahman-Ātman* as the ultimate reality which is eternal, early Buddhist thought opposed it by maintaining that there is nothing eternal except change.

Siddhārtha who belonged to the family of Gautama, is well known. Born into a princely family and the only child of his parents he renounced all his power and wealth, wife and child to seek the meaning of sorrow and suffering. He found that the doctrines of the Upaniṣads which required a man to practise austerities in his search for truth did not satisfy him. He wandered from place to place and finally found the answer to his question about the cause of sorrow and suffering while sitting in meditation under a Bodhi tree. The name Buddha means "the awakened one". He preached to the world the four noble truths which are that (1) there is suffering, (2) such suffering has a cause, (3) the cause of suffering is removable, thus removing suffering, and that (4) there is a way to remove this cause. But this does not mean that the teachings of Buddha were so codified even while he was teaching. He left no written documents and what we have now is what has been gathered by his disciples as his teachings. Consequently what he said originally is lost to us. What we know today as early Buddhism is a late compilation describing Buddhism in the early stages of its history.

All documentation of early Buddhism was done in Pāli which was a spoken dialect of Saṃskrit. Much of the writing is in the form of discussions and debates which were then the current method of establishing a doctrine. There was also a great deal of metaphor and allegory used to convey ideas. The first group of works are described as the *Tri-piṭaka*, the three baskets. These are supposed to be the utterances of Buddha himself. The first *piṭaka* consists of *suttas* which are aphorisms. The second *piṭaka* is the *Vinaya* which deals with the ethical discipline and the third deals with philosophical discussions and is known as *Abhidamma.* Like the Upaniṣads these *piṭakas* were also couched in difficult and terse language, so full of analogies and metaphors that their meaning got lost over the years. The followers and disciples of Buddha, gave each his own interpretation of Buddha's teachings. This resulted in a divergence of views amongst his followers. We can trace two broad developments known as Hīnayāna and

Mahāyāna. The Hīnayāna means the lesser way and the Mahāyāna means the greater way. Of these the former was older. Their doctrines are widely opposed to each other. As we shall see later, the two schools of Hīnayāna, the Vaibhāṣika and the Soutrāntika were schools of realism while the Yogācāra or the Vijñāna vāda and the Mādhyamika or Sūnya vāda which belonged to the Mahāyāna branch were schools of idealism.

About the period these Buddhist schools developed, several Buddhist works written in Saṃskrit or translated from Pāli, came to be written. The wealth of material at this time speaks of the opposition and conflict which developed between the Buddhist schools themselves and between them and the orthodox schools of Hinduism. Those who were responsible for the codification and propagation of the Vaibhāṣika school are the two great Buddhist logicians known as Dinnāga and Dharmakīrti. The former wrote *Pramāṇa Samuccaya* while the latter not only interpreted Dinnāga but wrote a very interesting treatise on logic called *Nyāya-Bindu.* This was later commented upon by Dharmōttara. This school was known as Vaibhāṣika because they swore their loyalty only to the *Abhidamma Piṭaka* and a commentary on it known as *Vibhāṣa.* The name also means that they considered the doctrines expressed by all other schools to be *viruddha* or absurd and that their own philosophical standpoint was different from all of them. Kumāralabdha is known to be the founder of the Soutrāntika school, whereas Vasubandhu and Asanga are reputed to have taught the Yogācāra or Vijñāna vāda school. The great work of Vasubandhu is known as *Abhidamma kōśa.* The *Lankāvatara* is another work belonging to this period. The last of the Buddhistic schools of idealism, the Màdhyamika, was fathered by Nagārjuna and his work is known as *Mūla-Mādhyama Kārika* which was commented upon by his famous disciple Candrakīrti.

We shall close our account of Buddhism by stating the main outlines of early Buddhism as supposed to have been taught by Buddha and propagated by his immediate disciples. In spite of the fact that Buddha rejected the Upaniṣadic theory of Being and concentrated purely on a practical solution to the problem of evil in the world, we find that there are many parallels between the two streams of thought. Just as in the Upaniṣads, Buddhism also rejects the belief in a personal God. While in the Upaniṣads the *Ātman-Brahman* is said to be knowable only in a negative manner, Buddhism eliminates the Self altogether. In spite of such resemblances, early Buddhism was not a metaphysical system. It was pragmatic and positivistic in outlook. As already stated, the purpose of Buddha's teachings was to find a way out of the suffering and misery that people were undergoing. Although he taught no metaphysics explicitly it is still possible to infer metaphysical ideas from his teachings. It is these that have given rise to later development into schools of differing metaphysics. We can make out three important factors of metaphysics in early Buddhism.

1. The Doctrine of Momentariness or *Kṣaṇika vāda*: This doctrine stresses the impermanence and mutability of things. All things are bound by time which is itself a flux. Therefore things exist only for one moment and they are not the same in the next since the factor of time is different. Two moments of our cognition are similar and not identical. Similarity is mistaken for identity. Every successive phase is, however, not entirely a new phase as the potentialities of the former exist and manifest themselves. There is continuity between the differing phases, although there is no identity of the material. What is permanent is only the name and the form, *nāma* and *rūpa.*

2. The Doctrine of No-Self—*Anatta vāda*: This is the logical conclusion of the above argument. Just as no identity is acceptable in regard to material things, so also no identity is acceptable in regard to *Ātman* or Self. The Self is also a momentary existence. The momentariness indicates the changing components of a thing. Therefore man, the whole, is also the whole of a living continuous complex. So-called "individuality" is an unstable state. Rhys Davids says, "There can be no individuality without putting together, there can be no putting together, no connection, without a becoming; there can be no becoming without becoming different, and there can be no becoming different without a dissolution, a passing away, which sooner or later will be inevitably complete."[1] Thus according to early Buddhism, there are neither permanent things, nor selves. The world is a continuous becoming. There is no "thing" that becomes. There is only the process.

[1] *The Religious Systems of the World,* p. 142.

3. The Law of Dependent Origination—*Pratītya samutpāda*: The becoming that characterises all existence follows a definite law. This law is the most vital contribution of Buddhism and all further developments of Buddhist thought take this as the corner-stone on which to build their philosophies. Hitherto change was explained as either accidental or of divine origination. Buddha rejected both these explanations and maintained that the principle underlying succession is a necessity. But necessary succession does not imply an internal teleology. It only means that production takes place when certain external conditions are fulfilled. The usual example given is that of the flame series. The flame will continue to exist as long as the conditions which are necessary for its origination such as the wick, oil, the necessary temperature, and other environmental conditions continue to exist. The flame goes on and on till one of the conditions is either withdrawn or ceases to exist. Thus the law, while universal in application becomes applicable only when certain external conditions co-operate with it. So the name *Pratītya samutpāda* is translated by Rhys Davids as "That being present, this becomes; from the arising of that, this arises."[1]

It was a knowledge of this principle of dependent origination that flashed into Lord Buddha's mind as he sat meditating under the tree. That the world is enmeshed in suffering is indubitable. But nothing can come into existence and continue to be if the factors which gave rise to it cease to be. So, if man were to find out what causes suffering and remove even one single link in it, then the whole edifice of misery in his life vanishes as though it were a house of cards. The efforts of man, therefore, must be directed to the elimination of such a cause and not in renunciation only.

More than the theoretical teaching outlined above, the practical teaching of early Buddhism is more valuable. If nothing is permanent, then all desires, including the love of the Self for the Self is purely a mirage and an illusion. When the Self itself is negated, then selfish and narrow desires must disappear. Therefore it is a belief in the self-identity of the person as well as the thing that is responsible for all sorrow and suffering. This is a wrong belief. Ignorance of the truth is the root cause for all suffering. So

[1] *Buddhism*, p. 89.

right knowledge must be acquired so as to remove wrong knowledge which is the root cause of suffering. Now that the cause of suffering is said to be ignorance, it requires to be shown how such ignorance can bring about suffering. It is only when the process is known that it can be stopped. This process is said to be a causal chain. The various links of this chain are known as *nidānas*. As this is only a particular application of the doctrine of dependent origination, we should not consider that these are the only links. These are links which cause human suffering and sorrow. The first one is *avidya* or ignorance. This is primal ignorance when man considers that things are permanent when actually they are momentary and transient. The individual feeling of "I" accompanied by its correlative of permanence is due to *avidya*. Out of this *avidya* is born *saṁskāra* or action. An action may be good or bad. It binds all the same. Such a binding is possible, because actions involve consciousness or *vijñāna*. It is only when the subject and object are opposed that action is possible. But the opposition involves the consciousness of the subject which is aware that the object is different from itself. It is this awareness that comes into being at the same time as the objective world and is invested with a name and a form. The activity of the sense organs depends on the arising of the awareness and this activity gives rise to impressions or sensations. So if the five senses and mind together with their objects are known as *ṣadagātmā*, then the contact between the senses and the objects is *sparśa* which results in *vedanā* or sensation. As a result of all this activity arises desire or *tṛṣṇa* and the clinging to existence, *upādāna*. This gives rise to the idea that there is a becoming, *bhāva*. It is these that lead man from birth to birth, *jāti*, and which ends invariably in old age and death, *jarā-maraṇa*. This whole chain starting from ignorance and ending with old age and death is that which causes sorrow and suffering. It is sometimes called the *bhāva cakra*, the wheel of existence. There is a way to remove this suffering for it is possible. This way is the famous eight-fold path preached by Buddha which will be explained in the chapter on the principles of morality.

The next school which did not accept the authority of the Veda is the well-known Jaina school. Both Jainism and Buddhism deny any creator or first cause to this world. Just as Buddhism is the name derived from Buddha, the enlightened one, so also

Jainism is the name derived from Jina, the victor. The founder was one who conquered his passions and became victorious over himself. The founders of both schools were kshatriyas, who, it is said by scholars, were mainly responsible for the rebellion against too much ritualism of the Vedas.

Vardhamāna, known as Mahavīra, the great hero, was said to be the last of the Jaina teachers. Tradition says that he was the twenty-fourth prophet. The twenty-third prophet was Pārśvanātha who is believed to have lived about the eighth century B.C. Nothing much is known about any of the teachers prior to Vardhamāna, although their names are mentioned in the Vedas and Purāṇas.[1] Ṛsabha, Ajiṭanatha, and Ariṣtanemi are found in *Yajur Veda* as those who preached the philosophy of Jainism. Vardhamāna belonged to a princely family and was the second son of the king of Magadha. Scholars maintain that he lived between 599 B.C. and 527 B.C. At the age of twenty-eight Vardhamāna renounced his princely life and entered upon *sanyāsa* or a life of renunciation. After having spent twelve years in rigid austerity, sometimes even going about naked, Vardhamāna is said to have conquered and became a prophet to his followers. At the end of this period he is said to have attained perfection and was known as a *Kevalin.* The Jaina prophets including Vardhamāna, were known as *Tīrthāṁkaras.* The word means, "one who has discovered the way to cross to the other shore" of this troubled ocean of life. He was also the Jina, one who has conquered. After Vardhamāna became a *Tīrthāṁkara,* he spent the rest of his life preaching his doctrines to the people. He founded both a lay system and a monastic order. The latter consists of two branches. One of them renounced everything in this world including even one's clothing and the other group stopped short of such extreme renunciation and considered clothing as necessary as eating. But such clothing was always to be simple and pure. So these were known as the sect of *Ṣvetāmbaras,* the white-robed ones, while the former were known as *Digambaras* or the sky-clad monks. There is not any appreciable difference in their philosophical canons.

As usual, much of the Jaina teaching was handed down from teacher to pupil through the generations. Naturally, during the

[1] I am indebted for much of this information to Dr. S. Radhakrishnan, *Indian Philosophy,* Vol. I.

process much was lost and much new material was added. About the beginning of fifth century B.C. a council of Jaina teachers gathered at the ancient city of Pātalīputra to codify and formulate the teachings. This took definite shape only in about A.D. 454 under the guidance of a renowned Jaina teacher, Devarddhi. Forty-one *sûtras* which were made up into different parts, were said to codify the teachings of the Jainas completely. The language used was the same as that used in the early Buddhistic canonical writings which was *prākṛtic* or *ardhamāgadhi*. But later writings were all in Saṃskrit. Some of the most important works of later Jaina literature are *Tattvārthādhigama Sūtra* by Umāsvati (after the third century A.D.), *Nyāyāvatāra* of Siddhasena Divākara (fifth century A.D.) *Ṣaddarśanasamuccaya* of Haribhadra (sixth century A.D.) and many others. However the system did not spread its teachings beyond the shores of India as Buddhism did. In fact today most of its followers are to be found in the western and southern parts of India.

While we are discussing the non-orthodox systems, we should lay a special emphasis on the materialist school of Cārvāka. There were many who were opposed to the sacrificial religion of the Vedas and who foreswore any faith in the scriptures and institutions which preached such a religion. Both Buddhistic and Jaina works refer to numerous schools which were different from Vedic religion. These, which were anti-Vedic, were referred to as *nāstikas* or heretics. This attitude developed and gained momentum as the ages passed and its priests were known as Śramaṇas as opposed to the Brāhmaṇās who were the Vedic priests. That these were a force to be reckoned with was a historical fact recorded by foreign travellers like Megasthenes. The attitude of the Śramaṇas was that there is no God, no soul and the Vedas are not the ultimate authority. They ridiculed the notion of a final cause. Famous names like Sanjaya the sceptic,[1] Ajita Keśakambali who rejected knowledge by insight and maintained that man was nothing but the elements which disintegrate on death, Gōśala who was a fatalist who believed that man was just a toy in the hands of nature, and many others who were thorough-going materialists. All schools of thought which came into existence during this time are believers in the impermanence of things and in the fact that

[1] I am indebted to Dr. S. Radhakrishnan's *Indian Philosophy*, Vol. I, for much of the information regarding the heretical thought of this period.

sorrow and suffering exist. Many of these teachers were known as *svabhāva vādins* or naturalists. The most important of these naturalists were the Lōkāyatas or the Cārvākas. The former name is derived from the fact that they consider only this world *lōka* as real and all supernatural or transcendental entities as utter fiction. They are realists of extreme convictions. They are also known as Cārvākas because they preach a sweet philosophy. The word actually means "a sweet tongued one" (*cāru vāka*). For them, pleasure and pain are the only realities and man has to shun the latter as much as he desires the former. It preaches an extreme form of Hedonism as can be gathered from their belief that passions are nature's legacy to man. If pleasure is mixed with pain, that cannot be helped for who will throw away the grain because it is covered with husk. So the advice given is to ignore pain and enjoy life to the utmost: "Who knows what is to come tomorrow? So let us enjoy everything now" is their watchword. They were naturalists with a vengeance for they denied even the law of causation and believed that everything happened in this world only accidentally. Hence they are known also as *Yadṛccha vādins* or *animitta vādins.* Both words mean accidentalism.

The founder of the Lōkāyata system is said to be Bṛhaspati. But there is no extant literature to prove this except that Madhva in his *Sarvadarśana Saṅgraha* gives a summary of the beliefs of Naturalists and says that their teacher was Bṛhaspati.

The development and practice of such materialism indicates the declaration of the ancient Indian of his spiritual independence. He was not cowed down either by weight of authority nor by any ridicule from orthodoxy. It was an effort at the removal of all dogmatism and all that goes with it. We find that later systematic development of Indian philosophy was very much influenced by this rebellion.

The period which followed the Purānic age was a period when much speculation and systematisation took place. During the Purānic age, as we have already stated, the absolutism of the Upaniṣads became merged into a personalism of a religious variety. We shall deal with this philosophico-religious development at the end of this book. Now it is necessary to take a peep into that vast amorphous literature known as the *Kalpa sūtras.*

These are divided into *Śrouta*, *Grihya* and *Dharma sūtras*. The first one codifies the sacrificial religion outlined in the *Brāhmaṇas*. The *Grihya-sūtras* tells of the rituals and practices to be followed by the head of the family in managing his household. The last one, the *Dharma sūtras* talk about the laws that should govern the life of man as a member of society. It lays down the norms for social and legal behaviour. All the three are in the form of aphorisms. Of these the *Dharma sūtra* of Manu is of great interest. Manu was not the maker of the law but only its codifier. This means that he made into a law whatever were the practices of the day. It is popularly known as the code of Manu or *Manu-dharma śāstra* or *Mānavadharma śāstra.* It seems that the main purpose of this code was to glorify the traditional customs and conventions when it was found that these were in jeopardy due to the rapid advancement of anti-authoritarian naturalisms. It was about this time that the caste system became rigid. What was conceived as a convenient division of labour, slowly sank into a hereditary practising of different types of works. The position of women became degraded from one of freedom and liberty to one of dependence and limitation to household duty and child-bearing. While *sanyāsa* or renunciation is proclaimed as the highest ideal for man, the stages of a *brahmacāri*—student—and that of a *grahastha*—family man—were also extolled. In these *āśramas* or stages of life, it was maintained that *śruti*, *smṛti*, *ācāra* (custom) and conscience were the authorities. Of these while the first three maintained the existing order, the last gives room for intelligent and rational changes.

The next stage in the history of Indian philosophy is the most significant stage. Philosophising develops whenever an existing theory is found inadequate and is attacked as such. That there was such a revolt is indisputable as evidenced by the rapid development of the non-Vedic schools of thought such as Buddhism, Jainism and Cārvāka. The floating beliefs which had their birth in the Upaniṣadic thought and which were vehemently attacked both by Buddhism and by Cārvāka had to reorient themselves to the prevailing agnosticism and scepticism. The believers were compelled to codify their views and present them in a more logical form and give up their doctrinaire attitudes. It was this necessity that gave rise to the period usually known as the *sūtra* period.

A systematic presentation of a view of philosophy was given the name *darśana* which literally means "sight". In this context, it is maintained that these philosophical truths were directly experienced and known by the sages and savants who first promulgated them. These were not arrived at by an analysis of empirical experience as in the west. But they were truths "given" to the sages when they went in search of them. The word *darśana* has a more relevant connotation for philosophising. It means that one should not be merely content in logically understanding the truth about Reality but should live in accordance with such convictions. Philosophy in ancient India was not only a logical appreciation of truth, but it was a way of life. This takes us immediately to the next point which is that at this time, philosophy found itself wearing the mantle of logical appraisal and was not content merely to rest itself on authority. *Ātma vidyā* or a study of the nature of ultimate reality as the Self became supported, defended and criticised by *Ānvīkṣaki* or the science of enquiry. Critical reason took over from intuition and regular philosophising began to flourish in an atmosphere of honest and keen enquiry. But this did not mean that these systems of philosophy denied the authority of their sources. On the other hand such authority was accepted but subjected to severe scrutiny. Thus we have a group of philosophies known as *darśanas* which owed allegiance to Vedic and Upaniṣadic thought. These were known as *āstika darśanas*. The characteristic of an *āstika darśana* was not only that it believed in the authority of the Veda, but also it believed in the eternity of the soul and in the idea of *mōkṣa* as freedom from sorrow and suffering. Of these *darśanas*, we find that six became very famous and we have plenty of extant literature on them. These were Nyāya founded by the sage Gautama, Vaiśeṣika, by the sage Kaṇāda, Sāṁkhya of Kapila, Yōga of Patanjali, Pūrva-Mimāṁsa of Jaimini and Uttara Mīmāmsa of Bādarāyaṇa. All these systems were first expressed in the form of *sūtras* or aphorisms. These were cryptic short sayings which did not permit of any doubt and which excluded all that which is superfluous to the presentation of the central idea. Perhaps such presentation was necessary, for in those days everything had to be committed to memory. There is no doubt that the sages whose names are associated with these systems were not actually the founders of these systems. These ideas must have been floating about for a long period prior to their codification by these sages. Generally these *sūtras* are assigned the time between A.D. 200 and 500. But it is evident that they are more antiquated than this. These were only the dates when such floating ideas took a more definite shape. The purpose of such codification was two-fold. In the first instance it was meant to establish a particular doctrine and secondly it was meant to refute all others which were critical and different from it.

The literature of every school, as time went by, became vast. The *sūtras* themselves were always accompanied by commentaries known as *bhāṣyas*. The *bhāṣyas* enlarged upon the cryptic sayings, for otherwise they were incomprehensible. The *bhāṣyas* gave interpretations of the original aphorisms. These were subjected to commentaries again and again, so that a vast literature was soon formed round a particular system. In spite of this divergent literary growth all the six systems accept certain essential points. We have already stated that all of them pay homage to their Vedic heritage by accepting it as an authority. However, we do not find blind acceptance of the Vedic authority and more often than not, it is subjected to critical thinking. This is evident by the fact that although all systems accept the Vedas or *śruti* as a means of knowledge, still the importance given to this means varies from system to system. In addition it is not the whole of the Veda that is accepted. Only such of the portions, interpreted to suit each system's philosophical predilections, are accepted as a means of knowledge. This will become evident while we study the theories of knowledge propounded by these systems. In addition to *śruti* or *śabda* as a means of knowledge, *pramāṇa*, all systems accept perception and inference also as valid means of acquiring knowledge. All the systems argue that there is something called soul or *Ātman.* But the connotation of the term is as varied as materialism varies from idealism. To the Nyāya-Vaiśeṣika systems the Self or soul is material, though this matter is of a different variety from crude matter. To the Vedāntic thinker the soul is of the very nature of consciousness. Thus while the same terminology is used by the different systems, the meaning of the term varies considerably from system to system. Similarly all the systems accept the condition of *mokṣa* but the nature of *mokṣa* is different for each system. While it is agreed that *mokṣa* is a state of freedom from sorrow and suffering yet the nature of freedom is not the same for all systems. All the systems, including the heterodox systems, agree that this sorrow and suffering are the result of wrong conception about the nature of reality. While the wrongness of the conception is emphasised by all schools, the nature of such conception differs from school to school. Evil is made out to be a metaphysical wrong thinking rather than moral evil. At the same time there is no difference at all between the systems in regard to the emphasis they lay on an ethical and moral life as a prerequisite for philosophical studies. A morally depraved person, a mentally immature person and a person whose emotions govern his actions are declared to be unfit for a philosophical study.

We shall now take up the six systems and study them in some detail. Customarily these systems are grouped into two because they either supplement each other's thought or fulfil each other's objectives in philosophising. Thus Nyāya and Vaiśeṣika are clubbed together because while the Vaiśeṣika provides the metaphysics, the Nyāya gives the logical bulwark for such metaphysics. The Sāṁkhya and Yoga are clubbed together because the latter while accepting the evolutionary approach to reality formulated by the former provides the necessary modes of mental control required to achieve the goal set by the former. The Pūrva Mīmāṁsa and Uttara Mīmāṁsa come together only because their philosophy is purely oriented to expounding the Vedic and Upaniṣadic teachings and providing for them a logical basis. The words pūrva and uttara mean posterior and anterior and when these are affixed to Mīmāṁsa, which means enquiry, the natural juxtaposition of these schools becomes meaningful. While the former two pairs would be treated as such in consequent chapters, the schools of Mīmāṁsa would be treated separately under different headings. At present, however, let us take a closer look at the literary development of these schools.

The Nyāya and Vaiśeṣika schools are the analytical schools of Indian philosophy. They felt that having mere faith in Upaniṣadic statements was not enough. It was as a protest against such blind faith and its attendant evils that Buddhism raised its flag of rebellion. Buddhists started philosophising from the empirical and rational standpoints. It became necessary to show that the conclusions of Buddhism which were nihilistic in nature were not the only logical conclusions that could be drawn starting with an empirical analysis. The burden of showing this fell to the portion of the Nyāya and Vaiśeṣika systems. Of these the Naiyāyika swears by reason and is prepared to accept as true whatever is established by reason. The Nyāya and Vaiśeṣika systems take up the things of the world and analyse them and come to conclusions about their real nature and validity. While the Nyāya deals exclusively and elaborately with the mechanism of knowledge, means of valid knowledge, the nature of valid knowledge and all other aspects of the mental process, the Vaiśeṣika deals with an analysis of experience gained from the external world. In this effort the Vaiśeṣika has given us one of the ancient accounts of the atomic constitution of this world.

The Nyāya system is also known as *tarka vidyā* or the science of debating and *vāda vidyā* the science of argumentation. Discussion or debate was an ancient method since these were used even in the Upaniṣadic times to arrive at truths. In those days, logic was mostly dialectics. Just as ancient Greek philosophy used the method of dialogue and discussion so also we find that the Upaniṣads use this method. A refinement of this was achieved in the Nyāya system. Gautama, like Aristotle, systematised the method of reasoning and gives us the multifarious modes of sophistry that usually accompany all reasoning. The first *sūtras* of Gautama are divided into five sections each of which is again divided into two parts. These five sections follow the method of enunciation, definition and criticism of all categories. The *Nyāya Sūtras* are usually allotted the third century B.C. The *bhāṣya* on the *Nyāya Sūtra* is attributed to Vātsyāyana who was supposed to have lived round about A.D. 400. Uddyōtakara's commentary of *Nyāya Bhāṣya* is known as *Nyāya Vārtika* and it is a defence of the Nyāya standpoint against the criticism of the Buddhist Dignāga. He belonged, according to scholars, to the time between 608 and 648 A.D. and must have had the patronage of the great scholar king Harṣavardhana. Vācaspati Miśra, who lived about A.D. 841 and who was a very great scholar of Advaita has written a commentary on the *Vārtika* called *Tātparyatīka*. There are more commentaries written by many scholars like Udayana, Jayanta Bhaṭṭa etc. By about A.D. 1200 Gangesōpādhyāya from Bengal wrote a book called *Tattvacintāmani*. This marks the beginning of a new epoch in Indian logic. From now onwards, the importance of Nyāya as a system of philosophy declined giving place to Nyāya as pure logic. Of the numerous writings which quickly succeeded the earlier works, the *Tarka-saṁgraha of* Annambhaṭṭa and the *Bhāṣāpariccheda* of Viswanātha, both of about A.D. 1650 are well known. The *Vaiśeṣika Sūtras* did not have the same prolific growth as the Nyāya had. Its first commentary or *bhāṣya* was by Praśastapāda who lived about fifth century A.D. Udayana's *Kiraṇāvali* and Śrīdhara's *Kāṇdalī* are both famous commentaries on the *bhāṣya.* Sivāditya's *Saptapadārthī* which is a work belonging to the syncritised school of Nyāya-Vaiśéṣika belongs to this period and is a well known simple exposition of both the metaphysics of the Vaiseṣika and the logic of the Nyāya systems. Today it is this Navya Nyāya (later or new Nyāya) that is popular amongst Indian philosophers.

It is interesting to note how the names Nyāya and Vaiśeṣika came to be given to these systems. In popular language the word Nyāya means the Right or the Just. In technical language it means reasoning. But such reasoning is to establish what is right and just. Therefore combining both the meanings, Nyāya literally means that by which the mind is led to a valid and right conclusion. The various names by which it was known through its history make this point evident. It was called *Anvīkṣikī* because it tried to harmonise between empirical knowledge and scriptural testimony. In other words, if scriptural testimony proved to be contradictory or opposed to empirical knowledge, it was probed into, analysed and an effort was made to find out how far it could be reconciled with canons of reasoning. Nyāya was also known as *pramāna mīmāmsa,* a science of demonstration in regard to the means of knowledge; as *tarka śāstra*, the science of inference; *hetuvidyā*, the science of reason or cause in an inference. All these names emphasise the fact that the Nyāya system was primarily a logical system. The name Vaiśeṣika is derived from *Viśeṣa* which means particular or individualistic. The system reduces, by the use of rigorous analysis, all things into atomic particles known as *aṇu* or *paramāṇu.* These particles are distinguishable from each other because of their particular qualities. Hence the system is known by the adjectival form of *viśeṣa*, which is Vaiśeṣika. Its propagator is known as Kaṇāda. His real name was Kāśyapa. Kaṇāda means "eater of atoms". Because the system considers atoms as the primary realities, the systematiser was nicknamed as the "eater of atoms".

The next group of two systems whose background we have to study are the Sāṁkhya and Yōga systems. It is claimed that Sāṁkhya is a very old system for there are references to it in the later Upaniṣads. In the *Svetāśvatara Upaniṣad,* there is a reference to one Kapila as the founder of the Sāṁkhya tradition. This is refuted by scholars and sages. Saṃkarācārya in his *Sūtra Bhāṣya* critically examines this claim and refutes it. The work *Sāṁkhya-Pravacana Sūtra* claimed as the product of its originator, is not available now. *Sāṁkhya-kārika* of Īśvarakriṣṇa is the earliest available work on Sāṁkhya and it belongs to the fifth century A.D. It is claimed that this Īśvarakriṣṇa was a contemporary of Kālidāsa the great Saṁskrit dramatist and poet. Equally important is the *Sāṁkhya Pravacana Bhāṣya* by Vijñana Bhikṣu who lived about A.D. 1600.

The system is a frankly evolutionary system. Its name is derived from the word *sāṁkhya* which means both "number" and "knowledge". It is *Sāṁkhya* because it derives the universe from *Prakṛti* which is the combination of three elements namely, *sattva, rajas* and *tamas.* It also maintains that ultimate reality is a duality. Both matter denoted by *Prakṛti* and spirit denoted by *Puruṣa* are the ultimate realities. The system is openly atheistic for it does not recognise the need for a God either as a creator or as one whose grace is required to acquire release from sorrow and suffering. This bondage is caused by the activity of *Prakṛti* and a knowledge of the distinction between *Prakṛti* and *Puruṣa* gives rise to *mōkṣa.* It is a dualistic system.

Sāṁkhya is usually combined with the more popular system of Yōga. The word *yōga* is used to mean various things. It means simply a method, specially a method of control, of both the body and mind. It also means yoking together, or putting together in harmony. Patanjali the founder of Yōga, uses the word to mean effort or strenuous endeavour to find perfection. He also uses it as discrimination between the Self or *Puruśa* and *Prakṛti* or matter. Thus the different meanings of the word tell us that the main purpose of the system is not to give a new system but to establish the method by which man can attain perfection or *mōkṣa.* It accepts the metaphysics of the Sāṁkhya. But Yōga is more theistic than Sāṁkhya. However its theism is not of the usual variety, for God here is not an object of worship and veneration only, but an aid for concentration.

The *Yōga Sūtra* of Patanjali is the oldest work of the system. It consists of four parts. The first deals with the nature and purpose of *samādhi* or meditation, the second deals with the means for *samādhi*, the third deals with the intermediary results which are the supernormal powers and the last part deals with the nature of *kaivalya* or *mōkṣa*, to be attained by following the methods laid down. This was commented on by Vyāsa in fourth century A.D. and this is a standard work on Yōga. The *Tattvavaiśāradi* which is a commentary on the *bhāṣya* was the work of Vācaspati Miśra who lived in the ninth century and is a work of equal importance to scholars. The special feature of the Yōga system is its practical discipline. While other systems maintain that peace of mind is essential for renunciation or for acquiring true knowledge, this system gives the actual methodology to acquire such peace of mind. The Yōga system maintains that by gaining a progressive control over the body and mind, the roving mind and its activities can be controlled and sublimated, resulting not only in the acquiring of peace of mind, surpassing ordinary understanding, but also to a state of mindlessness which is *kaivalya* or *mōkṣa*. There is another aspect of the system which is better known than what has been stated above. The system maintains that with the control of body and mind, certain latent capacities of man come into the foreground. These are what are usually known as extra-sensory perceptions and psycho-kinetic capacities. But the aspirant is forbidden to indulge in these for any gainful purpose, for they would mislead him away from the goal of *kaivalya*.

The next two systems have to be considered separately. Although they bear the common appellation of Mīmāṁsa with *Pūrva* and *Uttara* as prefixes, they deal with different types of philosophy. Pūrva Mīmāṁsa, as its name suggests, is prior enquiry. Its enquiry is prior logically and not chronologically. The system swears by the Vedas as revealed truths. But such truths have to be expressed in language. So it is a Mīmāṁsa or enquiry into the principles according to which the Vedic texts are to be interpreted. This means that to understand such revelatory texts, reason is essential. Again by using reason man must go to the idea behind language. In short the main purpose of the system is to analyse the relation between the expressed word and the idea which the word is supposed to express. At the same time the system considers that not all parts of the Vedas are worthy of enquiry. It ignores the *mantras* which are the first portions of the Vedas and concentrates its analysis on the *Brāhmaṇās*. The *Brāhmaṇās* are the portions dealing with rituals and it is evident that Mīmāmsa considers this as of primary importance. Therefore it suppresses the later Upaniṣads as well. Hence its name Pūrva Mīmāṁsa, the prior enquiry.

The main purpose of Vedic sacrificial religion was to attain heaven or *svarga* where man was to enjoy all the physical and mental pleasures to a much greater degree than he does in this world. All rituals involved in such sacrifices had this as their goal. But in the Mīmāṁsa, this aim was replaced by the ideal of *mōkṣa.* The emphasis on ritual was secondary to the need to achieve *mōkṣa.* To this extent, the Pūrva· Mīmāṁsa school achieved a transformation of Vedic religion. The philosophic theory underlying this ideal is not directly taken from the *mantras* or the *Brāhmaṇās.* It does not also continue the tradition of the Upaniṣads. Yet it is not a *svabhāva vāda* like the Cārváka. It is materialistic, realistic and pluralistic. It is atheistic inasmuch as it does not accept a God for creation. It believes in a soul, but a soul which has modal transformations. It is a highly logical system where we find much kinship with the Nyāya logic.

Jaimini is said to be the first codifier of the *Mīṁāmsa Sūtras.* He is usually assigned the fourth century B.C. by scholars. Because we find references to Nyāya and Yōga principles in the *sūtras* these must necessarily be later than them. The most important commentary, *bhāsya*, on *Jaimini Sūtras* is that of Sábara Svāmin whose date is fixed at about A.D. 400. This *bhāsya* was commented upon in two different ways by two different scholars. Prābhākara (A.D. 650) and Kumārila Bhaṭṭa (A.D. 700). The former's work is known as *Bṛhatī* which is a critical commentary on Sábara's *Bhāṣya.* Much of the literature of this school is yet unpublished and much also has been lost. That which is available and is well known is the *Prakaraṇa Pañcika* of Śālikānatha Miśra (A.D. 800) which is an elaborate commentary of the teachings of Prābhākara. The Prābhākara theory is known as the *Guru mata,* teachings of the Master. Kumārila is believed to be a pupil of Prābhākara, for he often refers to the latter's teachings in his great work *Slōkavārtika.* While he has given to the world other works known as *Tantravārtika* and *Tuptīka* it is to the *Slōkavārtika* that scholars turn to for an exposition of his philosophy. *Nyāyaratnākara* by Parthasārathi Miśra is not only a famous woık but also a most lucid exposition of the Bhāṭṭa school of Mīmāṁsa. *Śāstra dîpika* is another of his works.

Thus we find that the Mīmāṁsa school had split into two main streams of thought commonly called by their proponent's names as the Prābhākara school and Bhāṭṭa school of Mīmāṁsa. While Mīmāṁsa as such has not much to contribute as a metaphysics, later Mīmāṁsikas have made notable contributions in the field of logic and epistemology. One important factor of their contribution is that they consider that all knowledge is valid knowledge, but it becomes false later due to extraneous circumstances. This they have used very skilfully to establish the eternal validity of Vedas. We shall examine this at great length later on.

The most important systems of philosophy which are a living force today are the three systems known generally as Vedānta. These are the Advaita, Viśiṣṭādvaita and Dvaita schools.The schools of Viśiṣṭādvaita and Dvaita are philosophies of religion and as such will be dealt with separately. The Advaita school is a metaphysical system of non-dualistic absolutism. All the three systems claim to be authentic commentaries on the thought of the Upaniṣads hence they are known as "Vedānta", which is a name by which the Upaniṣads are also known. For the same reason they are also known as "Uttara Mīmāṁsa" which means "later enquiry". It is "later" because the Upaniṣads form the "later" portions of the Vedas. Bādarāyaṇa's *Vedanta Sūtras* are the source for all the three systems. This claim would sound preposterous in the light of the fact that there is nothing common between the three systems. They range from the monistic absolutism of the Advaita to a realistic pluralism of the Dvaita. Yet, their claim can be defended because the *Vedanta Sūtras* are so sententious that it was possible to interpret them in various ways. Scholars maintain that one of the chief purposes which the *Vedānta Sūtras* tried to achieve was to refute the then current theory that the Upaniṣads taught a dualism as envisaged by the Sāṁkhya school. A more urgent purpose was to refute the ritualism preached by the Mīmāṁsikas who said that the important portions of the Vedas were those which dealt with *karma* or ritualistic actions and not *jñāna* as given by the Upaniṣads. To the Mīmāṁsika the portions of the Vedas dealing with *karma*, namely *mantras* and

Brāhmaṇas were of primary value. It is to refute this that Bādarāyaṇa gave us his *Vedānta Sūtras.* It is also known as *Brahma Sūtraṣ* for it expounds the doctrine of *Brahman.* It is called *Sārīraika Sūtra* for it deals with the Self which is imprisoned in the *śarīra* or body.

The chief commentators on the *Brahma Sūtras* are Śaṁkara, Rāmāṇuja and Mādhva, well known for their philosophies which are called Advaita, Viśiṣṭādvaita and Dvaita respectively. There are other well known commentators like Bhāskara, Yādavaprākāśa, Vallabha, Vijñāna Bhikṣu and others. Their philosophies are enlargements of either the absolutistic or theistic interpretations. We will not deal with these minor deviations, but will confine ourselves to the major philosophic school of Advaita and the philosophies of religion of Viśiṣṭādvaita and Dvaita.

Śaṁkara is given different dates by different scholars. These range between the end of the sixth century A.D. to about A.D. 820. He is said to have been a child prodigy. His teacher was a certain Govinda who was himself a pupil of the renowned Gauḍapāda. Gauḍapāda was an Advaitic teacher of high repute and his commentary on *Māndūkyā Upaniṣad* known as *Māndûkyā Kārika* is the first systematic exposition of Advaita philosophy. At a very early age Śaṁkara was fired by an enthusiasm to show to the world the Advaitic truth. He renounced the world, became a *sanyāsin* and went about from place to place preaching Advaita and converting everyone to the philosophy of Advaita. Tradition says that in the course of his wanderings, he met the renowned Mīmāṁsācārya, Mandana Miśra and converted him to Advaita after a straight contest in argumentation. He became a disciple of Śaṁkara and was known in later days, as Sureśvara. Śaṁkara established four *mutts* or religious sanctuaries at Sringeri in Mysore state, Puri in the east, Dvāraka in the west and at Badrināth in the north. The task that Śaṁkara set himself was not so much religious as philosophical. The great philosophical truths of the Upaniṣads were becoming shrouded by various theological and ritual beliefs. Sentiment and emotional outpourings were taking the place of real knowledge about truth. The scepticism and nihilism of the Buddhists and their opposition to blind ritualism had conquered many a heart. So Śāṁkara set himself to the task of reviving the teachings of the Upaniṣads, not merely by appealing to the gullibility of the common man, but by the strong irrefutability of his logic. He always attacked the philosophical tenets of the rival, but never attacked their religious principles. His logical analysis of other systems are a model of accuracy and philosophical acumen. While believing and preaching the reality of one *Brahman* and the illusoriness of everything else, while maintaining that the individuality of the soul is a misnomer, as there is only one *Ātman* which is none other than *Brahman*, we find Śaṁkara was also a great devotee, a *bhaktā*. There are many poetical works amongst his writings which are the outpourings of a devoted saint to his God. This apparent contradiction is because Śaṁkara's philosophy postulates levels of reality. While there is no doubt that *jñāna* or knowledge can alone make a man realise the ultimate nature of his self, still it is by utter selfless devotion that man trains his mind to rise from the mire of his selfishness and wanton desires.

Śaṁkara wrote commentaries on all the principal Upaniṣads and on the Bhagavad Gītā. His other main works are *Upadesa Sahāśrī* and *Vivekacudāmanī*. Some of the most popular devotional poems of his are *Ānandalahari*, *Soundarya-lahari*, *Sivānanda-lahari*, *Lalitā Sahasranāma* and a host of others. His disciples and followers split into two camps. Padmapāda, one disciple, was responsible for the school known as Vivarana school. The treatise of this school is *Pañcapādika*. This was commented upon by Prakāsātman (A.D. 1000) in his *Vivarana* which was in its turn explained by Vidyāranya (A.D. 1350) in his *Vivarana–Prāmeya-saṁgraha*. The other stream of Advaita was started by Vācaspati (A.D. 841) by his *Bhāmati* which was commented upon by Appaya Dīkṣita (A.D. 1600) in his *Parimala*. There are other general works on Advaita like the *Pañcadasi* of Vidyaranya which describes the divergencies noted above. While the "Vedanta-paribhāṣa" of Dharmarāja Adhvārindra is a systematic exposition of the Advaita doctrine, specially its logical and epistemological aspects, the "Vedānta-sāra" of Sadānanda (A.D. 1550) is almost like an easy digest of the important tenets of Advaita.

The main principles of Advaita will emerge as we progress from its metaphysics to its epistemology. However, we should not forget that Advaita was almost a countervailing system to Buddhism. Using the same techniques that Buddhism used, Śaṁkara tried to establish the existence of one supreme consciousness and the temporary existence of everything else. Inasmuch as both consider *avidyā* or ignorance as the source of all evil they are one. But the nature of this ignorance is different for both the systems. Due to many similarities of arguments and illustrations, Śaṁkara is derided by his opponents as a Buddhist in disguise, *Praccanna Bauddha*. Nothing can be farther from the truth. While both start from the same standpoint, namely the momentariness or non-eternality of this world and soul, one branches off towards the establishment of a nihilism, while the other reaffirms the truths of the Upaniṣads that *Brahman* alone is real and everything else, though apparently real, is not ultimately so.

CHAPTER II

METAPHYSICS

The original material dealing with Indian metaphysics is as large in quantity as it is intrinsically difficult. It is not possible in a book of this type to attempt an analysis of all the metaphysical theories of traditional Indian Philosophy. The treatment of these theories has necessarily to be a sketchy and meagre one whetting of the interest of the reader for further research. Thus the following pages deal with the topics of metaphysics more in an expansive fashion. However the main trends of the six orthodox and the three non-orthodox schools are covered.

It is a general misconception born out of ignorance and interested propaganda that all of Indian metaphysics is idealistic. It is maintained that what is other than idealistic is either dead and gone or that it is so unimportant as not to be counted for purposes of characterising. This is quite incorrect. All shades of philosophical speculation are to be found in the ancient literature. Each system of thought tries to establish its philosophy by criticising other systems. The metaphysical ideas range from the very outspoken, commonsense, materialism of the Cārvāka to the highly sophisticated logical absolutism of the Advaita and the nihilism of the Buddha. In between we have the various shades of pluralism, dualism, qualified monism, subjectivism and others. But very often the metaphysical is so mixed with the epistemological that it is difficult to sift the one from the other. This is so because the metaphysics of each system claims an *a priori* origin but requires to be substantiated by epistemological arguments. However such a sifting has to be done for purposes of clarity. We shall start with substance and proceed to God after discussing the nature of self or soul as presented by the different systems. This will have to be a cross-sectional study.

Substance

The word "substance" is more appropriate to describe the Indian concept. It is substance that is the source of everything else. Like the early Greek philosophers the ancient Indian philosopher was intent on finding the answer to the question "What is it that is the warp and woof of everything else?" It is evident that "objects" perish, yet they have a value. What determines their value? Religious and secular values were found to be intricately interwoven either negatively or positively with the existence of substance. So a study of the nature of substance began. The very first formulation of the question is to be found in the Hymn of Creation in the *Ṛg Veda.*

> "Who knows for certain? Who shall here declare it?
> Whence was it born? and whence came this creation?
> The Gods were born after this world's creation:
> Then who can know whence it has arisen?"[1]

The question is further pursued in the Upaniṣads. It should be noted here that unlike in the Greek philosophy, no definite answers are provided. It was considered good philosophising if pertinent questions were raised and cogitated upon. Thus while raising the question of the nature of "substance" as the ultimate, we have an analysis of the nature of matter in successive levels. A most important and lucid account is to be found in the discussion between Gārgi the woman philosopher and Yājnavalkya, the philosopher-saint in the *Bṛhadāranyaka Upaniṣad.* In answer to the question "What is that on which this universe is woven warp and woof?" the notion of substance as instanced by various things is discussed. Starting from water the answers moved in ever-widening concepts through the atmosphere around us to the sun, the moon, the distant stellar constellations and finally the indefinable *Brahman.* When Gārgi persisted in knowing the nature of *Brahman,* Yājñavalkya rebuked her sternly by saying "You are questioning too much about a divinity about which further questions cannot be asked." The importance of this enquiry for us is that it indicates the line of thought which these ancients pursued. Starting from the most obvious necessity of life, water, they proceeded to build up a theory of substance as that which is the most ultimate real.

Realism: Pluralism

When we come to the stage of systematic philosophising, we have definite organised theories of substance supported by sturdy

[1] S. Radhakrishnan and C. A. Moore, Tr. *Source Book in Indian Philosophy,* p. 23.

logical bulwarks. The Cārvākas may be termed as naive realists. Believing as they do that perception is the only means of valid knowledge, they could not go beyond that which is perceptible in their search for a nature of substance. Hence that which is known by sense perception viz., the world of matter, is the only reality. Such an experiencible world is made up of the four elements, earth, water, air and fire in different combinations. Mind and consciousness are accidental emergent qualities of this elemental combination. This is a school of very naive realism. If we understand the background of the development of this school, then we would understand that their position is a violent throwback from the ritual-ridden formalistic theories of the later Vedic age. In modern times, the theory of Hobbes comes close to the Cārvāka theory. Arguing against Cartesian dualism, he maintained that thought is an action of bodies which have motion, and thus succeeded in reducing the sacred to the secular, a job which was accomplished equally thoroughly by the Cārvākas.

There are other materialist schools which do not take this extremist position of the Cārvākaś. The whole Upaniṣadic philosophy was based on the fundamental assumption that the soul or *Ātman* exists and that it should be released from the shackles of its encasement, the body. A whole intellectualist philosophy which developed around this idea gave rise to a staunch opposition in Buddhism which for the most part, and in its early forms, was anti-intellectualist. They laid greater stress on ethical discipline and humanist attitudes for a worthwhile life, for they held that there was nothing that was permanent and eternal. All that exists is momentary and it is an illusion produced by our thinking that makes such momentary things eternal and ultimate. This doctrine of momentariness, *kṣaṇikavāda,* of early Buddhism had two consequences. One was the denial of permanency to all objects. The object exists only for a partless moment. Secondly, like the objects, the soul is also non-existent in that it is not an eternally permanent being. This is the negative side of their metaphysics. Positively speaking early Buddhism maintained that what is known as objects and selves are nothing else but aggregates or *saṁghāta* of *nāma* and *rūpa.* The words have a different connotation here from what they have in the Upaniṣads. By *nāma* is meant all psychical factors and by *rūpa* is meant all physical factors. That is, the person is described as nothing else but an aggregate of psychophysical factors. The explanation of material things is similar. The qualities or attributes which constitute our knowledge of the perceptible object is all that there is what we call an object. They are also merely aggregates of data. There is no permanent substance.

From positive and negative accounts of early Buddhism we learn that for the Buddhist nothing continues to be the same for two instants, but is constantly changing. Change also is real. This change is known as *saṁtāna.* Just as we can never step twice into the same stream of water, so also every object is a never-ending succession of happenings never to be repeated. The world is a process. The question is raised that if the world is a never-ending series of happenings how can we call them a series and how can we account for the consecutiveness between two states which are apparently similar? Buddha did not accept either chance or the intervention of a supernatural being as the cause for this process. He viewed cause neither as the teleological self-unfolding nor a chance occurrence. It was a necessary succession, but the necessity was a contingent one imposed by external conditions. The example given is that a flame series does not come into being till all the conditions such as the wick, oil etc. are all present. Once the series starts, it will go on automatically till one of the conditions responsible for it is withdrawn. Thus an effect undoubtedly originates from a cause, but the origination itself is dependent on external conditions. Hence it is known as the law of dependent origination—*pratitya-samutpāda* which literally means "from the arising of that, this arises". In its general form this law of causation is equivalent to the law of sufficient reason. Where there are sufficient and relevant conditions there causality becomes necessary.

With this basic knowledge of early Buddhism we can now proceed to study its later developments. If we understand by metaphysics the study of a permanent reality, then there is no such metaphysics in early Buddhism for it does not acknowledge the existence of any permanent reality. To make up for this, as it were, the later schools have put forth various shades of metaphysical speculations both with regard to the existence of matter and to the existence of the Self. The later Buddhist philosophy in its Hīnayāna form developed two schools which propound a belief in reality in some form or other. These are the Vaibhāṣika and the Sountrāntika schools. It is usually believed that Buddhism is idealistic and nihilistic. While this is true of the Mahāyāna schools of Buddhism, the Hīnayāna schools are more realistic and materialistic. While we characterise these schools as realistic and materialistic, we should not forget that these terms are to be understood in the framework of the earlier Buddhistic doctrine of momentariness, *kṣanikavāda.*

Both the Vaibhāṣika and the Sountrāntika schools not only admit the reality of substance but also that all external objects are the result of a combination of primary atomic units which are directly perceived. These are further indivisible and unanalysable. These are the substates of the four fundamental sensations of colour, smell, taste and touch. The gross external objects are made up of clusters of these primary particles, but the clusterisation is a mental act, a *kalpana*, for these foundational particles do not have the power of interpenetration.

Although the word "atom" has been used to designate the final reference points in external reality, actually there is no justification for the use of such a word with all its modern connotations. The word used in the Saṁskrit texts is not the cognate word *aṇu*, but the more meaningful word *svalakṣaṇa.* The *Nyāya Bindu*, a Buddhist treatise explains that the word signifies uniqueness and means "that which can be defined only by itself". The particle, if it can be called particle at all, is one which can be known only by its character or *lakṣaṇa.* But then, these are not permanent entities. Each *svalakṣaṇa* is generated by the previous one and in its turn generates the subsequent one. Apart from this dependent origination, these *svalakṣaṇas* are absolutely unrelated and unique in existence. It is so because all relations are mental and are imposed by the mind on these particles. The particles themselves are neither related nor possess relations. Yet at the same time they are apprehendable by the senses. It is here that the seeds of the Buddhist subjectivism are sown. Thus these *svalakṣaṇas*, may be termed, for want of a better word, the source material for bare sensation. But when it becomes an object of perception, it is determined, constrained and characterised by subjective factors which are (1) generality, *jati*, (2) quality, *guṇa*, (3) action, *karma*, (4) name, *nāma*, and (5) substance, *dravya.* In a way we may call these the "categories" by which the *svalakṣaṇas* become known. These are purely mental and it is with the help of these that we know an object as belonging to a class, having a name and qualities and characterised by relations. Thus the perceived *svalakṣaṇa* is categorised into an object. It is easy to see how the Vaibhāṣika cannot be characterised as a naive realist. He is a transcendental realist like Kant. But for Kant the thing-in-itself is unknowable although existent. Its existence is inferable only. But inasmuch as the categorisation of the thing-in-itself is responsible for our knowledge of the object as it appears, there is similaritye between the Vaibhāṣika realism and Kantian transcendentalism. The similarity becomes more marked when we come to the next realist school of Buddhism.

The Sountrāntika realist differs from the Vaibhāṣika realist in his notion of the perceivability of the *svalakṣaṇa*. The former maintains that the object as it exists can never be known at any moment of perception. The doctrine of momentariness maintains that any object exists only for one moment. During the second moment it has already become a thing of the past. Therefore for knowledge of the *svalakṣaṇa* to arise in the mind, directly, such a *svalakṣaṇa* must exist at least for two moments of time. But this is impossible according to their presupposition. So the Sountrāntikas criticise the Vaibhāṣikas in this aspect and maintain that a direct knowledge of the external object is never possible. So although the object as a *svalakṣaṇa* exists, our knowledge of it is always inferential because it is based on sensations.

Both these schools of realism go a step further and maintain that the distinction between substance and attribute is only of linguistic convenience. But unlike modern Western linguistic philosophers these Buddhists do not deny external reality to objects. For these the externality of the object means that the object is only qualitative and not substantive. There is no enduring substance as the basis for the qualities. Only qualities are real and external.

This cautious approach to externality of the real is due to their general aversion to universals. A universal becomes possible only when there is a continuity of substantive existence. Such substantive continuity is anathema to Buddhist metaphysics. This way of accepting a qualitative momentary real establishes the importance of the particular in their system of thinking. The universal is a construction of the mind, and not an existential precept. Thus we find that these Buddhistic schools can be designated realisms only by courtesy. Their concession to the externality of reality is forced by the logical muddle into which a combination of their doctrine of momentariness and their theory of perception has landed them. The escape route they had planned and accepted was to deny substantiality while accepting qualitativeness to that which is perceived. Of these two the Sountrāntika is more true to the doctrine of perception. For to perceive an object at least two moments of activity are essential and they are contemporaneous. This being impossible the only other alternative is to postulate an inferential knowledge of the past moment of existence of the object and to accept the continuity of the qualitative nature based on their doctrine of dependent origination. Qualities of the past originate qualities of the present according to their doctrine of dependent origination.

A more satisfactory school of realism is that which is known as the Nyāya-Vaiśeṣika school which is one of the orthodox schools. The emphasis which the Buddhists have laid on a reality which is purely qualitative and on relations being purely mental brought forth a good deal of criticism from other schools, the most vehement of which is the Nyāya-Vaiśeṣika school. This school takes its stand on empirical experience and accepts a bland realistic point of view. Objects in the world are real. We experience them as real and external because they are related to us externally. Their interrelation is also external. Such objects are known as *padārthas* which literally means "the meaning of a word "or more appropriately "that which is indicated by the meaning of a word". By implication a *padārtha* is any object which can be named. All things of experience whether they are material or spiritual, if they are nameable, are *padārthas*. Thus even in the beginning the stress is laid on man's experience which is expressible in language. A judgment which is in language is distinct and separate from that which it indicates or to which it refers. This is the crucial characteristic of a realist. If there is no separation between a judgment and its referential aspect then importance is switched over to the language aspects ignoring or leaving the referential reality to take care of itself. If a stress is laid only on the referential aspect of reality ignoring the language aspect then we are divorcing experience as given in language judgments from reality which is the source of such judgments. So to safeguard against these two possibilities the Nyāya-Vaiśeṣika defined all objects as *padārthas*. These are substantive categories derived from a careful analysis of experience and thus form a metaphysical classification of all objects which can be given to knowledge. Like Aristotle, these philosophers were very conscious of the inseparable relation between a thing and its name. While classifying words, Aristotle also classifies things which are denoted by the words. For him substance is the *ens* while quantity, quality, relation, place, time, disposition, appurtenance, action and suffering are the predicables.[1] The Vaiśeṣika[2] philosopher gives a similar sevenfold classification of *padārthas* or categories. These are substance, *dravya*, quality, *guṇa*, activity, *karma*, generality, *sāmānya*, particularity, *viśeṣa*, inherence, *samavāya* and non-existence, *abhāva*.[3] Of these seven categories of *padārthas*, the first one, substance, *dravya*, lays the foundation for a realism. These substances are nine in number and are of varying shades of materiality. The definition of a substance is that it possesses action and attributes, and that it acts as a cause in combination with other categories. This implies that substance is the substratum of qualities and relations and is knowable. While substances are substrata of qualities and relations, these are not separable. Neither a substance, nor a quality is knowable without the other. The relation between them is a peculiar relation postulated by the system to account for the complete dependency of substance on quality and vice versa for them to become perceptible to us.

There are nine substances. These are earth, water, air, fire, ether, time, space, mind and soul. These nine substances and their characteristic qualities explain the whole of this universe. These substances exist in two forms: in their non-eternal divisible form, and in their eternal indivisible atomic form. One important diversion has to be made here. The Nyāya-Vaiśeṣika is a realist, but not a materialist in the sense in which the Cārvāka is a materialist. Normally a materialist is one who does not accept anything which is not material as ultimately real. If the Nyāya-Vaiśeṣika were to be classified merely as materialists then they could not accept mind and soul as real. On the other hand since they do accept the existence and perceivability of mind and

[1] Aristotle's Categories.

[2] We shall hereafter refer to this school as the Vaiśeṣika school for the metaphysical aspect is its contribution to the sincretist school.

[3] *Vai. Su.* I. 1. 15.

soul they have been classified as realists. We shall discuss the nature of these two substances later on, in the next section. All that is essential to point out here is that while the Nyāya-Vaiśeṣika are not gross materialists, they are realists of a sort. According to them materiality exists in different grades. Since they accept more than one thing as ultimately real, they are also designated as pluralistic realists.

The first four of these substances, earth, water, air and fire form one group. These do not refer to the things that are ordinarily experienced under these names, but to the super-sensible fine *paramāṇus* (atoms) of these substances which form the basis of their normal existence. These atomic subtrata, in combination, produce objects of experience like jars and tables. These four substances and *ākāśa* or ether are the *pañcamahābhūtas* (the five fundamental elemental substances) from which everything else comes into being. Each one of them possesses a peculiar quality, a *viśeṣa guṇa*, which is particular to that substance alone and and is not to be found elsewhere. Thus smell is the characteristic quality of earth, taste of water, colour of fire or light, touch of air and sound of *ākāśa*. Since these five qualities are also those by which a human being senses the world, the Nyāya-Vaiśeṣika believes that the respective sense-organs must be made up of these elemental substances. For example the sense of sight must be made up of light or fire particles for otherwise there could be no perception of colour; similarly the other sense-organs. The gross material substances are known as earth etc., not because they are purely made up of earth particles, but because their predominant component is earth substance. A word is necessary here to explain the substance *ākāśa,* usually translated as "ether". In the case of the other elemental substances both their qualities as well as the substances themselves are perceptible. But in the case of *ākāśa* only sound which is its quality is perceived. Usually the Vaiśeṣika prescribes two qualities for perceptibility. The object must have a perceptible dimension and a manifest colour. *Ākāśa* is neither limited nor coloured. Therefore it is argued that the existence of *ākāśa* as an all-pervading substance is inferred from the perception of the quality of the substance. Every substance must have a quality. Soundness is a quality which is not present in the other four substances. So it must belong to the fifth one, *ākāśa*, which is all-pervading. It is one of its kind. It is *sui-generis.*

Getting back to the first four substances of earth, water, air and fire, we are told that these exist in a two-fold form as atoms and as discrete objects which have their origin in the atoms. All objects of this world are combinations and complexes of these primary atoms. The notion of atoms or *paramāṇus* is very ancient in Indian thought. There are references to *paramāṇus* in the older Upaniṣads. However amongst the orthodox school the Vaiśeṣika was the first to formulate a viable theory of how these changeless, eternal particles come together to form the world of nature and experience it. However like Democritus and Leucippus of Greek philosophy, the Indian philosopher was interested in the atomic structure of substances only as a metaphysical explanation of reality rather than as a scientific theory. The process of arriving at the concept is an empirical and inferential process. All things in this universe are divisible. It is evident that such divisions cannot go on for ever. Since the objects of our experience are all wholes of parts, the ultimate parts which should be the primary basis of the wholes must be the atoms which are not further divisible. The Vaiśeṣika uses two words while referring to these particles. They are *aṇu* and *paramāṇu*. The former is a small particle but still a whole of parts. The latter is that which is no more divisible, invisible to the naked eye and eternal. By their very nature these ultimate particles or *paramāṇus* must be eternal. For, otherwise, all things of experience could tumble down any moment, being built on perishables. An important point to be noted about these *parāmāṇus* is that they were never created nor can they ever be destroyed. Of course this is implied when we say that these are eternal. However eternality can imply the idea that while they have a beginning they have no end. It is to avoid this confusion that the Vaiśeṣika maintains that the *paramāṇus* are neither created nor destructible. True to their pluralistic realism, the Vaiśeṣikas maintain that there are four different kinds of *paramāṇus* corresponding to the four fundamental elements. The atoms of the same substances are qualitatively similar while atoms of dissimilar substances are qualitatively dissimilar.

The Vaiśeṣikas do not favour the idea of Democritus that atoms can have only quantitative differences, nor do they agree that all qualitative variety is the outcome of quantitative arrangements. The reason for this is two-fold. First, quality is an inseparable aspect of substantiveness. The perceptibility of a substance is due to its inherent relation with quality. Secondly, to the Vaiśeṣikas all that is usually known as quantities such as size, number, weight are all qualities or *guṇas*. The Vaiśeṣika means by "qualitative", specially in this context, the particular qualities, *viśeṣa guṇas*, which are latent in the atomic form, but become patent as soon as combinations of atoms begin. The process of combination for the production of objects from these infinite and indivisible particles is as follows. The primary particles, *paramāṇus*, of the same substance first come together to form a binary, *dvyaṇuka*. Like the primary atoms these are also infinitely small and supersensible. Three such binaries again come together in a pattern of adjustment and are known as triads, *tryaṇukas*. These triads are the smallest visible particles. They are comparable, so the Vaiśeṣika maintains, to the smallest mote dancing in the sunbeam projected through an infinitesimal hole into a dark room. It is at the stage of the binaries that the qualities are produced in the object. As the combinations become bigger and more complicated, the various objects of this would arise. When destruction takes place, the same procedure is repeated in the same order. That is, first the binaries become separated and then the triads thus leading to a destruction of the object.

Bareidale Keith, a famous Indologist, maintains that the Vaiśeṣika atomic theory owes its origin to the influence of the Greek atomic theory. In support of his contention he cites the trade contacts that existed in the then known world.[1] Apart from the fact that such trade contacts are not sufficient evidence for the borrowing of ideas, the basic differences in the theories themselves do not support such a contention. As already stated the atoms of Democritus possess difference of size, weight, figure, and arrangement which are all quantitative differences. The Vaiśeṣika particles do not possess any such differences in the primary stage but develop specific qualities during the process of combination. Thus the earth atoms develop smell. However there is one common factor which is important. Both reject God as the creator of such atomic particles. The Greek philosopher makes his creation a matter of mechanical movement. He maintains that the atoms, being different in size, fall through space creating vortices between them, and these give rise to a further

[1] A. B. Keith, *Indian Logic and Atomism*, p. 17-18.

combination between them. The Vaiśeṣika, while not openly admitting a God, says that the moral law, *adṛṣṭa,* is as inexorable as a natural law, and causes the atoms to combine in the first instance. These and other minor internal differences do not permit us to accept the "borrowing" theory of Keith. Perhaps all that we can say is that when the human mind starts an enquiry into truth, it always develops on parallel lines, wherever it may be.

It is necessary to point out here one important aspect of Nyāya-Vaiśeṣika realism. They are not only realists but also rationalists. The world of objects is not only real, but also intelligible. An intellectual analysis based on logical principles is an adequate method to know reality. Intellectual analysis is defined as that knowledge which tells us which things exist and which do not exist, which are ultimate and which are not. The famous book of the Vaiśeṣikas known as *Padārthadharma-Saṁgraha* starts by maintaining that there is nothing *a priori* in such analysis. We have already said that that which is denoted by language is that which is the content of our knowledge. Hence the word *padārtha* denotes the category which is ultimately real.

In addition to the four substances that we have so far discussed there are others of which we should take note. Time (*kāla*), and space (*dik*) are realities. They are one in number, eternal and all-pervading. But space and time are inferable from our spatial and temporal cognitions. Cognitions involving the usage of referent words like "near" and "far", "present" and "future" are those which help us to infer the existence of these objects. There are two more substances, mind and soul, which would be discussed in the next section.

The categories or *padārthas* are seven of which we have so far discussed only the first one, *dravya* or substance. *Guṇa* or quality is the next on their list. A *guṇa* is defined as that which exists in a substance but in itself does not possess any quality or substance. It is that which determines the nature and character of a thing and not its existence. It is different from activity or *karma*, for it inheres in a thing and is passive. Such qualities according to the Vaiśeṣika are twenty-four in number. These are *rūpa* or colour, *rasa* or taste, *gandha* or smell, *sparśa* or touch, *śabda* or sound, *sāṁkhya* or number, *parimāna* or magnitude, *pṛthaktva* or distinctness, *sāṁyōga* or conjunction, *vibhāga* or disjunction, *paratva* or remoteness, *aparatva* or nearness, *buddhi* or cognition, *sukha* or happiness, *dukha* or unhappiness, *iccha* or desire, *dveṣa* or aversion, *prayatna* or effort, *gurutva* or heaviness, *dravatva* or fluidity, *sneha* or viscosity, *saṁskāra* or tendency, *dharma* or merit and *adharma* or demerit. That the enumeration and limitation of the qualities to these twenty-four is very arbitrary is evident. The purpose of these qualities is to state the fundamental fact that substance always exists along with qualities and that these are inseparable as one cannot be cognised without the other. These twenty-four *guṇas* were what the Vaiśeṣikas thought to be simplest and irreducible.

The next category is *karma* or action. It belongs to substance but is different from both substance and quality. All such actions can only be found in *mūrta dravyas* or corporeal substances such as earth, water, fire, air and mind. They cannot exist in all-pervasive substances like ether, time or space. This is so because action is the cause of conjunction and disjunction and these are possible only between discrete substances. Similarly it does not reside in time, space or soul which are incapable of motion. Motion is a form of action. So *karma* is also translated as motion. *Karma* or motion is an existent, having knowability and nameability. It exists because it is known and can be expressed by a word.

The next category accepted by the Nyāya-Vaiśeṣika school takes us away from concrete things like substances and qualities to more abstract realities. While they are abstract in nature they are not purely conceptual in existence. They have an ontological existence. *Sāmānya* or generality or universality is the first of them. That the notion of universal is essential for human knowledge and communication is evident. Such a universal is the objective basis of the notion of "commonness" of many particular, individual existents. While it is one, it exists in many individuals. Hence it produces the notion of inclusion and has an objective existence. It is the universal class-essence existing in many individuals. As such it does not cease to exist while it comes into existence in a newly born individual. It exists simultaneously and continuously in many individuals. When a perceived object is compared with a remembered one due to the revival of the remembered impression it is due to the recognition of a certain common character among them which inheres in all of them. This common character is the *sāmānya*. It is different from the particular which forms its substratum. The particulars are responsible for a discriminative cognition while a universal gives rise to an assimilative cognition. Nyāya-Vaiśeṣikas have differentiated between an accidental universality and a natural universality. Commonness arising out of language, race, and religion is only accidental whereas man-ness is a natural universal existing in all men irrespective of any accidental universals.

We have seen how the Buddhist does not accept the reality of universals. The Nyāya-Vaiśeṣikas criticise the Buddhist view on the following lines. If the universal were not a perceived existent, then each individual would be perceived as different. A cow is perceived as a cow and not as a horse and in addition, all individual cows are perceived to be alike. Thus universality helps not only in the perception of things in which it resides, but also to distinguish them from others which are different from them. The Buddhist realists regard such universality as a characteristic of cognitions, while the Nyāya-Vaiśeṣikas regard it as characteristic of objects.

The name of the system "Vaiśeṣika" is derived from the term *viśeṣa*, particularity, which is recognised as a category by this system. None of the other systems recognise this as a category. *Viśeṣa* or particularity is the distinguishing characteristic feature of eternal substances and is a unique contribution of the system. These eternal substances, as already pointed out, are the atoms of earth, water, fire, air, ether, time, space, self and mind. Not only is it necessary to distinguish one kind of atom from another, but also one atom from another of its own kind. That is, they are self-distinguishing. This character of being self-distinguishing is due to the presence of *viśeṣa*. Hence *viśeṣas* are many and as countless as there are atoms. One thing to be noted here is that this particularity has no generality of its own. The particularity is one which resides only in eternal substances and is different from differences which exist in composite groups of things. The existence of a particularity is inferred from the ultimate distinction of eternal substances. Without the existence of particularities, they would be indistinguishable from one another. The next category which is a unique contribution of the system and which is also an intellectual category is that of *samavāya* or inherent relation. While all other relations such as conjunction and disjunction are brought under qualities, the relation of inherence alone is treated as a separate category. This is an inseparable relation between two entities neither of which can ever exist by itself. For example, a whole cannot exist apart from its parts. A quality cannot exist apart from its substance. We shall have occasion to revert to this discussion of *samavāya* while we discuss later the causal theory of the Nyaya-Vaiśeṣika school.

Non-existence or *abhāva* is yet another category postulated by this school of pluralistic realism. This category is explained from four points of view. Being a system which believes in the creation of new things, it is necessary to state that a thing was non-existent before it came into being and similarly it is non-existent after it is destroyed. If there were no mutual non-existence then there can be no distinct things. Unless we say that being a cow excludes being a horse and vice-versa, it is not possible to have any knowledge of things. There are eternal things such as atoms, mind and soul which are absolutely not their products. That is there is absolute non-existence of all products. Thus we have the four ways of expressing non-existence. Such negation is known in the first instance by perception and secondly by inference. The perception of the negation of a jar depends upon the perception of its counter-entity, the presence of the jar itself. The non-existence of fire is inferred from the non-existence of smoke. Thus non-existence is perceived as a counter-entity and inferred as a correlate.

While it is not possible to find exact parallels for these categories in Western philosophy, we can say that these ideas have been present in some form or other from medieval times. The argument about the existence or non-existence of the universal is present throughout the history of philosophy in the West in some form or other. Such discussions always include within their scope the nature of the particular as well. The discussion about the impossibility of pure negation involved the discussion of the possibility of negation itself by Spinoza. The treatment of non-existence or negation by modern existential thinkers is well-known.

The Mimāṁsa school is one of realism like the Nyāya-Vaiśeṣika school. Both believe in the plurality of the real. They believe in the existence of permanent *dravyas* or substances which are the basic substrata of changing modes. The substance alone endures while its changing modes may take very many forms. Such substances are many.

The change that is characteristic of reality is never-ending. Hence it has no beginning. This idea implies that as the universe of things has no beginning, there is also no creator for it. The Bhaṭṭa Mīmāṁsika, a school of Mīmāṁsa says, "There was never a time when the universe was seen to be different from what it is now."[1] Although substance as such is static, self-evolving is its characteristic.

Of the two schools of Mīmāṁsa, the Bhāṭṭa school is close to the Nyāya-Vaiśeṣika school as they also accept the nine substances accepted by the Nyāya-Vaiśeṣikas. All categories are divided into two; those which are positive, *bhāva*, and those which are negative, *abhāva*. The latter are similar to the four aspects of *abhāva* or non-existence, accepted by the Nyāya-Vaiśeṣika school. There are prior, posterior, mutual and absolute non-existences. The positive categories are also similar to the Nyāya-Vaiśeṣika categories and they are substance, quality, action and generality. Of these we shall discuss substances and some of their characteristics. The Bhaṭṭa school accepts all the nine substances accepted by the Nyāya-Vaiśeṣikas namely, earth, water, air, fire, ether, time, space, self and mind. They add to this list two more substances which are darkness and sound. While the monistic philosophers of Greece tended to make one of these substances the ultimate, these Indian realists conceived reality not only as substantive but also as pluralistic. Just as Aristotle conceived fire, air, water and earth as four important substances having their own location and movement so also both the Nyāya-Vaiśeṣikas and the Mīmāṁsikas considered the substances as being separate entities having their own characteristic qualities. Again, like in Aristotelianism, all concrete objects of this world are combinations of various degrees of these and other elements.

For both the schools of Mīmāṁsika and Nyāya-Vaiśeṣika one important factor which determines what is to be considered as substantive is that such a substance must be perceivable. Thus while the Nyāya-Vaiśeṣika considered *tamas* or darkness as absence of light, the Mīmāṁsika gives it a special status of substantiveness, because it is perceivable. Sound or *śabda* belongs to the category

[1] Na kadacit anidsam jagat.

of substance for the same reason. But it has no substratum and is perceived directly by the organ of hearing. To the Nyāya-Vaiśeṣikas sound is a quality of ether and is perceived directly. The Mīmāṁsika is interested in maintaining that sound is eternal and is only manifested by the manifesting organ, the vocal chords. The reason for this we shall see in the next chapter where we discuss sound or *śabda* as a means of knowledge or *pramāṇa*.

The other school of Mīmāṁsa, the Prābhākara Mīmāṁsa recognises only eight categories. According to this school as well as the Bhaṭṭa Mīmāṁsikas the existence of external reality is an undeniable fact, for it is the foundation of all experiences in life. If there were only ideas, they would be meaningless as there would be nothing to which they could be correlated to fix their meaning. Thus the Prābhākaras accept eight categories of substance; quality, action, generality, inherence, force, similarity and number. The first three are explained on similar lines as the Nyāya-Vaiśeṣikas do. Generality or *sāmānya* is not inferable as the Nyāya-Vaiśeṣikas maintain but it is perceived in each individual along with its individuality.

Sāmavāya or inherence is also known as subsistence or *paratantratā*. It is a relation between two entities which are inseparable. But this relation is only inferable and not perceptible. Like all realists, the Mīmāṁsika had to explain why the causal relation is a necessary relation. The necessity of this cannot be explained on an empirical basis unless the necessity is reduced to one of associationism between cause and effect as Hume had done. Even then this associationism must follow a pattern invariably. Faced with this problem the Prābhākara Mīmāṁsika says that there is a potency or *śakti* in the cause which is responsible for the production of the effect. This is an imperceptible energy by virtue of whose presence the substances produce effects. Nothing much is said about the other two categories: similarity or *sādṛsya*, and number, *saṁkhyā*.

Thus we come to general conclusion that the systems of Nyāya-Vaiśeṣika and Mīmāṁsa are pluralistic realisms. Their realism is not mainly a materialistic realism like that of the Cārvākas. They believe that even categories like universality and relations are real, thus making them rationalists rather than realists.

Dualisms

There are two important and well-known schools of Indian philosophy which are dualistic in their assessment of reality. These are the Jaina and the Sāṁkhya systems. The school of Jainism belongs to the heterodox branch which had forsworn Vedic testimony while Sāṁkhya accepts the Veda as a *pramāṇa* or as a source of authoritative valid knowledge. Let us study the Jaina system first.

Jainism brings all reality under two categories, the conscious, *jīva* and the unconscious, *ajīva* and maintains that each can be understood only when it is contrasted with the other. The subject which is consciousness must be opposed to an unconscious object for it to function as subject. These two, subject and object are dichotomously related terms each depending on the other for its meaningful existence. The category of the unconscious substance, *ajīva* is again divided into two main classes, those which have form, *rūpa* and those which do not possess form, *arūpa*. The substance with form is matter, *pudgala,* and the formless substances are space, time, movement and stability.[1] They are essentially different from *jīva* in that they lack life and consciousness. *Pudgala* or matter possesses the qualities of colour, smell, taste and touch. Sound is not a quality but a mode of *pudgala*. It is *pudgala pariṇāma*. *Pudgala* is in the form of atoms primarily and all things in the world are the result of the combinations of these atoms. These are eternal and are supposed to be the bodies for souls. Such atoms have neither a beginning nor an end. They are supersensible and formless in their original state. However they have weight, because we find that some of them fall downwards and some travel upwards. These atoms combine to produce the world of objects because they are subject to the power of movement and stability provided by space in which they exist. This causes them to be attracted towards each other and thus combinations are born.

Umāsvati, a famous Jaina philosopher, defines substance as that which is characterised by birth, death and persistence.[2] This does not mean that substance is created and destroyed. It only means that while in its atomic form it is eternal, its modifications

[1] The Saṁskrit words used for the latter two are *dharma* and *adharma*. But they do not mean "merit" and "demerit" as in orthodox schools.

[2] *Tatt. Su.*, V. 29.

in the form of the objects of this world come into being, persist for a while and then change into another modification. These modes are called *paryāyas.* This idea of reality as always changing is something like the Buddhist idea, but it is not the same. For the latter there is no constant element like the atoms underlying the change. To the Jaina, reality is one-in-many. There is always unity in diversity. This is the result of human experience. We can never postulate anything that is in opposition or contradictory to experience.

It is a very important fact to notice that the term *dravya* or substance is used to denote both *jīva* and *ajīva*. One is a conscious substance while the other is an unconscious substance. We shall discuss *jīva* later, more fully. Of the other *ajīvas*, time or *kāla* is infinite. It exists in the form of two cycles. Each cycle is an era and is a complement to the other. While in the *avasarpiṇī* stage or descending stage, all morality and virtue are downgraded gradually, in the *utsarpiṇi* stage which is the opposite the reverse process in regard to the moral life of the people takes place. Like a wheel, these two eras go on moving and changing one into another. Space is also conceived in two parts, one where movement is possible. Since *dharma* and *adharma* are the principles of motion and stability these are always to be found in that portion of space where movement is possible.

All these *dravyas* including *jīva* and excluding *kāla* are also known as *astikayas.* The word means that they exist, *asti*, and are to be found with the constituent parts, *kayas.* In the whole of this universe there is something enduring which we come to know through its changes as given in our experience. While this is permanent and eternal the forms it assumes come into being and are perishable. Thus for Jainism both permanence and change are equally real. Matter exists in two forms. One the simple, eternal atomic form which is Being and the other the complex, perishable form manifested in all perceivable objects. The latter are known as *skandhas.*

It is from this metaphysical basis of reality that the Jainas derive their theory of *syādvāda* which is their most significant contribution to Indian philosophy. The basic tolerance exhibited by their philosophy to the contradictory theories of Being and Becoming and the most effortless manner in which they had reconciled these two contradictions in their theory of *syādvāda* is really amazing.

The word is made up of two different words, namely *syāt* and *vāda.* The first word *syāt* is the potential mood of the Saṁskrit word *as* which means "to be". When it is expressed in its potential form, "to be" becomes "may be". Hence the meaning of the whole is "may-be theory". The significance of this view is that we can never say dogmatically that the nature of Reality is either totally Being as the Upaniṣads say or that it is only Becoming as the early Buddhists maintained. Such dogmatic assertions are meaningless according to Jaina seers, for the world of experience tells us that reality exhibits both the characteristics. All affirmative propositions being only partial views lead to dogmatic metaphysics and hence are erroneous. They illustrate this by the story of the elephant and the blind men. Each man touched one part of the elephant and went away with the conception that that part alone constituted the whole elephant. Thus the Jainas point out that statements of absolute negation and absolute affirmation, give us only partial truth and never the whole. While every statement gives us a partial truth, no statement can give us once and for all the true nature of reality. However, we can come to know the multifaceted nature of reality by expressing it in different statements each of which conveys a partial truth. These statements, taking into consideration the various possibilities, are seven in number and are known as *saptabhangī naya*, the seven-fold statements or judgments. These are:

1) Maybe is — *syat asti*
2) Maybe is not — *syat nāsti*
3) Maybe is, and is not — *syat asti nāsti*
4) Maybe inexpressible — *syat avaktavyaḥ*
5) Maybe is, and yet inexpresssible — *syat asti ca avaktavyaḥ*
6) Maybe is not and is inexpressible— *syat nāsti ca, avaktavyaḥ*
7) Maybe is, is not and is inexpressible — *syat asti cā, nāsti ca, avaktavyaḥ.*

All these seven statements can be illustrated by taking any one object. The object may exist as A and not as B. The particles of earth may now exist in the form of a cup and later on, on some other occasion they may come into existence as a saucer. The particular form of its existence is therefore true only in a limited sense. The object thus can be characterised as both "is" and "is not" in successive stages. But when the same idea is expressed in a simultaneous manner with reference to the same object there is an obvious subversion of the fundamental law of thought, namely the law of contradiction. Thus in the fourth step it is maintained that reality, from any one standpoint is inexpressible. The other steps follow from this. What Jainism is intent on driving home is that there is no enduring self-identity in things as commonly assumed. The permanence in reality is due to the existence of eternal atoms and the changing things or *skandhas* come into being and perish. Their dualism consists in the recognition that the *jīva dravya* or soul substance is different from the *ajīva dravyas* or non-soul substances. The former is characterised by consciousness whereas the latter does not possess either life or consciousness. We shall discuss the nature of *jīva* later.

The Sāṁkhya dualism enjoys a great deal of popularity. Its popularity is perhaps due to the fact that it is more acceptable to the normal human being to think that matter is different from soul or spirit and that each cannot be reduced to the other though both co-exist. If soul were considered to be material, then the factors of willing and feeling remain unexplained. If matter were to be explained as consciousness then human experience, which does not find material things possessing consciousness becomes erroneous and can no more serve as the measuring rod for arriving at the truth. Therefore Sāṁkhya philosophy is accepted as basic by many philosophers, the most important of them being Viśiṣṭādvaita. Like Descartes the Sāṁkhya philosopher also believes that all reality can be divided into two fundamental categories, *Puruṣa,* the spirit and *Prakṛti*, the matter. Both these are fundamental realities and are the uncaused causes of the whole universe of nature and living things including man. A very important point that must be noted even at this stage of discussion is that *Prakṛti*, though translated as matter or substance, is not really that matter or substance which is in time and space. Time and space are evolutes of *Prakṛti.* Such a *Prakṛti* is also not material in the sense in which the Nyāya-Vaiśeṣika uses the term, namely atomic reality nor is it a spiritual substance as the Jainas believe. *Prakṛti* is substantive, unconscious and non-spiritual. *Puruṣa* alone is the conscious non-substantive spirit.

The *Sāṁkhya Kārika*, a very early commentary on Sāṁkhya aphorisms enumerates the following arguments for the acceptance of *Prakṛti* as source-matter.[1]

[1] *Saṁ. Kar.*, S. S. Suryanarayana Sastry's trans., verses 15 & 16.

1. All the objects of this universe possess certain common characteristics, thus indicating a common source. The Sāṁkhya system maintains that no element is so completely different from the other as to exclude a common source.

2. The process of evolution of things including life indicates an active principle which manifests itself in the process but is not exhausted by any one of its stages while it is immanent in all its stages.

3. All things of our experience are limited and finite. That which is so finite cannot give rise to the infinity which is the universe. The finite is itself dependent on something which is other than itself and thus cannot be the source of evolution.

4. The effect must be different from the cause as otherwise the principle of causality becomes meaningless. As such the world of objects, as an effect, cannot be its own cause.

5. The obvious unity exhibited through varying degrees of similarity suggests a single cause of this universe.

The above arguments of the Sāṁkhya philosopher to establish *Prakṛti* as the sole material cause of this universe resembles the usual arguments given by most materialist philosophers. But to the Sāṁkhya philosopher, *Prakṛti* is not simple matter, substantive in nature and possessing the potentiality to have qualities. On the other hand, the Sāṁkhyas emphasise the idealistic aspect of evolution rather than postulate a material source for it. If by materialism we mean that reality exhibits the characteristics opposite to that of teleology, that it is non-supra-sensuous, and that it is corporeal, then the *Prakṛti* of the Sāṁkhyas is non-materialistic. *Prakṛti* evolves for the purpose of liberating the *Puruṣa* from its bondage. Its evolutes are not only the material elements, but also the psychic elements. To the extent that *Prakṛti*, by itself is unconscious though its actions reveal a purpose, we may characterise *Prakṛti* as material in a very wide sense.

Prakṛti is the primordial cause and this universe is merely a transformation of this cause into its various effects. Thus there is envisaged a continuity from the lowest to the highest evolute and from the beginning till the end. The cause, *Prakṛti* cannot be less real than the world of objects, its effect. As Descartes said, the ultimate cause must contain within itself, all the reality, values, and purposes that are exhibited by the effects.

A difficulty about considering *Prakṛti* as the final cause is usually said to be the non-perceptibility of *Prakṛti* itself while its products possess the new quality of being perceptible. To the Sāṁkhya this is not a momentous objection. In the first instance perception can be no criterion for the existence of things, since we cannot perceive things which are either too near or too far away from our sense organ of sight. Then if the organs of sensation are defective, perceptible knowledge cannot arise. The *Sāṁkhya Kārika* says that the fineness of *Prakṛti* makes it supersensible and not nonperceptible.

Such a *Prakṛti* is a constituent of three *guṇas.* This word *guṇa* has two different meanings in Saṁskrit. It means a strand, a rope and it also means a quality and a characteristic. The former meaning is what we have to take here, for the latter meaning makes *Prakṛti* a quality residing in a substance and this is not acceptable to the Sāṁkhya philosopher. These *guṇas* are strands whose complex is *Prakṛti.* They are three in number, namely *sattva*, *rajas* and *tamas. Sattva* is potential consciousness and pure existence alone. When consciousness is made manifest it produces pleasure. The root *sat* means existence. It also means goodness, happiness, light and white colour. *Rajas* is that which indicates energy, activity, movement, force, and in terms of human beings, feverish enjoyment, sorrow, suffering, restlessness. It is supposed to be red in colour indicating brightness and ceaseless restlessness. The third *guṇa* is *tamas.* It is the inertia which dampens all activity giving rise to a sort of apathy leading to lazy tolerance. It is ignorance or lack of understanding, lack of energy and it is said to be dark in colour.

These three *guṇas* are never separate. *Prakṛti* is not something in which these *guṇas* subsist. These *guṇas* are themselves *Prakṛti.* They are like the strands of a rope. The strands by themselves are not the rope and the rope is a whole of these parts. It is the relation of inter-twining between the strands that gives us the rope. The rope is not different from the strands and yet in a way it is different. The origin of such a conception of *Prakṛti* is evidently based on an empirical and psychological analysis of experience. The three qualities represented by the three *guṇas* are to be found in all objects of empirical experience. Evolution itself is possible only when these three qualities representing equipoise, action and resistance come into a clash and get resolved. At no time are these *guṇas* conceived as existent exclusive of one another. They are either dominant or recessive.

Prior to the starting of evolution these three *guṇas* exist in a state of equilibrium. It is a state of rest. But actually it is not a state of rest at all. The Sāṁkhya philosophers believed that if there is a cessation of motion at any one time, then it would be difficult to conceive its reappearance at another time. So even in the supposed state of rest, while there is no change into the diversity of modes, there is, however, a change involving production and reproduction of itself, thus maintaining the principle of perpetual motion as a necessary ingredient of reality. The stage of internal motion is known as dissolution whereas the stage of external modal change is known as evolution. The external modality is the result of the influence and presence of an alien principle which is *Puruṣa* according to the Sāṁkhyas. *Prakṛti* starts the process of evolution automatically when the presence of the conscious principle *Puruṣa* is felt. Such a presence is said to upset the balance of the *guṇas* and the imbalance so produced starts off the course of evolution. Thus the things of this world are only produced but never created. Production is the manifestation of the basic *Prakṛti* in its different models. The variety and multiplicity of this world is accounted for, in the first instance, by the interaction of the *guṇas* themselves, and secondly their nature is accounted for by the predominance of one or the other of the *guṇas*. The *guṇas* are mentioned separately not to emphasise their exclusiveness so much as to emphasise the predominant aspect of any product. All the *guṇas* are always present in all things. But only one is more predominant than the other two in any given product. Such a product may be either a physical or a mental object.

Thus the Sāṁkhya philosopher deduces the being of *Prakṛti* from rational grounds. An analysis of all that we have said in the foregoing paragraphs reveals two important principles based on which this deduction is made. The first of these principles echoes the dictum of Aristotle which says that something cannot come out of nothing. The implication of the acceptance of this principle is the postulation of the theory that cause and effect are only the latent and the patent forms of the same substance. Thus causation, being incapable of giving rise to anything new, only presents the primordial matter in different or newer forms. The second principle which helps in the deduction of *Prakṛti* is that the finite implies always the infinite. The "finite" has a special meaning to the Sāṁkhya philosopher. It means not only that which is limited but also something which is not self-sustaining. The process of evolution reveals that the species is limited in the sense that it is dependent on a more pervasive, wider genus. We can go on enlarging this backwards till we come to one final self-sufficient and all-pervasive *Prakṛti.*

After thus establishing the existence of *Prakṛti* and defining its nature, a scheme of evolution is outlined by the system. Such an evolution is envisaged at two levels, one the primary and the other the secondary level. The first evolution concerns itself with the evolving of the twenty-four primary principles or *tattvas.* These are the physical and the psychical elements out of which the whole of this universe evolves. Of these the first evolute is *mahat,* the great. Its synonym is *buddhi.* Since evolution starts due to the disturbance in the balance of the *guṇas* this first evolute indicates the predominance of *sattva guṇa.* This is a very expansive, homogenous, single entity which is the basis for all physical and psychical elements in their cosmic aspect. Its synonym *buddhi* refers to the psychological aspect of the same intelligence appertaining to each individual. Such an evolution of both physical and psychical elements from a non-physical matrix like *Prakṛti* may appear contradictory. But when we remember that evolution starts only when the cosmic intelligence *Puruṣa* becomes reflected in the cosmic matter *Prakṛti* and that all products of evolution share both these characteristics, this contradiction will get resolved. This *mahat* or *buddhi* is not the incorporeal *Puruṣa* who is pure consciousness and intelligence. In its non-material aspect it is that universal capacity by means of which we distinguish between objects. It is that subtle substance without which no mental activity is possible.

We have stated that evolution starts due to the disturbance caused in the balance between the *guṇas* by the proximity of *Puruṣa.* This must be explained a little more. While *Prakṛti* is the non-intelligent and unconscious substantive matrix, *Puruṣa* is the conscious intelligence. In *Prakṛti* there is the *sattva guṇa* which has been described as fine matter, of the nature of light, etc. This *sattva guṇa* becomes predominant in the first stage of evolution for it is capable of reflecting the intelligence and consciousness that is *Puruṣa.* For such a reflection to take place, the Sāṁkhya philosopher maintains that the mere presence of *Puruṣa*, *sānnidhya mātra*, is enough. We shall come back to the evaluation of this relation and its consequential evolutionary processes a little later, after giving the whole process first.

The second evolute is egoity, *ahaṁkāra.* This is the sense of individuality. There is also a dual reference here. There can be no sense of individuality unless the sense of "otherness" is also present. The Self of man cannot be conceived as separate and its individuality cannot be established unless it is contrasted with the non-self, the object. The potentiality for such egoistic individuality on the psychical side and the development of the objective individuation on the physical side is implied by this evolute, *ahaṁkāra.* This evolute is more circumscribed and limited than the first one, *mahat.*

From here the development of two parallel series is conceived. One is the specifically psychical and the other is the specifically physical. Thus far the *sattva guṇa* has been the predominant factor. Now the next two also become active. When *sattva* and *rajas* combine suppressing the *tamas* principle, the psychic aspects of existence start evolving. Similarly when *rajas* cooperates with *tamas* suppressing *sattva*, the physical aspect starts evolving. The psychical series starts with the coming into being of *manas* or mind and proceeds towards the evolution of the five sensory organs of knowledge, *jñānendriyas* and the five organs of action, *karmendriyas.* All these are due to the dominance of one *guṇa* or other, while the rest of the *guṇas* are subservient.

It is necessary at this stage to pause a little to consider the fact that all the systems so far considered maintain that the mind is either materialistic or an evolute of matter. This seems to be a common idea accepted by all the schools. At the same time it is not gross substance. It is super-sensible matter and is of the nature of energy, light, and purity. Being *sāttvik* in nature and supported by *rājasa guṇa* it is capable of very quick movements. This factor helps it in its activity of perceiving objects. But, at the same time, we should also not forget that according to Sāṁkhya, all these evolutes denote essences and not objective factors of existence. This is significant from the human point of view. Intellect or *buddhi* is necessary before any individualism or egocentricism can develop. With the birth of ideas of "mine" and "thine" the concept of "mind" is born. Mind is, as it were, the door-keeper, while the sensations may be considered as doorways.[1] The existence of sensations of perception, implies the existence of a co-ordinating mind. Apparently the Sāṁkhya philosopher was motivated to postulate this scheme of evolution on an analogy with empirical activity by his observation of the latter. In deliberate action, thought comes first and action next. Thus the postulation of the instruments of these two activities are also made out on parallel lines. The organs of action are the hands, feet, tongue and those of evacuation and reproduction. The functioning of these, at one time or another, has to be directed and organized by the thinking capacity, the mind. The sensations imply that the mind is the organiser and also that the specific functional needs are fulfilled by these motor organs. These sensations, we must remember, are not the finite sense-organs. But these are their generic natures, and their capacities. It is out of a combination of all these that later secondary human psychic organs including the mind are evolved.

After this we have the evolution of the external or objective elements. These are derived from the human point of view and named after the human perceptions like the sound-essence, *śabda-tanmātra*, touch-essence, *sparśa-tanmātra* etc. The word "essence" or *tanmātra* means the most necessary factor which still can be defined and characterised as possessing that particular characteristic by which we ordinarily know it. It was recognised as early as when the *Sāṁkhya Sūtras* postulated that the human being's relations with the external world is normally limited to sense-perceptions. Thus only such elemental essences, *tanmātras*, which are the potential objects of sense-perceptions, can be the first objective evolutes. From these essences the later infinite and still supersensible elements, *bhūtādi*, are evolved. The whole of the universe is the result of the permutations and combinations of these elemental substances. The whole series of evolutes starting from *Prakṛti*, number twenty-four. The first one is *Prakṛti* which is only the cause and is not caused by anything else. All

[1] This idea is from *Sam. Pr. Bh.* Garbe's trans., verse 27.

the other twenty-three are both causes and effects. For those higher than themselves they are effects while for those lower, they are the causes. All these twenty-three are limited in magnitude. Each evolute is finer and purer than the one succeeding it. At the same time, there is nothing new that comes into existence. Evolution is merely the manifestation or unfolding of what is already there in a latent form. The sum total of *Prakṛti* is neither increased nor decreased by the process of evolution taking place within it. The whole of evolution can be schematically shown as follows.

1. *Prakṛti*
2. *Mahat* (*buddhi*)
3. *Ahaṁkāra*

4. *Manas* | *Five sense-organs* (5—9) | *Five motor organs* (10—14) | *Five tanmātras* (15—19) → *Five bhūtas.* (20—24)

The five *bhūtas* emerge as follows. *Śabda-tanmātra* or sound-essence emerges as *akāśa*, ether, with sound as its quality. From the combination of *śabda* and *sparśa tanmātras* we get air with its quality of touch and its capacity to convey sound. When the *rūpa-tanmātra* joins with these two we have fire or light with the three qualities of sound, touch and colour. The *rasa-tanmātra* when conjoined with the above three produces water with the four qualities of sound, touch, colour and taste. Lastly *gandha-tanmātra* along with the other four produces earth which has all the five qualities of sound, touch, colour, taste and smell. All these elements exist both in the form of discrete particles known as *paramāṇus* and of their universal essences. It is when these atoms combine that the whole universe of objects comes into being.

The whole scheme of Sāṁkhya evolution depends on two fundamental principles. One, which we have already mentioned is that nothing is ever created anew. Whatever exists must have already existed in the form of its cause prior to its becoming manifested as effect. Another name for *Prakṛti* is *Pradhāna* which means exactly this. It is that which is the first or is something which is presupposed. The second postulate is also something which we have already mentioned. That is the finite always implies the infinite. To be able to think of an infinite, the finite must be given. As Kant says, the human mind can imagine infinity in numbers only when he is aware of the finite series of numbers. The finite transcends itself into the infinite as Hegel would put it. This is all the more so when we recall that for the Sāṁkhya philosopher what is finite is not that which is limited by time and space, but that which cannot sustain itself. Each finite thing indicates something higher than itself which sustains it and by which it is sustained.

Inspite of all the above arguments which give a sort of validity to the Sāṁkhya theory of evolution, it becomes difficult to find any rationale behind it. That it is based on observances of human nature and activity and that it is this element of analogical anthropomorphism that has suggested the whole scheme is evident. But the order of psychological awareness need not be the order of metaphysical reality unless the subject as consciousness is conceived as the supreme one. Hence we find the Sāṁkhya philosophers getting into the difficult situation of not only accepting the one supreme *Puruṣa*, but also forced to accept the individual *Puruṣas* by the very logic of their theory of evolution. Otherwise the chronological succession of the evolution of intellect, egocentricism and mind become inexplicable.

A criticism of the Sāṁkhya evolution has to be taken still further back. The whole of it is suggestive of teleology. The conscious principle *Puruṣa* is reflected in the *sattva guṇa* of *Prakṛti*. This reflection triggers off the process of evolution. When there is dissolution, the *Puruṣa* becomes disentangled from this process and regains his purity of existence. In terms of individual subjects, the very aim of life is to achieve such disentanglement. This is the metaphysical aim. This aim seems to have become confused with a psychological analysis of human activity leading to the postulation of an analogical evolutionary process. It seems that a teleological aim is purposely superimposed on a natural evolutionary process.

But such teleology does not follow from the definition of *Prakṛti* and *Puruṣa*. *Prakṛti* being unconscious is completely mechanistic and incapable of teleological activities. *Puruṣa*, being conscious, is capable only of teleological activities. But the consciousness of *Puruṣa* is a non-active consciousness. So no activity at all, whether it is teleological or mechanical is possible to *Puruṣa* by itself. But *Prakṛti* is unconscious; so cannot evince any purpose, for unconscious purposiveness is a contradiction in terms. Thus it is difficult to account for the existence of teleology in this system if we consider the nature of their two fundamental realities only.

The Sāṁkhya thinker is aware that without a mover, who is himself not moving, the process of evolution is impossible. It is usually said that *Prakṛti* is blind and requires the guidance of *Puruṣa* to work out its manifold acts of production. The guidance of *Puruṣa* is merely mechanical, since no volition but mere proximity is involved. Thus the *Puruṣa* of the Sāṁkhya is comparable here unmoved Mover of Aristotle but with an element of purpose thrown in. The Sāṁkhya is admittedly an atheist doctrine, for in it the *Puruṣa* is not God transcending the activity of *Prakṛti*. *Puruṣa* is as much incomplete and inactive as *Prakṛti* and requires the activities of *Prakṛti* for its freedom and existence.

Monisms or Idealisms

So far we have examined pluralistic and dualistic explanations of reality given by some classical Indian philosophers. In this section we shall go a step further in our analysis of the nature of substance and consider some monistic and idealistic interpretations. We shall again start with the non-orthodox school of Buddhism. We have already seen how Hīnayāna Buddhism gave a realist interpretation of the nature of substance. All such realisms have to answer the fundamental epistemological question of how a knowledge of such an external real is possible. The only means of explaining any perceptual confrontation between the subject and the object is by using the means of the sensations. Unfortunately such an explanation leads to further difficulties. If we depend on our senses alone for a knowledge of reality then the existence of such a reality depends upon our sense-perception. In other words one can easily be reduced to the position of Berkeley who maintained that "*Esse erst percipii*".

Hence from an epistemological standpoint the logical conclusion of a realist metaphysics is subjective idealism. This is the position taken by the Yogācāra school of Buddhism. If ideas need a cause for their existence, then such a cause need not necessarily be external. Like Berkeley the Yogācāra also had to establish that there need be no unknown absolute matter which acts as the cause for the ideas and he also tried to show that matter itself is merely an idea of the mind. Berkeley's criticism of the primary and secondary qualities is very well known. Like him the Yogācārin also maintains that substance as the bearer of these qualities is an illogical postulation. This they do by arguing that both the externality and the substantiality of a substance as the source of our ideas is unwarranted. The other idealist school of Buddhism, the Mādhyamika school leads to a nihilistic explanation. While the Yogācāra maintains that consciousness alone is real, the Mādhyamika denies even that.

By criticising the representative realism of the Sountrāntika and the Vaibhāṣika, which we have already discussed, the Yogācāra postulates his theory. He is known also as the Vijñānavadin which name emphasises the metaphysical theory of the school. However unlike the Berkeleyan subjectivists, the Vijñānavadin holds that neither the subject nor the object is real. But only knowledge is real. All that one is aware of is neither the subject nor the object, but only a stream of ideas which are momentary. The specific nature of the cognition or the idea is not due to any external stimulation but due to the impressions of past experience, *vāsanas*. Each *vāsana* goes back for its formation to a prior one thus going back endlessly. It is an undeniable fact that the knowing subject realises its identity as an existent only when it is opposed to the known object. Similarly it is the subject whose consciousness bestows on the object its identity of existence. Therefore the whole of the subject and the object do not obtain their identity because of their own opposition in the knowledge situation; such knowledge of identity is the result of a continually changing pattern,, each taking its clue from the previous one. Yet for all these imaginary entities, there must be some substratum. This is said to be a stream of consciousness, *ālaya vijñāna*. Each personal consciousness is but a part of this *ālaya vijñāna*.

The Vijñānavādin rests his presuppositions on certain arguments. The most obvious one is that of dream analogy. In dreams there are no objects corresponding to experiences. There is only an appearance of externality. Similarly in waking empirical experience what is really a cognition appears to be an external object. Next the Yogācāra argues that there is always an invariable concomittance, *sahopalambaniyama,* between the cognition and its content. At no time do we have things without thoughts. Therefore there is no need to complicate matters by separating them and maintaining that things are different from thoughts. They may as well be considered as different aspects of one and the same stream of consciousness. Lastly the very argument used by realists to emphasise the reality of the object is turned against them. Objects are seen to impress different people differently. Therefore the objects have to be independent of the impressions caused by them in the knowing subject—so argues the realist. The Yogācārin counters the argument by saying that since the fact of different impressions is indubitable, they cannot be caused by an identical object having a separate existence. Hence all knowledge is self-caused and self-validated. While the positive contribution of this argument is almost ridiculous, the negative logic of it seems to be indisputable. The indemonstrability of the realist position is made apparent by this argument. The Vijñānavādin also gives a polemical argument. Granting that the object exists, it cannot be known directly without its qualities. He pursues the problem, "Does the external object apprehended by us arise from any existence or not? It does not arise from an existence, for that which is generated has no permanence; nor does it not arise from an existence, for what has not come into being has no existence."[1] Again if matter is a whole of parts, then the question is which of them are cognised as object, the whole or the parts? If matter is atomic then it is not perceivable for atoms are supersensible.

Thus while the Vijñānavādin admits of psychological distinctions between subject and object, he denies all metaphysical reality to such distinctions. The Yogācāra subjectivism is open to all the usual criticisms that are offered against subjective idealism. Being a subjectivist, there can be no possibility of knowing anything that is trans-subjective. To be so completely satisfied by one's own subjective knowledge is not a true account of experience. Fichte went a step further and said that all finite

[1] *Sar. Sam.*, p. 24.

selves are the products of one eternal principle which forms the core or essence of each individual mentality. Thus there is a striking resemblance between the Vijñānavāda and Fichtean ego-centricism.

The Mādhyamika Buddhist carries this argument of the Vijñānavādin to its logical conclusion. Generally, in the west, all Buddhism is associated with nihilism. This is only true of the Mādhyamika Buddhist. It is also known as *śūnya vāda* and is the most well-known of Buddhist schools. Nāgārjuna the founder of this school is one of the world's most astute dialectitians. His logical acumen was so great that later schools of philosophy like the Navya Nyāya school and the school of Advaita derived much of their argumentative form from the methodology of Nāgārjuna. The philosophy of Nāgārjuna is known as Mādhyamika, because it follows a middle path in metaphysics just as early Buddhist philosophy offered a middle path between asceticism and worldly life.

The usual idealist position is as follows. The material objects of this world are seen to be changing all the time. If such a world were real, then it should be, at its core at least, an unchanging Being. The existence of such a Being implies that everything that can be is already present in it and that it is the most perfect. The Mādhyamika maintains that if reality is conceived in this manner then all striving for perfection is meaningless because such perfection is already in each of us the essence of our Being. Therefore such absolute perfection cannot be attributed to the world. The world is an ever-evolving and ever-changing flux. This does not mean that the world is a nothing, but that its existence is only momentary. The Mādhyamika does not accept the reality of the world either as a pluralism, dualism or monism. If it is a Being of such a type then he is bound to accept all the determination that goes along with such notion. Nor does he accept that the world is a non-Being. For this would mean the Cārvāka position of having no basis for their ethical and spiritual seeking. Hence Nāgārjuna maintains that objects exist only in the form of their *dharmas*, their essential qualities. An object is merely a collection of *dharmas* following one another without a break. But these are all perishable as they can exist for only one movement. If the reality of a thing is denied because there can be no sufficient reason for its assumption then neither external objects nor the inner stream of consciousness can be real. The unintelligible is unreal. Therefore even consciousness or *vijñāna* is unreal because it depends on relations which are themselves unintelligible. Consciousness must necessarily exist for it is the only means of knowing the relations which make the subsistence of the world as an idea in consciousness possible. This is the argument of the Vijñānavādin. The Mādhyamika says that this is not possible, for relations themselves are not intelligible. Nāgārjuna takes the relation of motion or *gati* and after a brilliant analysis points out that it is utterly unintelligible. Almost like Zeno's arguments about the moving arrow, Nāgārjuna argues that the idea of passing a path is ridiculous. "We are not passing a path which has already been passed. Nor are we passing that which has yet to be passed. The existence of a path which has neither been passed nor is yet to be passed is beyond comprehension."[1] To continue the argument, as passing is incomprehensible the passer of such a passing also becomes incomprehensible. The passer cannot be considered identical with passing, since the agent cannot be identical with the act. If they are different then we are saying that these two can exist separately. That is the act of passing can be without the passer and vice versa. Thus these two can be neither identical nor different. From this argument follows the conclusion that all these three namely, the passer, the path and the act of passing are all unreal. But Nāgārjuna is particular in saying that while from a logical and metaphysical point of view the objects are all unreal, from a practical and empirical point they are to be considered as real. Their reality is provisional, *smṛti satya*, only to be scrapped by the logical arguments. To those who cast doubts upon the possibility of such a reality, the Mādhyamika points out that even in ordinary experience we come across such elements. For example universal characteristics like cowness have no objective reality and yet we say that they have an existence.

All objects exist only in the form of their qualities which constitute their essence. The existence of things as essences is known because of the possibility of their being defined. An object that cannot be defined cannot be known. Taking space, *ākāśa* as an example it is asked, what is space? If we know it prior to its differentia or *lakṣaṇa*, then the differentia become unnecessary.

[1] *Ma. Su.*, ii, 1, as quoted by Dr. S. Radhakrishnan in *Indian Philosophy*, Vol. I, *op.cit.*, p. 648.

If the existence of *ākāśa* comes into being after it is defined, then its existence becomes a conventional existence and not an essential one. Thus it is only the experiences of fleeting qualities that give rise to the impression that there is a real object.

What then of the Self that experiences? To the Vijñānavādin, the Self as consciousness alone is real. To this the Mādhyamika objects and says that the general principle that there can be no substance apart from its qualities applies here also. There can be no soul prior to the acts of seeing, feeling and willing, for there is no way of knowing about the existence of such a soul apart from these acts. If it is said that the soul comes into being after these acts take place, then such acts could take place independently and the postulation of a soul becomes unnecessary. If it is said that they are simultaneous existents then we have to accept that they are independent existences which can so exist and this position is meaningless. Therefore there can be no soul apart from such activities. The reality of the soul is as much a contingent reality as the reality of the object. Both are useful for practical purposes and have no ultimate relevance.

It may seem that Nagarjuna has destroyed everything by using a negative method. But this is not so. The usefulness of the negative method lies in the demonstration that the nature of reality cannot be captured by empirical modes of thought. The dialectic of Nāgārjuna has three movements in it. The first movement shows up the inevitable clashes involved in dogmatic theories. The second movement shows that because of their very inherent contradictions they can at best only falsify reality. Thought is discursive. As such, affirmations and negations belonging to the world of intellect cannot portray the nature of reality. The third movement establishes the idea that reality, paradoxically, can only be known when thought itself is negated.[1] Thus we cannot say that Nāgārjuna was a phenomenalist. *Śūnya* does not and cannot mean "nothingness". It can only mean that there is no discrete individuality either subjective or objective.

The positive contribution of the Buddhist idealism lies in the fact that they give us levels of experiences and degrees of truth and reality. It is necessary here to define the connotation of the

[1] Dinnāga, *Pramāṇa Samuccaya*, Tr. Stcherbatsky under the title *Buddhist Logic*.

word experience or *anubhava* and knowledge or *jñāna*. Generally all Indian systems of philosophy accept these two words. They usually mean all empirical experience and knowledge and not merely valid experience and knowledge. The function of knowledge is to lead to experience. The truth or falsity of knowledge is then tested by the pragmatic implications of experience. Till this is done, from an empirical standpoint, there is no way of saying whether knowledge is true or not. From this point of view *jñāna* or knowledge refers to all kinds of knowledge situations including illusions and hallucinations. It is just a relation between a knowing mind and the object. This relation does not guarantee its logical validity. Hallucinatory objects are evanescent for they are not bound by space and time. But space, time and the relations between them are all unreal as already explained. So, inspite of their appearance of reality, objects limited by space and time are really one step removed from hallucinatory objects. Each implies the other and is implicated by it. The third stage of *sūnya* is that where all *dharmas,* qualitative and quantitative, have no place. Thought, conditioned by relations, has no place here. This is the final experience of *śunyatā.*

Next we have the monistic idealism known as Advaita, Nondualism whose chief exponent is Śaṁkarācārya. Śaṁkara, like the other Indian philosophers of his time, starts with an analysis of experience. The purpose of philosophy is to evaluate the facts of experience and draw inferences as to their ultimate meaning for human beings. Merely a study of facts is science, but a study of the implications of these facts for human values is philosophy. This is exactly what Śaṁkara has done in his *Sūtra Bhāṣya,* his major Advaitic work. Like Kant, Śaṁkara does not question the existence of scientific or psychological experiences. But like Kant, he evaluates the meaning and worth of such facts from the human standpoint. This is done by an examination of subjective and objective experience.[1] These two must finally converge to a focal point, if life and experience are to be free from contradictions and if life is to be free from the consequent pain and suffering. Such pain and suffering is the result of the contradiction between what actually is and what we want. When we think that some things are eternal when they are not and behave accordingly, it leads to contradictions. Such contradictory

[1] *Śaṁkara's Commentary on Br. Su.,* Thibaut, 1.1. Intro.

experiences lead to sorrow and disappointment. In this section we shall explain how the Advaitin conceives of the world of nature and experience and then examine his metaphysical theory of the nature of reality.

The word *Prakṛti* used by the Sāṁkhya system is also made use of by the Advaita system. But the meaning given by the two systems to this word is entirely different. While to the Sāṁkhya, the word refers to the primal matter made up of *sattva*, *rajas* and *tamas* characteristics, to the Advaitin it is the principle of superimposition of the manifold of sense on the supersensuous. The word "supersensuous" here means that which is not given directly to our perceptions. We cannot deny that we know only our sensations and anything beyond that is not known directly. The Advaitin is not only a monist but also an absolute idealist. For him there is only one reality. This reality is seen as many in experience. However let us first see how the Advaitin accounts for the world of nature which forms the subject matter of our empirical experience.

Creation is evolution and it is orderly. The first element is *Prakṛti.* It is this that forms the basis of objectivity and it is from this that the first evolute *ākāśa* (ether)[1] arises. From this is evolved air, from air comes fire, water from fire and earth from water. The inherent quality of ether is sound. Air has the qualities of sound and touch. Fire has for its qualities sound, touch and colour. Water is qualified by sound, touch, colour and taste, whereas earth has sound, touch, colour, taste and smell for its qualities. In this scheme the primary element is ether and the primary quality is sound. All other elements are born out of this. These five elements are called *tanmātras* meaning essences. These elements are not gross. They are only conceptual existences. That is why these are also known as *sūkṣma-bhūtas* (subtle elements). The gross objects of this world like earth, water etc., are evolved from combinations of these subtle elements. These objects possess all the qualities of the subtle elements and are

[1] The following is the comment of Thibaut on the translation of the word *ākāśa* into *ether*: 'The Vedantins do not clearly distinguish between empty space and an exceedingly fine matter filling all space, and thus it happens that in many cases where we speak of the former they speak of *ākāśa*, i.e. the all-pervading substratum of sound; which howsoever attennuated is yet one of the material elements, and as such belongs to the same category as air, fire, water and earth", in his translation of *Ved. Su.*, on the word occurring in II, 3, 1.

said to combine in a systematic manner known as *pañcīkaraṇa* (quintuplication).[1] In their turn these gross elements modify themselves into different kinds of objects.

The process of creation does not stop with the evolution of such material objects. Like the Sāṁkhya the Advaitin also recognizes the three *guṇas*, namely *sattva*, *rajas* and *tamas*. The working of these *guṇas* is not the same here as in the Sāṁkhya system. In the latter *ahaṁkāra* is *tamas* dominated. When this is stimulated alternately by *sattva* and *rajas*, the evolution of the elements takes place. But in Advaita as we have already seen, the elements are the result, evolved straight from *Prakṛti*, (also known as *māyā*), whose components are the three *guṇas*. The dominance of one or the other constituent *guna* is to be found only in the products of the elments.[2] From the five elements mentioned before, in association with *sattva guṇa*, arise the five sense organs, *indriyas* and mind, *manas*. Thus the human body is a combination of elements in different proportions. Such is the process of evolution of inorganic nature. Life is also an evolute of these elements. But with the entrance of life on the stage, consciousness also becomes manifest to a lesser or greater degree depending on the stage of evolution.

Śaṁkara gives this account of creation in his major work, the *Śūtra Bhāṣya*, to explain the world of objects which are objects of experience for human beings.[3] It is necessary to remember that any theory of creation is at best only a surmise and a theory based on a logical analysis of observable facts. The only authenticity that such theories enjoy is one which they derive from the application of cold and calculated logic. Empirical experience can never be denied. But an analysis of experience brings about a knowledge of wider and wider ranges of uniformities which lie, as it were, behind the multitudes of our experiences. This makes Śaṁkara postulate a theory of reality which maintains that, in the last resort, reality is only one although we experience it as many. This metaphysical position is Advaita or non-dualism. All philosophers, whether in the East or in the West, have to face a fundamental problem. If he starts out with the theory that the

[1] *Vedāntasāra* by Sadānanda. The process involves the compounding of the subtle elements in a definite ratio. For example, in the gross element earth, there are all other elements in the ratio of 1 is to 5.

[2] *Ved. Par.*, S.S. Suryanarayana Sastri's trans. Note on chapter 8, Verse 23.

[3] *Sū. Bh.*, II 1. 3.

observable plurality is the ultimate reality, then he has to explain the almost compelling search of philosophers for a uniform principle of explanation of the source of this universe. This also seems to be the motive force for all scientific enquiry. If on the other hand he starts out with a theory that there is only one reality then he has to explain the nature of the multiplicity and the fact of multiplicity that is the content of all empirical experience. Śaṁkara is no exception. He also had to face a similar dilemma. Before we go on to explain the solution offered by Śaṁkara following the traditional ideas of the Upaniṣads, it is necessary to explain the usage of words like existence and reality. Radhakrishnan says that it is the distinction between these two which provides the justification for the separation of metaphysics from physics. That which exists possesses existence though it may not be real, like the illusory snake. A thing may be real, though it does not exist at the time of perception like the rope seen as a snake. The function of the philosopher, according to Śaṁkara is not to dabble with that which exists only. That is the field of descriptive sciences.[1] The philosopher has always to be conscious that there is a real which may or may not be given in that which is seen as the existent. The existent is not the whole of the real. At the same time what is other than the existent is not the non-existent and what is other than the real is not unreal. Indian philosophers like the Nyāya and the Sāṁkhya, would object to this position of Śaṁkara and say that what is not real can only be unreal. This is where the unique contribution of Śaṁkara to Indian philosophy arises. Just as Kant revolutionised philosophy by trying to bridge the gulf between empiricists and rationalists so also Śaṁkara has given a solution which bridges the gulf between the one and the many in a unique manner. Between the real which is the truth and the unreal there is an intermediate existence which is caused by *māyā*. Objects belonging to this category are neither real nor unreal. This position is very difficult to explain in ordinary Western terminology. There is no word cognate in meaning with the word *māyā*. It is not unreal, because it is not purely subjective imagination. It is not illusion, for unlike illusion it gives rise to knowledge and has truth status although to a limited extent only. To use the word appearance is more satisfactory, but unfortunately

[1] This is the problem of Kant in his *Critique of Pure Reason*. He tries to separate the appearance from reality and makes an effort to study the nature of such reality.

the word is often confused with illusion and as such, a lot of misunderstandings arise. But we have to use one or the other of the above words. Whatever word we use we must remember that it refers to *māyā* which is neither real nor unreal. Let us examine this concept more closely.

In Western idealisms, reality is defined as that which is beyond contradictions and is self-sufficient. The Advaitin accepts the same definition. But, he asks, at what level does contradiction cease to exist? What is existence? If existence is the characteristic of that which is experienced, then, is all that is experienced existent? In answering these doubts, Śaṁkara critically examines each type of experience to find out if it is beyond contradictions. First, the illusory experience. Let us say, a rope is mistaken for a snake. There is no knowledge at all of the rope. Is the snake then the real object? The usual test that is applied is non-contradiction. The snake-experience is real now but is sublated under different conditions and becomes the rope-experience. There is no doubt that both are experiences. If we say that reality is that which is experiencible, then both the snake and the rope, having the same locus of perception must be real. This is obviously impossible. So the Western philosopher makes use of two criteria to judge these two experiences and to determine which of them is truly real. First the criterion of non-contradiction is used. The illusory experience is seen to be contradicted by the later experience; hence that experience which is thus sublatable cannot give rise to knowledge of a real object. What is self-contradictory cannot be real. There are many flaws in this argument. According to the Advaitin, the most important of them is as follows. In both the experiences, i.e., the experience of snake and of rope, the "this" of experience persists. What is sublated is only the predicate aspect of the judgement, "this is a snake". What is contradicted is only the conceptual side of the judgement, leaving the referential "this" unsublated. So the snake must be real as it has got an unsublated, unsublatable perceived locus viz., "this". Only the snake aspect of the "this" is sublated when we say "this is a rope and not a snake". Hence the experience of the snake is illusory experience and does not refer to real existence. Only we interpret it wrongly. Thus Śaṁkara would maintain that the illusory is neither absolutely non-existent, nor absolutely unreal.

The second criterion by which the Western philosopher judges such experience to be unreal, is rather an inferential criterion.

Empirical-experience of an object shows its non-contradictory nature by the fact that it is public and accepted by all normal people. That is, the evidence is public and pragmatic. These arguments, however plausible they may be *prima facie*, do not stand the test of critical analysis. The nature of the empirical object, as philosophers like Berkeley and the Vijñānavāda school of Buddhism have shown, is entirely dependent on the perceiving individual. At the same time, the solidity, the colour, the form and the other characteristics are experienced as belonging to the object. Even the scientist today maintains that we can know the nature of the object as external only inferentially and that there is no way of proving its existence apart from this.[1]

In other words the phenomenal world of objects is not what it seems to be. There is self-contradiction even here. The other reason for postulating the empirical world as real is the notion of public or common experience. Let us examine this a little. Any judge in a Court of Law will testify to the fact that there are as many accounts of an incident as there are witnesses to it. There is always a great deal of rationalisation of sense impressions present in what is called common experience. Interpretation is an all-important factor in accounts of public experiences. Thus there are enough self-contradictions in our empirical experience to make us doubt if the objects of such experiences have any independent true existence at all. The empirical object is valid only pragmatically. For by our definition, whatever is self-contradictory cannot be ultimate. Thus to the Advaitin there are three levels of existence which are all real in some degree or other. The illusory object is characterised by apparent existence *prātibhāsika sattā*, the empirical object has pragmatic existence, *vyāvahārika sattā*, while the final truth has real existence, *pāramārthika sattā*. Before we go on to deal with the third type of reality, a note of warning is necessary here. Although Śaṁkara derives his reality from an analysis of epistemological experience, still he cannot be called a subjective idealist of the Berkeleyan brand. To the subjective idealist reality is nothing other than mental impressions. To Śaṁkara, while reality is one *Brahman*, it appears as many due to ignorance. Non-self-contradiction, as a criterion of reality, leads Śaṁkara even beyond the empirical experience to something more than that.

[1] Henry Margenau, *The Nature of Physical Reality*, Chapter 4 discusses this idea thoroughly.

Thus, to the Advaitin the empirical world of substance, time and causality is all real, but its reality is of a limited nature; like the pragmatist, Śaṁkara says that as long as the world serves our purposes we have to treat it as real. But there are purposes and purposes. The scientific purpose of knowledge is to arrive at a dispassionate study of the nature of reality. Hence the common man's ideas about reality do not serve the purposes of a scientist. The scientist's ideas of reality fall short of the philosopher's hypotheses. So Śaṁkara argues that each level of experience deals with one level of existence, but all these become sublated from a higher level of experience.

We are already acquainted with the nature of *Brahman* as the sole ultimate reality as expounded by the Upaniṣads. It is this idea that is logically expounded and established by Gauḍapāda and his most famous disciple Śaṁkara. We have discussed in the above paragraphs that Śaṁkara considers metaphysics as that which is implied in experience. Facts of experience can never be questioned. But what we have to evaluate is the presuppositions of such facts. It is based on such an evaluation that Śaṁkara arrives at degrees of existence. The only reality is *Brahman*. What is the nature of reality? We have already indicated that it is akin to the *Brahman-Ātman* identity of the Upaniṣads. This is the unlimited, incomprehensible consciousness implied by our empirical knowledge, or it may also be that infinite Being presupposed by all finite experience. But this does not mean that it is empirical knowledge or finite experience, nor does it mean that these exhaust or stand for *Brahman*. It only means that neither intellect or finiteness can exhaust *Brahman* while pointing to it. *Brahman* can never be an object, *dṛk*, of what is perceived, *dṛśya*. It is only when man grasps the distinction between the empirical and the finite as the object perceivable, and the transcendental and infinite which can never be such an object, that he can start comprehending *Brahman*. While direct description of *Brahman* is never possible, it can be pointed out indirectly with the help of appearances. Such an Advaitic *Brahman* is not only indefinable it is also unknowable in the ordinary sense of the term. The moment it is said to be knowable it becomes limited to the categories of the understanding. In this case *Brahman* is as it appears to us and not what it really is, in itself. That is why it is described as *nirguṇa* in the Upaniṣads and is accepted so by the Advaitin. *Nirguṇa* means devoid of all characteristics.

But it is not pure negation. Śaṁkara says in his commentary on *Chāndogya Upaniṣad* that it is only the dull-witted *manda buddhi* that would consider the Absolute as pure negation. For negation itself is a mental category and we cannot attribute it to *Brahman*, nor can there be complete negation without a positive implication.

Brahman is consciousness, real and bliss. *Sat*, *cit* and *ānanda:* each of these means that *Brahman* is not an unconscious Being, that it is not unreal and that it is not of the nature of pain. If this is the only real entity then what is the place of this world and our empirical experiences in the scheme of things? It has already been explained that this world of empirical experience is as phenomenal from the point of view of ultimate reality as the illusory experience is phenomenal from the point of view of empirical experience. These are different levels of experiences, and each is true within its own parameters. Then the question is, does this not lead to a multiplicity of reals? Does it not mean that both unity and multiplicity are equally, though under differing contexts, real? Judged from the criterion that the real is that which is eternal, and non-sublatable, we have shown that *Brahman* alone can be real. What then is the status of the world? The world is said to be unreal since it is sublated by true knowledge. Again according to Śaṁkara, what has a beginning also has an end and thus is unreal. How did such an unreal world come into being in the first instance?

Śaṁkara is very well aware of the logical impossibility of establishing any precise relationship between the Reality, *Brahman*, and the world whose reality is illusory and thus is only an appearance. This seeing of the many and experiencing it as real while the one *Brahman* alone is the real is called *māyā.* Generally the Vedāntins use the terms *avidya*, *ajñāna*, *māyā* and *Prakṛti* almost synonymously. For our purpose here we shall also do the same. All these words generally mean the fact that under the influence of *māyā* the Absolute One appears as the many.

Māyā as used in the Veda denotes a kind of magic power. It is said that Indra the Vedic God, assumed disguised forms with the help of *māyā.* In the *Svetāśvatara Upaniṣad*, which is primarily a theistic Upaniṣad, we have the statement that *māyā* is the nature of the world *Prakṛti* and that the Great Lord, Maheśwara is the Master of *māyā.* However when we come to Advaita this *māyā* is treated as a principle of explanation of how the one becomes the many. Sadānanda, the famous exponent of Advaita maintains that *māyā* is "something positive, though intangible, which cannot be described as either being or non-being, and which is antagonistic to knowledge".[1] We have to examine this definition in the course of which we shall learn about its nature. We have already stated that from the point of view of *Brahman* the world is illusory. From the point of view of the world *Brahman* is incomprehensible. *Māyā* cannot be a relation between these two, for a relation can exist only between two relata which are both real. Therefore the question of the nature of *māyā* expressing a relation between *Brahman* and the world does not arise for Śaṁkara. The plurality of the world is imaginary only from the standpoint of *Brahman* knowledge. So we cannot shift our ground and ask, how can the world of plurality be unreal? *Brahman* is non-different from the world and therefore the question of a relation between the two does not arise.

It is not also possible to say that the infinite, real, *Brahman* is the cause of the finite unreal world. The notion of causality is not possible here for two reasons. Causality assumes the reality of both the cause and the effect which is not possible here. Cause and effect have to be two distinct and separate things. Again to say that infinite cause submits itself to the category of cause involving time is to say that that which is eternal and timeless becomes limited, which is contradictory. Therefore the world is neither evolved nor created although it seems to be so. This "seeming so" is due to *māyā* which is ignorance. The discursive mind of man can never grasp the unity of reality. Therefore it thinks that the plurality is real. This is due to ignorance. This ignorance is *māyā*. This *māyā* has two functions. It conceals the true nature of the real as one and shows up the false plurality of the universe as true. It conceals the real and projects the unreal. We must, at this stage, sound a note of warning. *Māyā* is neither a second nor a third something. It is just a principle which is embedded in the human intellect and due to which we see the appearance of the many in one. The very definition of *māyā* as that which measures the immeasurable[2] explicates the function and role of *māyā*.

[1] *Ved. Sa.*, 34. As quoted by Swami Nikhilānanda in his *Self-knowledge*.
[2] *Miyate anena iti Māyā*: "That which measures is māyā."

Māyā is also described as that which is neither real nor unreal. It is *sadasadvilakṣaṇa.* It is also something which is indeterminable, *anirvacanīya.* It is real because its product, the world, is experiencible. It cannot be ultimately real, because it is sublated by a higher knowledge or experience of *Brahman.* Therefore it is different from both that which is real and that which is unreal. But a thing can only be either real or unreal and it is impossible for thought to grasp something which is neither. Therefore it cannot be determined. We shall see in a later chapter how all this is explained from an epistemological point of view.

Nature of Self

Before starting on this section, I would like to clarify the meaning of the term "Self" in general. In Western philosophy, specially classical philosophy, the terms "mind" and "self" are used to mean the same thing, viz., the conscious, thinking person. When Descartes gave his famous dictum "Cogito ergo sum" he maintained that the thinking substance is the Self of man. Similarly when Hume rejected the mind as the causal source of thought, he was implicitly expressing the idea that mind and Self are identical. Such an identification between mind and Self is not acceptable to Indian philosophy. Mind or *manas* is different from Self or *Ātman* and as such the nature of these two have to be discussed separately. But this does not mean that these are two entities which exist independently as individual entities in the human body. These are always seen to be acting as one. But they are not identical and at empirical levels, can be conceptually studied as different things. In this section we shall discuss the nature of Self as the agent of the knowing processes and as the conscious awareness. The nature of *manas* or mind as the psychological instrument of acquiring knowledge will be discussed in the next chapter.

It is often said that Indian philosophy is spiritualistic and phenomenalistic. Whether this characterisation is applicable to the entire field of Indian philosophy is doubtful. It is, however, surely applicable to the very early Indian philosophical thought found in the Vedas and Upaniṣads. Since Vedic thought goes back almost into the limbo of oblivion, it is not surprising that these early Vedic Indians were entirely anthropomorphic in their ideas about the nature of the Self. The Vedic Indian was entirely dependent on the whims and fancies of nature for his sustenance.

He could not explain in any rational manner these whims and fancies except in an anthropomorphic way. Hence he bestowed every hill and dale, every tree and creeper, the seasons, the sky and the earth, every natural phenomenon with a spirit and worshipped it. The spirit of such worship was always pragmatic and depended on mutually satisfactory results for these *devas* and men. It was conceived only as some spirit infesting the natural phenomena and not the personal God, although it was a spirit that had to be pacified by sacrifices. Inspite of this compelling need to postulate spirits anthropomorphically, the ancient Indian was very careful not to personalize these forces completely. Descriptions of these gods abound with partial personification, leaving the essential characteristics of the corresponding natural phenomena intact.[1] This helped the ancient Indian to remember that these gods were, after all, his own creations.

That such arrested anthropomorphism was a conscious effort of the Vedic Indian becomes clear by their later speculations. Slowly such fanciful speculations were given up. We find the Vedic Indian struggling to find a more basically permanent stuff which could in its turn explain all natural phenomena. Witness the struggle in his mind when he asks questions like:

> Who hath beheld him as he sprang into being, seen how the boneless One supports the bony?
>
> Where is the blood of earth, the life, the spirit?
>
> Who may approach the man who knows, to ask it?
>
> Unripe in mind, in spirit undiscerning? I ask of these the God's established places; For up above the yearling
>
> Calf the sages, to form a web, their own seven threads have woven.
>
> I ask, unknowing, those who know, the sages as one all, ignorant for sake of knowledge.
>
> What was that One who in the unborn's image has established and fixed firm these world's six regions.[2]

1 For example the epithets for Agni, the fire-god, are "His flames are fierce; never aging are the flames of him who is beautiful to behold. . . . Agni eats with his sharp jaws, he chews, he throws down the forests as a warrior throws down his foes. . . . " Tr. Hermann Oldenberg, 1. 143.

2 *The Hymns of the Ṛg Veda, Tr.,* R.T.H. Griffith, 1. 164.

In the same hymn, a monotheistic suggestion is also given when the ancient one says, "To what is one, sages give many a title: they call it Agni, Yama, Mātarīśvan". It is highly significant that the word *Iśvara* or God is not applied to these denizens of nature. God here is conceived only as a "giver" to man. We find references to father, mother and teacher also being equivalent to the devas, because they also "give" to the best of their ability. Thus the process of making gods in the image of man started.

Very soon, the Vedic Indian becomes dissatisfied with this huge pantheon of devas. As a first attempt to introduce some order and meaning, all the gods were classified into three groups, namely, gods of the earth, gods of the heavens, and the gods of mid-air. From out of this grouping emerged the concept of "all-god" (*Viśvedevāḥ*) which referred to the universal spirit behind all nature. Yet, due to the fact of arrested personification, mentioned earlier, the Vedic Indian was never unaware of the fact that these gods were only conceptualisations of glorified natural phenomena. Thus the fact that these gods were not the final answer to their quest was forever present with them.

The next stage of development of the idea of God has been variously referred to as "henotheism",[1] and "opportune monotheism".[2] But such a characterisation involving the idea that the Vedic Indian raised one god at a time, as need and opportunity arose, to the position of supremacy, is not correct. On the other hand, such a tendency was the result of the uncertain mind groping to find a single plausible answer to the quest of the meaning of nature. The *Ṛg Veda* abounds with passages where god after god was tried as an answer to this riddle, but none proved satisfactory to the searching mind of the seeker. From out of this trial and error process develop the concepts of "the creator of this Universe", Viśvakarma, and "the Lord of this creation", Prajāpatī. These were conceptual, although anthropomorphic, personalisations and not personifications of nature. The plurality of the gods also had by now, disappeared and many names were given to this one final cause, the monotheistic deity.

Intermingled with these monotheistic notions, an idea of monism was also developing. In the song of creation,[3] all the opposites

[1] Max Mueller.

[2] Bloomfield.

[3] Referred to by Hiriyanna in his *Outlines of Indian Philosophy*, p. 42.

such as death and life, good and evil, being and non-being are all viewed as developing within a fundamental principle which is referred to as "that one" (*tad ekam*) and the universe is not seen as the product of a creative process, but as a spontaneous unfolding of a suprasensible first cause.

Such a mature explanation of the nature of the spirit is the foundation stone for a most profound development of the nature of the Self in the Upaniṣads. In the Vedas there is not much specific discussion of the nature of the Self, it is always in contrast with nature that the Self of man is assumed to exist. We have already said that the Upaniṣads are the end-portions of the Vedas. This is so not only in a literary sense, but also in an ideal sense. The ideas of the Vedas, find their culmination in the Upaniṣadic thought.

In these Upaniṣads, the torch of enquiry turned inward and questions like "By whom impelled soars the mind projected?"[1] are raised and answered. Reality is sought to be analysed not only from an objective standpoint, but also from the point of view of the experiencing subject. This Self, who is the experiencer is called the *Ātman.* The word *Ātman* has three derivative meanings, to breathe, to move and to blow.[2] However, there seems to be a progressive change in the meaning of the word with the increasing knowledge of the people. In the *Chāndōgya Upaniṣad* there is a story which establishes this fact.[3] Indra and Virocana, the representatives of the gods and the demons respectively, went to Prajāpatī, the Lord of all beings and the divine seer and requested him to instruct them about the nature of the Self. The answer provided is through four stages of the development of the notion of the Self. The First and most obvious answer is that the physical body is the Self. Indra, the representative of the gods raised a fundamental objection and said that the Self cannot be conceived as lame or deaf when the physical body is so afflicted. Hence there can be no identity between the two. The next answer identifies the Self with the dreamer of dreams. This also did not prove satisfactory, for Indra pointed out, the dreamer does not suffer the drawbacks inherent in a physical body, nor do the imagined privileges of a dream-body affect the natural physical body.

[1] *Ke. Up.*, 1. 1-3 Hume's trans.
[2] Monier Williams, *Sanskrit-English Dictionary.*
[3] *Ch. Up.*, VIII, sections 7, 8, & 9. Hume's Trans.

The Self is also not affected by the dreamer's peculiarities, hence they cannot be identical. The doubt arises which is the true Self, the waking or the dreaming Self? Beset with such difficulties, Indra seeks further clarification. The Self is now equated, by the master, to the person who is enjoying deep sleep without dreams. But Indra, getting very exasperated, points out that this is no answer at all, as the person who is fast asleep has no experiences at all: "He becomes (as) one who has gone to destruction".[1] Prajāpatī confirms this and says that just like air, lightning and thunder, which are by themselves formless, assume form and shape when associated with space, so also, the Self which is not really the experience, becomes so when associated with a body having a form and a shape. It is that which while being not identifiable with the body, can still only be known through the body. It is the only true subject which can never be known as an object. Thus these several stages of the argument given by Prājapatī states the important truth that the body which is subject to birth, growth and death, the dream states which are apparently independent of the waking experiences of the body are not the basic Self or *Ātman.*

The method of instruction used by Prajāpatī in the above story is generally the method used in the Upaniṣads. It is a method of progressive abstraction of non-essentials. When any philosophic question is cluttered up with non-essential answers which appear credible, it becomes difficult to reach the core of the answer. So the non-essentials are stripped off and the nature of the Self is shown to be that which exists continuously through all the changing experiences like a string passing through multi-coloured and multi-shaped beads.

The same idea is expressed in various ways in several other Upaniṣads also. In the *Māndūkya Upaniṣad*, which is a later Upaniṣad, the seer arrives at a definition of the soul after an analysis of the various experiences of man. The most obvious startting point is the waking experience. Man feels and wills through the necessary adjunct of the body. The contacting point between the Self which possesses knowledge of the objects, and the world of objects which are thus known, is the physical body. The physiological body is not the knower as evidenced by the fact that there is no knowledge of all the sensations that have an impact

[1] *Ch. Up.*, 11, 1-3.

and come into contact with the body. The Self knows only that which it wants to know thus ignoring the rest of the material. Therefore the existence of the soul or, *Ātman*, is a necessary prerequisite for the activity of the body. Again in the *Bṛhadāranyaka Upaniṣad* there is a reference to this aspect of the Self when such questions as "By which one knows all this?—whereby could one know that? by what means could the knower be known?"[1] Although there can be no direct proof of the subject, yet it is always referred to as the *Puruṣa* in these treatises. The etymological meaning of this word is "what lies in the citadel of the body".[2] However the fact that the body is not the soul and that the waking experience is not the sole experience of man is never forgotten. Hence the Upaniṣadic seer, next analyses the state of dream experience.

Dream experience must have attracted quite a deal of attention in those ancient days, because we have a large number of references to dreams in the literature of the times. It is accepted that the experiences of the dreamer are no doubt based on the experiences of the person during waking life. But the difference lies in the non-awareness of such a dependence during dream experience. The limitations imposed by a physical body are not present in dream experience. Similarly natural laws do not have any enforcing inhibition on the experiences of the dream world. Hence, the Upaniṣad says, a contradiction is involved between the waking and dream states which, somehow has to be resolved. This resolution cannot be arrived at if these two worlds are examined separately. But viewed in juxtaposition, we arrive at the concept of the *Puruṣa* who necessarily must be the co-ordinating agent of such diverse experiences. Hence a search for this *Puruṣa* leads the Upaniṣadic seer to an investigation of the experience of the dreamless state, *suṣupti.* Here there is not only the non-existence of any dream states which are based upon psychical states, but there is also the non-existence of the presence of the physical awareness based on the existence of the physical body. But there is something else that is ever present in all the three states and whose existence becomes better known in the deep sleep experience. This is the Self or soul. The Self is quiescent at this stage, since the adjuncts such as the body and the mind are not active. The Self, although not active, is not non-existent. It

[1] *Br. Up.,* II. 4, 14.
[2] Hiriyanna, *Outlines of Indian Philosophy,* p. 66.

has to be aware of its own existence at least for otherwise, statements like "I slept so well that I did not know anything else" will not have any meaning. Nor can such a state be described as one of complete unconsciousness. We recollect, after waking up, not only that we are the same person who went to sleep, but also, how peaceful and pleasant that state of sleep was. Since it is in this state alone that the Self exists untrammelled by its appendages of body and mind, the Upaniṣadic seer maintains that it is in this stage that we get a glimpse of the true nature of the soul or *Ātman.* From these three stages of man's experience, it is possible to derive a sort of an understanding of the nature of the soul. It is that which is the source of deep happiness for man. When it is associated with and functions through a body and mind, the waking experiences of man are the result. When it functions only through mind, dreams are the result. It is *that something* without which body and mind have no meaning or unity.

The above argument that the soul exists and that its nature is pure consciousness or awareness may be unacceptable to many modern western philosophers.[1] But there has not been given any conclusive proof for the non-existence of the soul. The answers that they have tended to give to the question: "What is the soul?" have always roamed round and above the question but have never touched the core of the problem.[2] We shall have to discuss this problem at greater length later on. But here, I would like to point out that the behaviourist and neo-realist schools forget that they are seeking a meaning for a behavioural pattern. The pattern by itself does not suffice. It is the meaning behind it that is sought. Such seeking is indicative of the fact that there is something more than behavioural patterns. However it is important to remember that the nature of the Self is one of the most important, fundamental ideas discussed in the Upaniṣads.

It is also interesting to note that the Vedic Indian did not stop his enquiry into the nature of reality by only analysing the nature of the Self as the subject. There is no doubt that the emphasis has been an enquiry into the subjective self, but the meaning of

[1] Specially analysts, neo-behaviourists, neo-rationalists and others of the same breed.

[2] As an example of such discussions, one may quote A. C. Ewing, *The Fundamental Questions of Philosophy*, pp. 112-118.

an empirical self becomes possible only when it is encased, as it were, in a body. This body is part of the world of objects. In addition, we have to assume by inference, the existence of other selves, encased in other bodies. Hence an examination of the world other than the Self is launched upon. In the *Taitiriya Upaniṣad* this reality is examined from a humanistic standpoint. Following the pattern of Upaniṣadic instruction, the father gives the framework of the concept of reality to the enquiring son. The source of the reality of the external world is said to be "that whence beings are born, that by which when born they live, that into which on deceasing they enter....".[1] The son, known as Bhṛgu tries to discover that which would fulfil such requirements. All the changing multiplicity of things and objects in this world have a name and a form, *nāma* and *rūpa*. Apart from this, the question is, is there anything else that forms the common basis? The most obvious answer is that it is matter, *anna*. To this, the most obvious objection is that it does not cover all the aspects of life and thought. No doubt, matter is an essential component. But it is not all. Hence the next answer provided by the father is it is life, *prāna*. It is the presence of life that tanslates inorganic matter into the pulsating organic units. But, breath or life by itself does not explain thought or consciousness, which is a significant aspect of reality, and which is present not only in man, but also in most of the animal and vegetable kingdom, to a greater or lesser degree. So next, mind, *manas*, is postulated as the nature of ultimate reality. *Manas* here does not mean Self. It means that capacity of the Self by which perceptions are received and culled togtheer to form meaningful concepts, what Bosanquet would call the "constructive" capacity of the human being to put together atomic sensations into meaningful wholes. Bhṛgu argues that mind, being the most important evolute, ought to be at the core of reality. But a doubt is expressed. There is yet another aspect of reality that is not exhausted by mere perceptual consciousness. This is *vijñāna*, the capacity to understand, to correlate and establish relations. In terms of Kantian philosophy, this may be called the capacity to postulate the categories of the understanding. No doubt this is a finer reality, but it still involves a subject-object relationship. The existence of such a duality implies an imperfection, for reality which is one is still being seen as subject and object. Can this fulfil the requirements of Reality

[1] *Tai. Up.*, III, 1-6.

with which we began our discussion? Apparently not, as Bhṛgu gives a further answer: bliss, *ānanda*. This is the highest state of existence and experience where man is not conscious of any jarring dualities. Here, there is the experience of only peaceful contentment born out of perfect balance. It is not possible to give a single definition of such *ānanda*. All that we can say is, it is the "fullness of fullness". It is neither abstract nor negative. This is made clear when we scan the different steps by which we arrived at this concept. Each higher concept is more affirmative and pervasive than the lower which it includes and transcends. At the same time, it is not the highest in any mechanical or organic sense. It is the logical highest conceivable from the human point of view of reality. Perhaps this may be comparable to the Hegelian absolute which includes and transcends every known aspect of reality and which is not exhausted by any one of these. This is called *Brahman* from the root *Bṛ* which means "to grow".[1]

Here we have two streams of thought viz., the subjective and the objective (the *Ātman* and *Brahman*). The subjective element *Ātman*, which we have discussed in detail before, came to mean in the course of time, the central essence of man which is called the Self or the spirit. A very characteristic mode of thought native to the Vedas and even to the later philosophic and religious literature in India is the establishing of correlates anthropomorphically between the human individual and the universe. Perhaps this is in evidence of the most compelling need of mankind, namely, to explain the unknown in terms of the known. This is brought out very skilfully in the famous *Puruṣa Sūkta* which compares representative man with the cosmic man *Puruṣa*.[2] This tendency is also to be found in the Upaniṣads. Thus the different conceptions of *Brahman* correspond with the different conceptions of *Ātman*. In the state of *ānanda*, *Ātman* is at its purest and thus becomes identical with the concept of *Brahman* as the highest reality. This blending of the objective and the subjective into the "that one" principle of the Vedas, becomes commonly, known as *Brahman* in the Upaniṣads and forms the subject of philosophical enquiry throughout the ages. The *Ātman* doctrine conceives

[1] Various meanings are given to the word *Brahman*. It means that which swells or grows. It also means prayer or supplication. But for our purpose here the meaning "that which grows or breathes" is to be taken.

[2] A song which occurs in the *Ṛg Veda*. It is also known as *The Song of Creation*. A good translation of it is to be found in *Old Saṁskrit Texts*, J. Muir., Vol. 5, p. 356.

of the physical world as not-Self and thus discards it in its search for the essence of man. The *Brahman* doctrine includes and transcends the physical world, establishing that the not-Self is finally reducible to that which is the essence of the Self. Hence these two principles automatically fused together to become the one principle of reality, *Brahman*. The most significant development of such a fusion is the idea that there can be no break between man, nature and Reality. The rationale of such a *Brahman-Ātman* identity resulting in one *Brahman* concept is evident. The unity of *Brahman*, such as the objective reality, can only be a hypothesis. There can be no necessary compulsion involved in such a postulation. But the experience of such a necessary certainty is a sure characteristic of the person's experience of the Self as *Ātman*. There is another difference also. To start with, these two—the Self and the not-Self—are opposite facts. When these two are brought together into a logical whole dialectics asserts itself and we have a third something which is neither the one nor the other and yet is both. This is the absolute *Brahman*. It cannot be characterised either positively or negatively, for the Upaniṣadic seer maintains that such definition is a limitation by a process of exclusion. This idea of Reality or *Brahman* is known as the acosmic ideal, *niṣprapañca vāda*.

We had already referred to the habit of the Vedic Indian of establishing correlations between man and nature. So far we have stated that the highest and the purest existence of *Ātman* is identifiable with the purest and highest existence of the cosmos. The *turīya* is the fourth state for man and identifiable with the state of bliss, *ānanda*. But man has other aspects as well for which also correlates have been established. Man is a self-conscious, rational being. Corresponding to this, *Brahman*, the Ultimate Reality is postulated to be the self-conscious *Īśvara*, God. Reason in man can thrive only when there are opposing factors. Analogically, God is bestowed with all that is good and great, for ever warring with evil and sin.[1] The grace and goodness of God can only shine in contrast with cruelty and unkindness present in this world. It is thus that the notion of a God is born in the Upaniṣads.

Similarly the vital and the conscious man is correlated with the cosmic man *Hiraṇyagarbha*. He has the universe as His body.

[1] *Sv. Up.*

He is the totality of all created objects. He is the material cause of this universe. This concept of the cosmic man is lower than the concept of *Īśvara* or God. *Īśvara* is the self-conscious awareness personified and seen as a limitation of the *Brahman*, the ultimate reality while *Hiraṇyagarbha* is an anthropomorphically conceived person having the universe as his body and endowed with vitality and consciousness. While we are discussing these several correlates between man and the universe, we should always bear in mind that these are parallels effected for an easier comprehension of the nature of this universe. Similarly when the *Ātman* is identified with the physical body *Brahman* is stated to be the same as the *Virāt*, the spirit having the cosmos as its body. The description of this *Virāt* given in the *Muṇḍaka Upaniṣad*[1] states that His eyes are the sun and the moon and His ears are the directions etc.

Now we have seen not only that the essence of *Ātman* is identified with the essence of *Brahman* but also a parallel is drawn between every aspect of human existence and the existence of this universe. This is the Self or *Brahman*, the Supreme Reality as taught in the Upaniṣads.

Passing on from the Upaniṣadic concept of the Self as ultimate reality through the Puraṇas to the age of the systems, we find a definite movement towards ignoring the *Nirguṇa Brahman* concept and asserting the *Saguṇa Brahman* idea. *Brahman* as endowed with all good qualities is said to be the highest reality and man and his *Ātman* is explained as a dependent reality. Much ritualism grew up around these ideas. Amongst the *nāstika darsànas* which flouted the reality of the soul and of God, the Cārvāka is the foremost. We have already discussed the general position of Cārvāka in the previous section. It is but necessary here only to stress the fact that to this "sweet-tongued" philosopher the Self is only an evolute of the four material substances—earth, water, air and fire. It is the result of a chemical combination of these materials. When the body dies, everything else dies. The Self is an epiphenomenon.

This position of the Cārvākas is irrefutable. If the criteria for establishing the existence of anything is purely perception, then there is nothing one can do to show that the Self exists.

[1] IV. 4, 11.

The Self, according to Upaniṣadic tradition, is not perceivable. The question that the Cārvāka or the Lokāyata raises against the existence of the Self is, in a way, similar to those raised by modern linguistic analysts and behaviouristic psychologists. To the analyst the Self is merely a name given to several dispositions, both long-term and short-term and a way of referring to these.[1] The behaviourist maintains that all patterns of human behaviour including willing and feeling can be explained by the mechanical concept of stimulus-response.

In the seventeenth century, philosophers like Hume had already discussed the possibility of a permanent Self and had said that it is nothing but an association of ideas. "Each individual man is simply a certain region of material plenum and what distinguishes this region from the other regions is only the motions that take place there".[2] Thus the notion of a permanent Self has been agitating the minds of philosophers, both in the East and in the West, for a long time. But, even today, we are nowhere near the answer. The doubts are valid, but the felt certainty of the Self is also indubitable.

This speculation of the Cārvākas regarding the nature of the Self leads to the doctrine of the Buddhists. The central tenet of all Buddhism, whether it be the early canonical Buddhism or the later systematic doctrines is the doctrine of no-soul. The early Buddhism maintained that the body-soul complex is a part of the total becoming. It is the union of the mental and the material that makes for the individuality of man. Such a total is a *Saṁskāra*, an organised complex. The organisation, as we have seen already in the previous section, is one of dependent origination. Man never remains the same. He is an everchanging complex whole in which the change is due to the component parts which are never the same in two consecutive moments. It is repeatedly said that we have no consciousness of any changeless permanent entity called soul. All that we are aware of is only linkages of causes and effects. Making use of the Upaniṣadic idea that all objects are recognisable by the possessions of *nāma*, name and *rūpa*, form, the Buddhist stresses the point that apart from these two, there is nothing more that can be known. But this does

[1] Refer to *The Concept of Mind* by Ryle. Specially the chapter on 'Self Knowledge.'

[2] W. T. Jones, *A History of Western Philosophy*, p. 641.

not mean that the Buddha negated the existence of the soul. There are many instances where the Buddha refuses to answer the question: "What is the soul"? We can only understand that the Buddha felt that to posit a soul seemed to go beyond the empirical and descriptive standpoint which he was adopting. What we know and can understand is only the empirical self. We cannot say what lies beyond. This is characteristic of Buddhistic thought. Buddha's concern was with the immediate and not with something that is beyond the scope of the present. But he never actually denied the existence of the Self nor did he affirm it. This prevarication has lead the later Buddhist schools to adopt varying theories. Buddha himself must have felt that one's attention must not be diverted by metaphysical questions when one is involved in trying to find out the cause of suffering and misery and the means to get rid of it.

In later Buddhism we have both realistic as well as idealistic trends with regard to the existence of the soul. This was inevitable. The silence of the Buddha regarding metaphysical aspects, left the field wide open to his followers to pursue their own particular logical developments.

The Hīnayāna schools developed pluralistic realisms. The Vaibhāṣika school maintained that while change as an empirical factor is real, the basis of such change is also real. Cause and effect refer to the two phases of one thing. These phases are momentary while the substratum is permanent. The Vaibhāṣika school maintains that existence is independent of our perception.

Thus approaching the existence of the Self through epistemological arguments the Vaibhāṣika maintains that the perceiver or *upalabdhṛ* is the Self. But this Self is none other than consciousness or *citta* or mind or the capacity to discriminate. This is permanent. Its quality is memory. Thus while the Vaibhāṣika, in a way, concedes that there is no individual soul as a permanent substrate, their pluralism and realism compel them to accept a permanent consciousness or *vijñāna* of which all knowledge is a changing quality.

The second school of the Hīnayāna, the Sountrāntikas, like the modern critical realists, hold that the existence of reality is inferrable though not directly perceivable. That one end of this inferential process is consciousness is acknowledged. They argue that the moral responsibility implied by the great teachings of the Buddha and the cognitive experiences of man imply an active subject. Hence it was necessary to postulate the existence of a Self. However, both these schools of realism hold that such a Self is not eternal but is a manifestation of a succession of short-lived states. Even then the underlying person, in a way, persists. They have however religiously avoided the use of the word "Self" for this and used the word *vijñāna* with its cognitive overtones.

These two schools paved the way to the two idealistic schools of Buddhism. The representative theory of the Sountrantika led to the subjectivism of the Yogācāra or the Vijñānavāda school. Vijñānavāda is the theory which believes in the reality of thought relations. It is with this aspect that we are here concerned. Like Berkeley, the Vijñānavādin showed up the difficulties of assuming the existence of absolute matter which is knowable only through sense-perceptions.

The main argument of this school for the establishment of a Self or a mind is that if the mind were also unreal then all reasoning, thinking and arguments would also be unreal and none could sustain any position. Therefore the reality of mind at least should be accepted to make any philosophising possible. This mind or consciousness or *vijñāna* alone is real. This consciousness is self-subsistent since it does not require any external object in opposition to which its meaning could be established. This consciousness or mind is a store-house of all impressions and hence is called *ālaya-vijñāna.* Yet it is not an unchanging eternal thing like the soul or *Ātman* of the Upaniṣads. It is a stream of continuously changing states. All the possible mental activities are present here in the form of potentialities or traces which become patent in the individual in his day-to-day empirical life. This *ālaya-vijñāna* is the whole whereas the individual is the part. The parts are ever changing while the whole remains intact. This is comparable to the collective unconsciousness of Jung. The individual consciousness is only a fraction of this great store house. Dr. Radhakrishnan explains[1] that there are indications that this *ālaya vijñāna* was sometimes used in the sense of the absolute Self. When

[1] *Indian Philosophy*, Part I, p. 629.

the immanent principle of all existence is equated to the storehouse of consciousness, the Vijñānavādin is postulating an absolute consciousness, the universal Self. The world of space, time and objects is contingent on individual consciousness and has no separate existence. Thus it is a subjectivism that is taught by this school. The subjectivism is a result of their epistemology which maintains that apart from perceptual knowledge which is entirely based on our sense perception there can be no independent objects. The theory of *ālaya vijñāna* is a metaphysical postulation to explain the possibility of continuous knowledge based on a psychological analysis of consciousness. Thus the metaphysics of the Vijñānavāda school is a mixing up of the psychological with the epistemological aspects.

However the phenomenal world with its distinction of the subject and object is accepted by the Vijñānavādin. While psychologically this distinction is acceptable, critically, they said, these are but differences in one whole which is the *vijñāna* or thought. The world of space and time appears to be real because of imperfect understanding of the true nature of *vijñāna*. The consciousness which is originally free from the distinction of subject and object, still, due to the beginningless predispositions, does develop these distinctions when it becomes associated with the material components of the body.

One can very easily detect similarities between the philosophy of Fichte and that of the Vijñānavādin. For Fichte all experience is ego-centred and is self-conscious. When there is a perception or experience of that which is other than the ego, this otherness is merely a limitation of the ego. The absolute ego becomes differentiated into a plurality of finite egos and in the process conceives the "other" in opposition to itself and as the non-ego. This is the Vijñānavādin's theory.

The Mādhyamika idealism or nihilism maintains that there is no Being which can be characterised either as the Self or as the substance. All the other schools of Buddhism accept the reality of the world only conventionally, for empirical purposes but deny its permanence. The Mādhyamika stretches this logic and says that even the Self is only a conventional entity and that there can be nothing transcendental in it.

The first of the āstika schools which gives a realistic and materialistic explanation of the Self is the synchritistic school of Nyāya-Vaiśeṣika. The soul or Self is a real substantive possessing qualities like earth possesses the quality of smell. These qualities are pleasure, pain, knowledge, desire, aversion and volition. While quoting the scriptures to establish the existence of the Self,[1] the Naiyāyika proves its existence by inference. The argument is as follows: A man sees an object, remembers having seen it before and recognises it as such and such and desires to possess it. All this is possible only when there is a continuity underlying all the actions. This continuous thing is the soul. Uddyotakara says that if this were not so, every cognition would be a new cognition and no recognition would be possible[2]. This soul itself is unconscious, but consciousness or knowledge arises in it when it comes into contact with the object and as a result of the activity of senses. Such a consciousness is fleeting and as such cannot constitute the essence of the soul. Whatever may be the object of knowledge, whether it be the fleeting sound or the permanent jar, it is transitory.[3] If such consciousness were the essence of the soul, then the soul itself would be non-permanent. Therefore, the Naiyāyikas argue that the soul is different from consciousness because it is permanent and the latter can only be its impermanent characteristic.

This soul is not made up of parts, for whatever is a compound substance is destructible into its parts. The soul has no beginning, for what has a beginning must also have an end, and the soul is eternal. Nor is the soul limited in size, for what has limitations must also have parts and must be destructible. Though it is all-pervading, the activities of the soul appear to be limited, because it can only act through and in conjunction with *manas* or mind, which is atomic. Because of the fact that the feelings and thoughts of one individual are not the same as those of others, it is maintained that there are a number of souls.

Such a soul is bound up with body and mind. The body is made up of physical atoms and the nature of the body which comes to be associated with each soul is determined by the past actions of the soul and the body comes to be formed under the influence

[1] *Ny. Su.*, I. 1. 10.
[2] *Ny. Vār.*, 1. 1. 10.
[3] *Ny. Bh.*, III, 2, 1-2.

of an unseen force or destiny. With the destruction of the body and the mind, the soul losses all the six qualities which have already been mentioned. Therefore the state of freedom or *mokṣa*, for the Self, is that where it is free not only from pain, but from all qualities and limitations of the body. This state of the soul, which is the ideal to be achieved is known as *apavarga* or escape. This escape is from *moha* or delusion.[1] The delusion consists in mistaking accidental features of the soul such as the characteristics of knowledge, pain, pleasure, desire, aversion and effort as being permanent. It also consists of thinking that the body and mind belong to the soul, whereas actually they do not.

One fundamental difficulty is involved in the Nyāya-Vaiśeṣika conception of the soul. If the soul is different from body and mind, what makes them come together to act and produce knowledge? They cannot call upon God, for as we have seen already, God is not necessary for this system except as the primordial mover of atoms. So they have to rely on their conception of *adṛṣṭa*, the invisible potency which acts like Descartes' *Deus ex machina* to account for the interaction between body and mind.

In Indian philosophy the notions of the soul or Self are closely connected with the ideas of God, the former is usually known as *Jivātman* and the latter as *Paramātman*. Both are *Ātmans*, but while the individual self is the empirical or limited *ātma*, God is the transcendental or Supreme *Ātman*. The Nyāya-Vaiśeṣika system accords a very casual recognition to God. Even this came about only during the period when the two schools merged together. Annambhatta, the logician of the synchritist school treats of God as the Supreme Soul. But it is in the *Kusumānjali* of Udayana that we come across the so-called proofs for the existence of God.

The argument of the Naiyāyikas that the world is composed of complex particles which, due to their power of motion, come together, involves the postulation of God as a mover of these atoms. God is necessary as an explanation for the functions of matter which evolve into this world. The second argument is similar to the teleological argument. The universe is of the nature of an effect since it is made up of parts. Since there is an analogy to artefacts, there must be a creator who is an intelligent Being. This is God. It is difficult to say if this God is a person or not. The fact that volition is involved in the act of causation imparts a

[1] *Ny. Su.* IV.. i. 3-8.

certain notion of personality. Yet he is not referred to as *Paramātma* implying some kindred nature with human *Ātman.*

The second point that Udayana makes is that there is an observed physical order in the universe which speaks of a controller, and similarly the moral government of the world requires a moral governor. The history of western philosophy has shown how all such arguments depend on the presupposition of a causal relation between the empirical and the transcendental which is not admissible. Similarly these arguments accept the idea that an organisation requires an organiser who is intelligent. Even this is questionable. The whole scheme of the Nyāya proofs lies on the fact that no one has disproved God although most of them have ignored Him in their philosophising.

The *Nyāya Sutrās* make only a very casual mention of *Īśvara* while the *Vāiśeṣika Sutrās* do not even do that. They did not feel the need for a God in their systems, for whatever they could not explain by using the canons of their reasoning they said was done or was caused by that inexplicable something called *adṛṣṭa.* But the criticism levelled against them by other schools, made the commentators find a place for God and even provide logical reasons for the same.

As we have already stated, the Mīmāmsika is a realist and believes in the reality of a plurality of souls. The two schools of Mīmāmsa conceive of the *Ātman* or *Jīva* in different ways. Their main reason, though not overtly expressed is that the Vedic statements promising rewards in a heaven cannot be wrong and that such rewards can only be enjoyed by a soul which survives the death of the body. So a Self or *Ātman* distinct from the body, the senses and the understanding is accepted as real. Both the schools accept a plurality of selves based on the fact of variety of experiences. According to the Kumārila Bhaṭṭa school, the *Ātman* is both the agent and the enjoyer. This system comes close to the Nyāya-Vaiśeṣika in its conception of the *Ātman.* The soul, in addition to being an agent and an enjoyer also says that modal changes are possible for the soul. But such internal modality does not vitiate either the permanency or identity of the Self. *Jñāna* or knowledge is a mode of the Self. But since the *Ātman,* by hypothesis, is omnipresent, this *jñāna* or knowledge has to be understood to mean something different from its usual connotation.

The dualistic system of Sāṁkhya postulates that both *Prakṛti*, the primordial matter, and *Puruṣa*, the primal soul, are both real. *Puruṣa* means one who is bound by the body. *Puruṣa* is the consciousness in the body. The individual self is not the body, or the mind. It is that which knows, making use of the body and the mind. But the soul is not the active principle in knowledge. It is at the receiving end only. It is also the enjoyer, but not the doer of actions. While *Prakṛti* is the active agent in all knowledge processes, the *Puruṣa* is the passive principle. The existence of this *Puruṣa* is established by reason. Just as reasons are given for the establishment of *Prakṛti*, so also reasons are given to establish the existence of *Puruṣa*. The first argument is that the body which is insentient requires a sentient principle to enjoy it. Without consciousness there can be no enjoyment. The body made up of the elements is not consciousness. So, there must be a conscious principle which knows and enjoys. This *Puruṣa* is not the senses, for the senses are only instruments of perception and not the perceiving agent. Secondly, *Prakṛti*, which is a complex entity, implies the existence of something simpler which is the *Puruṣa*. All knowable objects are made up of the three *guṇas*. If their seer is also a complex of such *guṇās*, then there is the difficulty of stating which part knows which part. Therefore the seer must be without *guṇas* or parts. Thirdly man is always trying to perfect himself and achieve *mokṣa* or freedom. *Mōkṣa* is not for *Prakṛti*, for *Prakṛti* itself is the bondage. Hence from what can *Prakṛti* try to escape? So *Mokṣa* is for the *Puruṣa* who is bound by *Prakṛti*. Fourthly the argument from design which is so efficiently used by Western philosophers to prove the existence of a designer God is used by the Sāṁkhya philosopher to indicate not a designer, but one who profits from the design. *Prakṛti* evolves producing various things of this world. These things are for the enjoyment of someone else who is the *Puruṣa*. As an atheistic doctrine, the Sāṁkhya philosophy refuses to equate its *Puruṣa* with a God or *Īśvara*. To the Sāṁkhya, *Prakṛti* is organic and can and does develop on its own. It does not require any external cause. But still, the evolving activity of *Prakṛti* is not for its own sake, but for the sake of the *Puruṣa*. Therefore, there is a teleology implicit in the evolution of *Prakṛti*. Using all these four arguments the Sāṁkhya philosopher establishes the existence of *Puruṣa*. The relation between *Puruṣa* and *Prakṛti* is often described as the relation between a blind man and a lame man who are bent upon walking towards a goal. The blind man cannot see and has to depend upon the sight of the lame man. The lame man cannot walk and so has to depend upon the legs and walking ability of the blind man. Each guides and helps the other till both reach their goal. *Puruṣa* is the lame man, for *Puruṣa* cannot act by itself. *Prakṛti* is the blind man, for it has no consciousness and is not the seer. So wherever the *Puruṣa* desires to go, or whatever the goal set by the *Puruṣa*, that *Prakṛti* has to achieve.

We have stated before that the felt unity of a person's experiences and enjoyments would not be possible unless the Self as an existent in the body is postulated. In fact the whole of the Sāṁkhya argument for the existence of *Puruṣa* depends on the enjoying and experiencing nature of *Puruṣa*. From this it follows that there have to be many *Puruṣas* and not one *Puruṣa* as postulated in the beginning. If there is only one *Puruṣa* who is single and without parts then the plurality of selves or *jīvas*, each one experiencing and endowed with moral and intellectual capacities becomes difficult to explain. On the other hand if each of these selves are accepted as a separate entity in itself, then the idea that there are only two fundamental ultimates, namely *Puruṣa* and *Prakṛti* becomes difficult to maintain. This is the weak point of any dualistic approach to reality. The only way out of such an impasse is to maintain that somehow the one *Puruṣa* becomes or appears to be many. This is what the later commentators on the Sāṁkhya systems say. Vijñānabhikṣu in his *Sāṁkhya Pravacana Bhāṣya* maintains that *Puruṣa* associated with the *ahaṁkāra* is the *jīva.*[1] The pure *Puruṣa* due to its proximity becomes reflected in the *buddhi* or *Prakṛti.* Such reflection is possible, because *buddhi* is *sāttvic* in nature and is capable of reflection. This reflection is itself something associated with *ahaṁkāra* or egoism and this is the *jīva* or Self. Since there are many such reflections there are many *Puruṣās* or *jīvas.* It is due to this association that the unconscious *buddhi* appears to be the intelligent agent and the inactive *Puruṣa* appears to be the active *ahamkāra* or the ego.

The idea of *mokṣa* is for the *Puruṣa* to get release from these shackles of *buddhi*, *ahaṁkāra* and other products of *Prakṛti.* *Kaivalya* is, to be aloof from *Prakṛti.* The Self in this condition has no pain or pleasure or knowledge. The immediate cause of such separation is knowledge. But it is not enough if mere

[1] 6.63.

intellectual knowledge is present. This would mean that the *Puruṣa* is still associated with *buddhi* which is the instrument of intellection. When such knowledge is experienced then every experience serves to separate the Self from the bondage of *Prakṛti.* The Sāṁkhya system, as we know of it, does not anywhere explain in any systematic way the method of acquiring such intuitive knowledge. This seems to have been developed in a very elaborate systematic manner by the Yōga system. There is a mention in the *Sāṁkhya Kārika* that this knowledge of the separation between *Prakṛti* and *Puruṣa* is to be gained by *vairāgya* or detachment.[1] In the first instance such detachment is caused by the sorrows and sufferings of this life, which gradually is to be developed into a higher form of *vairāgya* where realisation of the distinction between *Puruṣa* and *Prakṛti* is achieved by the former.

The Yōga system specialises in delineating the methodology for the practice of detachment and meditation. The practice of detachment requires moral training and the practice of meditation requires training in concentration. By the practice of these two, the *Puruṣa* is able to achieve knowledge of the distinctness of the Self from *Prakṛti* which leads to a state of concentration known as *samādhi* where the Self can leave the body at will. At this stage the Self manifests extraordinary powers and is capable of dissociating itself from the body even while the body is alive. The stages of development of these capacities and final release are known to have been achieved while the Self is in meditation and is in a state of *samādhi* or concentration. There are two levels of this. The first one is while the Self is in concentration on an external object other than itself. The second one is while the Self concentrates on itself, to the exclusion of all otherness. These stages of concentration will be dealt with in another chapter.

We must make a special note here that while the Yōgā system accepts the dualistic approach of the Sāṁkhya, it resolves it into a monism in practice. For this system the Self alone is real while all other appurtenances are temporary and become resolved into their constituents in the last resort. The practical discipline laid down by the Yōga systematiser is accepted by almost all the systems as useful at one stage or other.

We have seen how the Yōga system, although not a metaphysical system, still reduces the Sāṁkhya dualism to a monism of sorts

[1] *Y. Sū.*, 64.

to suit its purposes. The Yōga system by implication conceives the ultimate as one Reality which is not only differenceless but is also of the nature of pure consciousness. In this respect the Yōga system is closer to the Advaita non-dualism which we have now to consider. While discussing the *Upaniṣads* we had shown how the central teaching of the *Upaniṣads* was the establishment of *Bṛahman* as the ultimate reality. We had also shown how this *Brahman* was described as *sat*—existence; *cit*—consciousness, and *ānanda*—bliss. While this is accepted as the sole reality by Śaṁkara he had to explain how this indivisible one Reality is seen, known and experienced as the many of this world. In addition to this problem Śaṁkara had to cope with the fact that an individual person is both a *jīva* as well as a body. That the body is a product of the elemental substances is not denied. But the existence of such a body is an appearance due to *māyā*. This we have already seen. Now the problem is to explain the combination of psycho-physical activity and the consciousness or awareness of the person, which are opposed to each other as light and darkness are opposed to each other. Therefore it becomes imperative not only to understand the metaphysically real Self, but also to make an enquiry into the nature of this empirical Self which is the psycho-physical-conscious organism. Śaṁkara observes: "The *Ātman* exists as the *Jīvātman* (empirical Self) who presides over the cage of the body and sense organs and through which he acts and enjoys the fruits of such actions."[1] Thus while accepting the individuality of the empirical embodied Self, Śaṁkara very carefully points out that the Self which is so embodied is eternal. It is not born, nor does it die. There is a continuity in its existence which is only put an end to when the soul attains release from the bondage of *māyā*. Nevertheless, the soul is intimately associated with the psycho-physical organism. Therefore empirically, the *jīva* is to be described as the knower, enjoyer and the agent of action. That is, he is the cognitive agent, conative agent and the agent of action. This triple agency has to be explained. One common factor for all this agency is that such an agency is not inherent in the nature of the soul. Hence this agency in the Self is due to superimposition resulting from *avidya* or ignorance. That is the Self acts as an agent only when it is in association with the limiting adjuncts, *upādhis* like body and mind. Such empirical

1 Astyātma jīvākhyah sarīrendrīya pañjarādhyaksah karmaphala sambandhi, *B. Su. Bh.* II, 3, 17.

jīvās are many, although the Advaitin maintains that the ultimate reality is only one *Ātman* which is pure consciousness. As the plurality is due to the limiting adjuncts, *upādhis*, there can be as many souls as the variability of such limiting adjuncts is possible. Since the differentia of a *jīva* is its habitation in a body, there can be as many *jīvas* as there can be bodies.

This theory of the Advaitin, taken in conjunction with his theory of *māyā* explains how the one *Brahman* appears as the many *jīvās*. But this theory must also be taken in conjunction with the theory of *kośās* or sheaths which are accepted by the Advaitin. An elaborate discussion of this is found in the *Taittirīya Upaniṣad*. Normally, we recognise, name and consider a person as a person only in his embodied stage. A disembodied person is not recognisable and a dead body is not a person. Therefore the physical body is considered to be important for it is through the body, which is the psycho-physical organism that man puts into practice his triple agency. This physical organism is a product of food that is eaten and digested. Hence the outermost covering of man, by using which he comes into contact with that which he considers to be other than himself and which is necessary for his existence, is called the sheath of food, *annamaya kōśa*. In the last chapter we have seen how the Upaniṣadic thinker drew parallels between the subject as Reality and *Brahman* as Reality. We saw there how just as the Self imprisoned in the body is recognised, so also the *Brahman* as Ultimate Reality is understood as embodied by this universe. This idea is expressed by the Upaniṣadic saying that food is *Brahman*.[1] This is a profound idea. Evolutionary thinkers are never tired of repeating that life is the result of evolution from inorganic matter.

To assume that life existed prior to its appearance in the organic levels is not warranted by evidence. But the living being, once it is born, is sustained by the same matter from which it took its origin. Similarly when death takes place, the body resolves itself into its original constituents. So without a living body there can be no *jīva*. Hence the most essential sheath is the *annamaya kōśa*, the sheath made up of substance and maintained by food. It must not be forgotten that it is not any physical form that constitutes the sheath. It is a body itself that is endowed with life, *prāna*. The soul or *Ātman* is manifested wherever there is life.

1 *Annam brahmeti vyajanāt*, *Tai. Up.*, III. 2.

Brahman who is *Ātman* is the imperishable Self. This Self manifests itself wherever there is life. "It is life that shines in all beings. One who knows this has the superior wisdom. No one else."[1] It is in man that such life becomes self-conscious and knows itself as the knower. It is only at this level of evolution man is aware that his body is not himself although it is necessary for his agency. Hence the *jīva* as *prāṇa* or life is called the *prāṇamaya kōśa.* The Self depends on the senses for the acquiring of knowledge. But the senses depend for their proper functioning, on breath or *prāṇa.* Life is not merely a sporadic event in the cosmos. It is that which indicates the cosmic unity of *Brahman* in which all beings share.

But all this is not enough. Have we not come across cases of people who possess both life and body and still cannot be classified really as people! Therefore the Advaitin, following the Upaniṣadic seer's probing into the matter, maintains that there is yet another important aspect or sheath which is an essential for *jīva.* This is the *manomaya kośa* or the sheath of intellect. With this we are coming closer to the *jīva* in the human being, for a mind which contemplates, observes, studies and analyses is a *sine qua non* for man. Matter apparently reaches into life and life fulfils itself in mind or consciousness. But then the Advaitic seer poses the question: what is the use of mere consciousness or awareness? If this is all that is the differentia of a *jīva* then the higher evolved creatures are no different from man. So, in man this consciousness becomes self-consciousness, self-awareness. Thus *vijṇānamaya kōśa*, discriminative knowledge, is the next sheath for the *jīva.* It is only at this level that the distinction between Self and not-Self, subject and object emerges. Śaṁkara in his *Vivekacūḍāmanī* says that the feeling of egoity, the idea of agency is innately bound up with this self-conscious awareness.[2] The last sheath is the sheath of bliss, *ānandamaya kośa.* This limitation of the pure Self indicates all that is best and good in man. It is a psychological fact that man seeks happiness and pleasure always in this empirical life. But such seeking is not free from pain. It is very well understood that there can be no happiness without pain, just as there can be no shade without the sun.

1 "Prānohy eśa yah sarva-bhūtair vibhāti vijanan vidvān bhavate, Nātivādi"—I am indebted to Prof. N. A. Nikam for this interpretation.

2 pp. 186-191.

Therefore seeking after such pleasures is not enough. Hence man seeks perfection wherein the contrast between pain and pleasure is avoided. This he does when he integrates his impulses, his desires with all that is true, good and beautiful. When man struggles towards love, peace and unity, man is trying to bring out the best in him. This is the innermost Self of him, limited only by the *ānandamaya kōśa*. By the postulation of all these *kośās* or sheaths the Advaitin expresses the idea that the body, mind, and intelligence are all instruments for the Self. This Self is the knower, by which everything becomes known. If the Self were not there, there would be no knowledge, no experience. The *ānandamaya kōśa* points in one direction to the lower Self and in the other direction to the knower, the one whose nature is *ānanda* or peace. There is still the empirical aspect as there is still the separation between the Self and the not-Self. The real is the pure Self which uses at the empirical level, the body and mind as instruments. As we have seen in the previous chapter, the Upaniṣadic seers establish the existence of the Self in various ways, the most important of them being the analysis of the stages of experience. The waking, dreaming, deep sleep and the fourth state experiences indicate the levels of experience each leading to the higher and ending in the *turīya*, the transcendental. This last is not one state among other states. It is the Self itself where awareness and being coalesce to reveal the Self as the real.

There is yet another aspect of the Self which arises from the epistemology of the Advaita, which we would do better to discuss here. Here the *jīva* is designated as the *sākṣin*, the witness. In every act of seeing and hearing and other sense-activities, we are aware of not only of the object that is sensed but also of the fact that we are aware. In other words, but for this fact of self-awareness as a component of the knowing process, there can be no continuity of the knowledge process. This is the *Sākṣin* which is the witness-Self. There is a slight difference in the conceptions of the *jīva* and the witness-Self. The *jīva* is the Self which is the subject in the knowledge process. The *Sākṣin* is the knower who is aware that he is knowing. According to Śaṁkara, this witness-Self is also contingent. There is no one who can doubt his own existence as awareness because even to be able to have such a doubt, there must be awareness. This is what, perhaps, Descartes meant by "I think, therefore I exist". The Advaitin would say "I am aware, therefore I am existent".

While the Advaitin maintains that *Brahman* alone is real, he concedes empirical existence to the *jīva* or Self due to *māyā.* The principle of *māyā* is already explained. There are some analogies which are used by the Advaitin to explain the notion of separate selves being real while *Brahman* is really the real (*Satyasya satyam*). In reality the sun is only one. But a person who does not see the sun but is cognisant only with the reflections of the sun in broken pieces of glass, thinks that such reflections which are many, alone constitute reality. This is like the myth of the cave of Plato. Just like the prisoners in the cave can know only the movement of the shadows and take such a shadowy world to be the real world, the empirically bound *jīva* thinks that he, the empirical self is the real one. This is due to his ignorance of his true nature as *Brahman.* The same idea is represented by another analogy. The atmosphere even when limited by a pot and by a cup is non-different from the atmosphere around, yet it is possible for us to view these atmospheres that are limited by the form and the shape of the containers as two different ones. Yet another analogy is that of the prince who was taken away by gypsies at a tender age and brought up as one of them. The prince is ignorant of his true identity and lives and experiences the life of a gypsy. Once the prince comes to know of his true nature, the identification he had established with the world of the gypsies is proved to be due to ignorance. Similarly the *jīva* bound by his ignorance thinks that his empirical self is that which is ultimately real. Once wisdom dawns and ignorance is shattered, such wrong identification ends and the *jīva* realises that its true nature is *Brahman.*

While such is the status of the *jīva,* what of *Īśvara* or God? Is He real? If *Brahman* alone is real what is the position of *Īśvara*? According to the Upaniṣads, we had found that the selfsame *Brahman* was considered both the qualified *Īśvara, Saguṇa Brahman,* and the non-qualified Reality, *Nirguṇa Brahman.* The Advaitin accepts in principle this description of *Brahman* as both the Ultimate Reality which is indescribable and as *Īśvara* with all auspicious and good qualities. From the moment *Brahman* is conceived as an object of thought, it becomes related to a subject and as such, determinate. Thought can know only that which possesses a differentia for definition. Thus the ideal of *Brahman,* when elaborated in thought and posited as a goal for achievement becomes limited by these attributes. In fact the Advaitin gives secondary place to the definition of *Brahman* in negative terms which is found in the Upaniṣads. It is thought that this definition culminates in the "nothingness" of the Buddhist. Śaṁkara, in his commentary on *Chāndōgya Upaniṣad* maintains that it is only the dull-witted, *manda-buddhi*, who can so conceive of Ultimate Reality.[1] It is true, as Spinoza maintained, that negation implies an affirmation. To indicate this the Advaitin gives a primary place to such descriptions of *Brahman* as are indicated by the statements *Tat tvam asi*—"That thou art". Thus while Śaṁkara considers the concept of *Saguṇa Brahman* inadequate, he does not reject it either.[2] He stresses that its importance is entirely empirical. The Advaitin considers the attribution of a name and form to the Ultimate Reality impossible, but when this is done by the human mind, it is only the ultimacy of such name and form that are denied and not that which appears under their guise.

We have seen how the Naiyāyika gives proofs for the existence of God. The very notion of "proving the existence" of God is contradictory according to Śaṁkara. Pointing out how the different proofs given so far conflict with each other, Śaṁkara demolishes them as inadequate since they depend on reason. In this Śaṁkara's philosophy closely resembles that of Kant. Śaṁkara rejects the argument for design. The world is an appearance, it exhibits a system. The mind and reasoning powers of man are part of such a system. The part cannot go beyond itself and witness the whole. If this can be done, then man ceases to be a part, and becomes something that is transcendental to the whole and thus to the universe itself. This is not the case. So, man with the limitations of his intellect, cannot prove the existence of a God as the systematiser of the universe. Thus the belief in God arrived at by an analysis of the systematic nature of the world is only a concept of the human mind and does not prove the existence of God. Similarly the cosmological argument conceives God as the cause of this cosmos. We shall see in the next section, how, according to Śaṁkara the very idea of causation is riddled with contradiction. As applied to God considered as the uncaused cause, it is pointed out, that the idea of an uncaused cause cannot be admitted within the realm of phenomenal experience, for here the

[1] *Ch. Up*. VIII, i, 1.

[2] Commentary on *Ch. Up*, VIII, i, 1.

rule of the causal principle, namely that every effect must have a cause, is absolute. Thus since cause implies the space time framework, *Īśvara* or God must also be within this framework, which is absurd.

All such counter-arguments are meant to show the impossibility of "proving" that *Īśvara* is the creator. We have already said that man's puny intellect cannot encompass the whole of this universe and establish a cause for it. We have to rely on the sacred scriptures which maintain that the world is created by *Īśvara* or *Saguṇa Brahman.* The Upaniṣads postulate this idea, because qualityless *Brahman*, being absolutely transcendental cannot serve to explain the experience of phenomena. Therefore a two-fold definition of *Brahman* is attempted. One definition is known as *svarūpa lakṣaṇa* or definition with reference to the essence and the other definition is known as *taṭasthalakṣaṇa* or definition with reference to accidentals.[1] Normally the purpose of a definition is to provide a means by which the defined can be marked off and recognised. The essential definition of *Brahman* does not come under this category. It only refers to the functional adjectives of *Brahman* such as *satyam*, *jñānam* and *anantam.* The functional adjectives are also imposed on the qualityless *Brahman* by the human mind. These three are not separate adjectives indicating three different types of realities. On the other hand these three adjectives, indicate indirectly *Brahman* which is not an object amongst other objects. Our interest here is in the second definition where *Brahman* is defined in terms of its accidental qualities. The world, as we experience it, is not purely a static Being. It is a changing, pulsating, teeming universe of becoming. This becoming must be somehow reconciled with the absoluteness of *Brahman.* The Advaitin does this by establishing that becoming is an accidental quality of *Brahman.* This is the principle of *māyā.* What the Advaitin does here is not to prove the existence of *Īśvara*, but to provide an explanation of his existence. While discussing *Nirguṇa Brahman*, the argument adopts a transcendental view. While describing *Saguṇa Brahman* the argument is from an empirical standpoint. These are known as *parā vidya* and *aparā vidya* respectively. The *Muṇḍāka Upaniṣad* draws a distinction between these two types of knowledge.[2]

1 *Ved. Par.*

2 *Mu. Up.*, I. 4 & 5.

Aparā vidya is the lower knowledge of all the sciences and arts, while *parā vidya* is the higher knowledge of the imperishable *Brahman*. Does this mean that these two knowledges are separate and opposed to each other? If this is so does it not follow that, that about which the knowledges are, are also opposed and separate? Does this not mean then that there are two realities and not one? To all these questions the Advaitin's answer is the same. There is only one reality which is *Brahman*. All the rest are appearances. Let us examine this position a little further. *Brahman* as the eternal, imperishable is said to be of the nature of existence, consciousness and bliss. This means that *Brahman* is awareness and as such is aware that it is the indestructible Reality. We have already stated earlier that conscious awareness and the realisation of such consciousness is the characteristic of the fully developed human being. Similarly consciousness as being aware of itself as indestructible is a way of describing *Brahman*. How does man arrive at this knowledge-description? It is by an assiduous cultivation of knowledge and a desireless search for the Ultimate. While doing this, he acquires an expert knowledge of all the sciences and of all the arts. Finding that these only tell him of the nature of Reality which at one time or other, in one form or other, is liable to destruction, he searches further afield and becomes aware that a knowledge of Reality is not a polar knowledge involving subject and object, but a knowledge which is pure awareness; this awareness is a joy and a delight. In this process of arriving at complete awareness, he comes to know and experience that *Īśvara* is the acme of all *aparā vidya*. As the subject-object orientation persists in this *vidya*, this cannot be a final knowledge.

Īśvara or God, therefore, for the Advaitin cannot be the final resting place. *Brahman*, due to *māyā* or ignorance, is experienced not only as this universe but also as God. The distinction between *Īśvara* as the infinite and *jīva* as the finite, is a distinction between the different members of a whole.[1] When *Brahman* is perceived through the veil of *māyā*, it appears as God, man and this world (*Īsvara*, *jīva* and *prapañca*). Fichte's Absolute provides for itself an "other" in the very act of its self-positing—the affirmation or positing of the Self is possible only by opposing it to the not-Self. Similarly in Advaita the conception of *Īśvara* as

[1] *B. Su. Bh.*, III. 2.31.

the God of worship is a self-limitation of *Brahman* which by its very limitation posits also the non-Self, the world. If *Brahman* itself were to change then it would cease to be *Brahman*. But from the human standpoint, the world of experience which is a becoming has to be explained. This is done by attributing Godhood to *Brahman* and reducing it to a name and form. The self-subsistent *Brahman* becomes the God or *Īśvara*, the principle which acts as the unifying force for all things in this universe.

Theory of Causality

There are four fundamental views of causality which we have to discuss here: the view of the Buddhist which is called the theory of dependent origination, the theory of the Naiyāyika which maintains that the effect is a new creation, the theory of the Sāṁkhya which holds that nothing new can be created because the sum total of Reality is constant, and the theory of the Advaitin who maintains that while causation may be empirically valid, metaphysically it is a self-contradiction and the effect is a mere appearance. Each theory is fundamentally rooted in the metaphysics of the school which upholds it and forms the basis of a ratification of the metaphysics. This is a peculiarity of Indian philosophy itself. An attempt is made to ratify the intuited truths about the nature of reality by intellectual means. Thus each *darśana* puts forward a particular theory to suit its metaphysical predilections.

We have already hinted at the doctrine of dependent origination held by all the Buddhist schools. Early Buddhism, (before the schools of metaphysics developed) tried to explain the law of causality. A causal theory is vital to their belief in becoming. According to them there is incessant change, but there is nothing that changes. However, such change is not chaotic. It is governed by a law. The law is not a natural law, but one where some sort of a necessity prevails between a series of similar states which provides the compulsion for one state of the series to be succeeded by another state. While the idea of an order pervading the universe is very old since it is to be seen in the concept of *ṛta* of the Vedas, such an order was then re-established on the basis of supernatural intervention. The order that was envisaged by Buddha excludes all such supernatural agencies. Nor is the order in the universe due to an inner teleology manifested by that which is considered to be the cause. On the other hand cause can never become active on its own. It is seen to be active only when certain co-operative conditions are present. So causality implies a necessity, but a necessity which is contingent on other conditions. For example: the flame series starts only when the conditions, which are the wick, oil etc. are present. The series goes on as long as these conditions are present. If even one of them ceases to be present the series ceases. The continuous existence of the series is dependent on the continuous association between the conditions. Therefore this theory of causal relation is known as dependent origination, *prātītya samutpāda* which literally means "arising in correlation with".

We must distinguish here between two notions of necessity. One is that which is involved in the natural law and the other is that which is implied in dependent origination. A natural law says that wherever the effect Q is found there the cause P must also be present. The relation between P and Q is conditional and implies the logical relation of "following from". This means that given the conditions P, the result Q must follow. The necessity implied is absolute, otherwise there can be no causal law at all. If under any circumstances, the chain becomes unstrung then causal law itself becomes defunct. In dependent origination this is not so. The "cause" becomes a "because" providing not only a causal relation, but also a notion of formal implication. By removing the dependency involved in the production of the effect, the causal series can be arrested. The causal factors being natural ones can be determined in their entirety. As they are knowable, they are also removable, thus removing the possibility of the occurrence of the effect. This theory was used first in the termination of misery by the Buddhists and then later came to be extended to all causal phenomena.

In later Buddhism causation is discussed as change which is total. It is argued that if all change were not total, then there would be a residual part which would be a permanent aspect; this is not acceptable to the Buddhists. In a causal relation between A and B, the cause A totally becomes the effect B, and such a becoming is perpetual. For example, a seed has the capacity to become a shoot. Such a capacity must be manifested all at once, otherwise the efficiency becomes suspended and this goes against the doctrine of becoming. The Buddhist does not accept the idea of potentiality dismissing it as merely another name for lack of efficiency in becoming an effect. A thing *is* only during the moment of its action and its action is its efficiency to produce the next moment of its existence in the series. The seed is thus never inactive. It is all the time becoming; it is continuously producing itself as the next in the series. When the shoot appears, what has happened is that a change has occurred in the series. The seed series, at some stage suddenly becomes replaced by the shoot-series. This happens because the conditions of the seed-series are arrested and the conditions of the shoot-series appear. Even in destruction, there is nothing that is destroyed. The series of that which is "destroyed" is replaced by the series of that which destroys it.

The Mādhyamika idealist explains this conception of dependent origination in a different manner. He does not believe in any origination, whether it is dependent or otherwise. Nāgārjuna maintains in his *Kārika* that all causality is illusion. It is based on the fact that all experience itself is an illusion, for it is the result of relations which are self-contradictory. The empirical processes of experience are all real only at that level and disappear when subjected to philosophic investigation. So the Mādhyamika Buddhist maintains that causation which is a relation is not a true relation. It is workable at the empirical level and possesses only a provisional reality, *samvṛttisatya.*

While the idea that the effect is different from the cause and that it is something which is entirely newly produced is the common link between the dependent origination of the Buddhist and the *asatkārya vāda* of the Naiyāyika, the latter approaches the problem from the point of view of its realistic metaphysics. The effect, according to this theory, is something that is produced anew. It was not already there but has come into being as a result of the causal activity. Hence the theory is known as *ārambha-vāda*, the doctrine of new creation. It is also called *āsatkārya-vāda*, the doctrine of non-existent effect, because the effect was non-existent prior to its creation.

While causal relation as such is not given as a fact, its existence is known by observation of facts and is ascertained from such empirical successions which are uniform and without exception. The Naiyāyika maintains that the effect should not exist without the cause and that an absence of the cause must mean an absence of the effect. Such an event which can be considered as a cause must be antecedent to the effect. Thus a general definition of cause emerges as that which is the invariable (immediate) antecedent of what is not a superfluity: *Ananyatāsiddha, kāryaniyata, purvavṛtti kāranam.*[1] The cause is something determined by the nature of effect. For example: if the effect is oil, the cause cannot be a stone. The cause must be something in which, through experience, we come to know the possibility of the existence of oil. Secondly, the effect which determined the nature of the cause must be such that it is not originated by any other cause. It must not only be immediately antecedent to the effect, it must also be invariable. It is only when all these conditions are fulfilled that an event can be considered as the cause of another event. This definition almost anticipates the definition given by J. S. Mill who maintains that a cause is an invariable unconditional antecedent of an effect.

Later Naiyāyikas found this definition faulty. There can be many things that are invariable and immediately antecedent to the effect and which are not the cause. For example, the colour of the potter's wheel is as much an invariable, immediate and antecedent factor of the coming into being of the pot, yet it cannot be the cause. Therefore these later Naiyāyikas maintain that for every effect there is a special cause which alone is the real cause. This is called *kāraṇam* and is defined as that special event which is not only invariable and antecedent but also that in which the causal activity subsists: *Vyāparavad asādhāraṇam kāraṇam karaṇam.*[2] Of the large number of events which can be described as cause, that event which is actively responsible for the production of the effect, is the real cause. This definition not only makes the nature of a cause precise, it also emphasises the fact that the effect is the result of a causal activity. The effect is different from the cause in form, potency and special position. Thus we find that the Nyāya definition of cause considers it as something that is responsible actively for the production of the effect. The attributes of a cause such as its colour, the cause of a cause such as the father of the potter, are excluded from the cause.

According to the Nyāya-Vaiśeṣika philosophers the logical relation between the cause and effect is a unique one known as *samavāya* or inherent relation. This relation is a contribution of

1 *Tar-Sam.*
2 *Tar-Sam.*

the Vaiśeṣika school and accepted by the Nyāya. It is a relation that exists between things which are inseparable. If the relation is severed, one of the relata at least will be destroyed. We may say that the relation is similar to an internal relation where the nature of the relation is integral and coheres in the relata. This approach of the Nyāya-Vaiśeṣika to causal relation is indicative of their intellectual approach to the problem. Causal relation is not something that is observable as a physical fact. It is the way the intellect of man understands a particular set of facts. Hence their relation, as understood, is an inseparable relation.

Such a cause is said to be of three types. The material cause, *upadāna kāraṇa* is understood in two ways. One is the *samavāyi kāraṇa* or inherent cause. This is invariably a substance. Thus the threads which are woven into a cloth are the inherent material cause. The other aspect of the threads, namely their conjunction in a particular manner is the non-inherent cause or *asamavāyī kāraṇa* of the effect, the cloth. The other cause is the *nimitta kāraṇa*, the instrument whose activity brings about the effect. Perhaps we may draw a very wide parallel between the Aristotelian division of cause into material, formal and efficient cause and the Nyāya conception of *samavāyī*, *asamavāyī* and *nimitta kārāṇā*.

Directly opposed to the Nyāya theory is the theory of the Sāṁkhya which maintains that nothing new is ever produced as a result of causal activity. Causation is merely a manifestation of that which already exists. It makes patent what was always latent. The implicit form is known as cause and the explicit form is known as the effect. They are the developed and the undeveloped states of the same substance. In production there is no new thing which comes into existence. Production is only a development of the undeveloped in a particular manner. They ask the Naiyāyikas how a new thing which did not exist before can come into being as a result of the causal operation. If this were possible, that is, if there were no similarity between cause and effect, if the cause were utterly new and different from the effect, then oil could be produced from stones! The causal relation cannot exist between things which are essentially different from one another.[1] Cause and effect are distinct, but not different, from each other. It is no doubt true that the qualities that the effect manifests are not the same as those that are present

1 *Tatt - Kau.*

in the cause. For example: a pot made of clay can hold water but clay itself cannot do this. Causal activity can take place and causal efficiency become active only in such things which possess the capacity to do so. For example: it is only threads and not wood that can be woven into cloth. The very fact that the potency becomes active means there is production of the effect. Again the Sāṁkhya thinkers maintain that if the cause had not already existed in a latent form in the effect, it could never be produced, even if a thousand artists were to try to do so.[1]

While cause is non-different from the effect in essence, it is different in practical use. This difference is due to the removal of certain factors from the cause. If these are not removed causal activity will not take place. These are known as concomitant potencies, *sahakāriśakti*, and are three in number. They are the place or *deśa*, time or *kāla* and form or *ākāra* of the thing. Cause is seen to be of two kinds. The material cause is common to both the states. The efficient cause is such that, while acting from outside, it helps in the removal of the concomitant factors and manifests the effect in a different space, time and form. The effect is the consequent of the antecedent cause and both are identical in essence.

The importance of this theory to the Sāṁkhya thinker lies in his metaphysics which maintains that the world around us is an explicit state of the original *Prakṛti*. Another name for this is *pradhāna* which means "what was presupposed". This requires a little clarification. It is observed that when objects of clay are all destroyed, they go back into the substance from out of which they have been fashioned. Taking this argument to its logical conclusion shows that all things of this world must be reducible to some common factor which, the Sāṁkhya thinker calls *Prakṛti* or *pradhāna*. This theory is also known as *pariṇāma vāda* or theory of change.

The theory of cause put forth by Śaṁkara in his Advaita is known as *vivarta vāda* or the doctrine of phenomenal appearance. While discussing the metaphysics of the Advaitin we pointed out how, for the Advaitin, *Brahman* alone is real while everything else including the *jīva* is an appearance. Such phenomenal appearance is explained by their theory of cause. The Naiyāyika

[1] "*Nahi nīlam śilpi sahasreṇāpi pītam kartum sakyate*"— "Even a thousand artists cannot make blue into yellow." *Tatt–Kau.*

maintains that the cause and effect is created anew every time. The Sāṁkhya while accepting that both cause and effect are real, is not prepared to accept the idea that the effect is a new creation. Instead he maintains that the causal process only manifests what was already pre-existent in the cause. The Advaitin wipes away the effect altogether by saying that while the cause is real the effect is not so. This makes the theory of cause a mockery. However, as Bradley does, the Advaitin points out that all relations, including the causal relation, are not ultimate relations. While its empirical validity is not questioned, the positing of the relation as a process of creation of this universe is not acceptable to the Advaitin. Let us examine this in more detail now.

In the last section while discussing the nature of *Brahman* as *Īśvara*, we pointed out how these are only two aspects of one and the same reality. We also speculated and found that the existence of *Īśvara* as a separate entity is unthinkable. Now we have to consider the creative aspect of *Īśvara*. It is claimed by certain Vedantins who are theistic in their approach to the *Bādarāyana Sūtras* that causation, as applied to creation is to be seen as *Brahma-pariṇāma*. That is, *Brahman* itself as the material cause of this universe, modifies and changes itself as this universe during the process of creation. To this the Advaitin says that such a definition of *Brahman*, attributing to it the causal activity of creation comes under *definition per accidens* and should not be taken as the definition of the essential nature of *Brahman*. A *definition per accidens*, *taṭasthalakṣaṇa*, is that "which serves to distinguish while not enduring throughout the same time as the defined".[1] That is, attributing of creative activity to *Īśvara*, does not make *Īśvara* really the causal agent but helps in distinguishing *Īśvara* as a source of this world appearance from *Īśvara* as *Brahman*. Such distinction is secondary and only temporary as there are really no two *Īśvaras*, but only one *Brahman*.

The Advaitin accepts that *Brahman* as *Īśvara* is both the material and efficient cause of this universe. *Īśvara* is partless, actionless, quiescent and without marks. How can such an *Īśvara* be the material cause of this world? If He is the material cause, then is there a real transformation or only an apparent transformation? Śaṁkara accepts, as a preliminary measure that there is real transformation, but argues against it and proves that such a transfor-

[1] *Ved. Par.*, VIII, 8.

mation is only illusory. The essence of a real *pariṇāma vāda* is that both cause and effect are equally real. Unless the Advaitin accepts this, he cannot accept the real transformation of *Īśvara* into this world as its real cause. Therefore the Advaitin, true to his metaphysics, argues that both cause and effect cannot be real. The effect is only an illusory transformation of *Īśvara* like the snake appearing in the rope. In reality cause and effect are not two distinct facts. They are not connected by the *samavāya* relation as the Nyāya-Vaiśeṣika holds. The Advaitin argues that if cause and effect are inseparably related, then cause cannot exist before the effect as the Naiyāyika holds. Therefore it is simpler to hold that there is an identity of essence between cause and effect. It is maintained that apart from the cause the effect has no existence. This is because the cause is immutable whereas the effect is evanescent. The snake is present in the rope only as long as the perceiver does not have the clarity of perceptual knowledge. But once he has this clarity the snake ceases to exist. The rope has always been there. Similarly, the world is an unreal effect of *Brahman* who is the cause. On the other hand the world is real for experience; if this were not so, we would all be in the world of Berkeleyan subjectivism. We arrive then at the absurd conclusion that the world is neither real nor unreal. We therefore have to consider the possibility of the world as an effect, partly identical and partly different from *Brahman* who is the cause. The question now is whether the relation between cause and effect is not one of identity-in-difference since both identity and difference are not acceptable as a relation between them? This is not acceptable to the Advaitin. Elsewhere Bradley has shown this hybrid relation to be full of contradictions. Similarly the Advaitin discusses this point at great length in the various texts. It is not possible to dwell on this at great length here. We shall confine ourselves to that aspect of the discussion which is pertinent to our present problem. There can be only two relations between things, identity or difference. If two things are identical, they cannot be different, and vice versa. If we are to postulate a relation of identity-in-difference between, say A and B, then, what we are maintaining is that A is both identical to B and different from B. That is, A is both B and not B at the same time. This is a self-contradiction and violates laws of thinking. The Advaitin maintains that the relation between cause and effect cannot be such a contradictory relation. The cause alone is real.

The effect is only a phenomenal appearance of the cause. Hence this theory of the Advaitin is known as *vivarta vāda.* According to this the cause, no doubt, produces the effect, but the cause does not undergo any change and the effect that is produced is illusory and transient.

While the above discussion outlines the metaphysical aspects of the causal relation, the Advaitin is very careful in maintaining that the phenomenality of the effect is valid only at the *pāramārthika*, transcendental, level and at the *prātibhāsika* or illusory levels. In ordinary empirical experience, one has to accept the law of causation as a valid law. However, all that is valid at the empirical level need not also be valid at the transcendental level. When we apply logical canons to our various beliefs at the empirical level, we find that they do not stand the test of such scrutiny. The position of the law of causality is the same. At the empirical level the Advaitin accepts change due to causality. At the transcendental level, there can be no change at all since *Brahman* is immutable.

CHAPTER III

THEORY OF KNOWLEDGE

The previous chapter has already shown how the need for a development of systematic theory of knowledge arose in the different schools of Indian philosophy. The necessity of such a theory of knowledge growing out of and being dependent on the ontology of each system has also been emphasized. In this chapter we are going to discuss the nature, starting point, forms and the validity of knowledge along with the means of attaining such knowledge. Wherever possible historical parallels between the Indian schools and Western systems have been drawn.

Nature of Knowledge

The most important question to be answered first is, what is the nature of knowledge? Is it empirical or metaphysical? Knowledge as empirical, would express the relation of one object to another. Metaphysical knowledge is the knowledge in and for itself and the knowledge pertaining to the nature of the thing-in-itself apart from its relations. In the modern day, the whole battle of epistemology is centred round this possible distinction in the nature of knowledge. Empirical philosophers maintain that a thing is never known apart from what it does or apart from its relation to other things. But idealist philosophers object to this and say that such an argument leads to a confusion between *doing* and *being*. An object not only does things but it also exists. When we speak of an object capable of various actions and relations we are implicitly accepting the different aspects of the object as doing and being. Being very much aware of such arguments, the schools of Indian philosophy analyze both these aspects of an object. This is because of the practical character of Indian philosophy. Every school of Indian philosophy traces the sufferings and sorrows of man, the evils of this world, and moral irresponsibility to a wrong knowledge of the true nature of the objects of knowledge. The highest purpose of man is to attain true knowledge. A removal of wrong knowledge sets man on the path to self-realization, *mōkṣa.*

The empirical aspect of knowledge can be distinguished into the psychological and the logical. From a psychological point of view, knowledge is an action where the external object is apprehended. The "object" is to be interpreted here to mean anything that is knowable. Hence the question of the cognition being right or wrong does not arise here. It is merely the act of knowing where the object is a presented object. Thus, knowledge includes all knowing states such as sensations, perceptions, imaginations, doubts and illusions. The difference between truth and falsity is of no concern here. Knowledge, thus understood, is merely descriptive of the act of knowledge.

As Russell says: "Whatever we are acquainted with must be something; we may draw wrong inferences from our acquaintance, but the acquaintance itself cannot be deceptive".[1] Thus when an object is known merely as an object in an act of knowing there can be no question of truth or falsity about the act itself. This distinction is important as certain Indian schools of thought discuss this in great detail, trying to fix the locus of validity in the various activities involved in the complex act of knowing. From a logical point of view knowledge must always be true. It is distinguishable from all penumbra, problematic and hypothetical cognitions. A knowledge that is true is accompanied always by the belief that it is true. But truth cannot be purely a subjective certainty. Hence knowledge, to be true, must conform to the nature of the object that is known. It is in this context that classical Indian philosophers discuss the nature of truth and the methods of arriving at such truth.

The metaphysical nature of knowledge is also of importance in this context. Questions about the status of knowledge as a real have to be examined. Is it a substance, quality or relation? If it is considered as a substance, its ontological status has to be defined. If it is a quality, then one possibility which we will be facing is the nature of knowledge as an action. We have stated that to classical philosophers in India action is a quality since it always inheres in a substance. In this sense knowledge enjoys an ontological status. Knowledge is also treated as a quality of a different sort. Just as colour is a quality of a substance, it is maintained by certain schools that knowledge inheres in the Self as its quality. The former theory of the nature of

1 Bertrand Russell, *Problems of Philosophy*, p. 119.

knowledge is accepted by the Mīmāṁsa and Bauddha schools, whereas the latter is acceptable to all the schools except the Advaita school of the Vedāntins. To this school knowledge is an existent reality and is, in its pure form, the soul itself.

Let us now examine these in detail. All schools of thought accept the fact that we do have a knowledge of things and objects as being external. Even the idealist schools of the Vedānta start with this assumption. But after showing how knowledge of these objects arises empirically they go on further to show that such an object has really no ultimate externality. The realist schools like the Nyāya analyse the processes of perception and come to the conclusion that knowledge can only be of objects that are other than the knowing mind. As such, all the schools have to make a start with the analysis of sense-perception. There is still another difference between the realist and idealist schools of India. The former emphasize that perceptual knowledge is dependent upon and arises as a result of sense activity and sense-object relation. The latter schools maintain that perceptual knowledge being direct, sense activity or sense-object relation is not a necessary condition of such knowledge.

Objectivism is carried to its farthest extreme by the materialist Cārvāka who maintains that knowledge is only the manner in which physiological reflexes to environmental situations occur. This view is in line with the interpretation of knowledge given by the modern behaviourism of Watson.[1] A parallel may also be drawn with the naive materialism of Hobbes. Both of them believe, as the common man does, that the objects are all real and "out there", and knowledge can only be of the perceptual type. Memory and such other things are dependent on perception and sensations. Knowledge is an activity of the body. There is no mind apart from this. There can never be a knowledge without sensations. Mind is only a function of matter, since, it is never seen to function apart from matter. Even memory is only "decaying sensation" as Hobbes would say. Thus there is a great deal of resemblance between the ancient Cārvāka theory and the theory of Hobbes.[2]

The position of the Cārvāka is not accepted generally by the other Indian schools. It did, however, catalyse their definition

[1] John B. Watson, *The Ways of Behaviourism*, pp. 80-85.

[2] F.J.E. Woodbridge (ed.), *The Philosophy of Hobbes*, p. 92 ff.

of the issues here as elsewhere. In criticism of it they show that this explanation is like putting the cart before the horse. They maintain that behaviour arises out of knowledge and presupposes knowledge as a prerequisite. All knowledge patterns involve subjective as well as objective aspects. Even if it is granted that the overt objective side of knowledge is behaviour, the subjective aspect is still left out of consideration.

The Nyāya school of thought is the culmination of post-Upaniṣadic logical thinking; it is also the basis for the later logical and epistemological period. As such it occupies a very important place in the history of Indian logic. The Naiyāyika, although a realist, still rejects the behavioural explanation of the nature of knowledge. He reminds us that even if knowledge is merely an activity, the nature of this activity has still to be determined. Such an activity can only be either physical or mental. It cannot be a physical force, as it is not measurable like any other physical force. The assumption that it is a mental action is questionable. It is only metaphysically that we can speak of knowledge as an action. In knowledge there is the object that is known, and the subject that knows. Knowledge is the accomplished fact which illuminates the relations that exist between subject and object. Although this is so, knowledge itself is not a relation. All that we can safely assume is that knowledge appears when a relation is established between subject and object.

Having understood knowledge in this wide sense the Nyāya school, then gives us the various forms of it. Presentational knowledge, *anubhava*, is the knowledge which arises out of immediate subject-object relation. Such knowledge is different from memory, *smṛtī*, which is recollected knowledge based on previous experience. Both presentational knowledge and memory can have valid or invalid forms. A valid presentative knowledge is *pramā*. Validity is judged by correspondence. When an object is truly presented in knowledge, we have *pramā*. This word *pramā* is used to mean only true cognition. Novelty is one of the conditions of true cognition. Such a definition of knowledge is generally accepted by the other schools of Indian realism such as Sāṁkhya.

The idealist schools of Indian thought present a different problem. Reality can be known only in experience. But a frank and sustaining analysis of experience always leads us to the situation that reality is that which cannot be known. To use the terminology of Kant, the thing-in-itself is the source of knowledge, but it can never be known as an object of knowledge.

This poses several questions. If we can never know the thing-in-itself, what happens to all our scientific and metaphysical knowledge? Is it real and true? Such questions can only leave us with a confused scepticism. In recent Western philosophy some of the logical positivists like Carnap tell us that such questions should not be asked, because they are irrelevant and do not provide any answers, and as such are nonsensical.[1] The Vedāntic idealist when posed with the same problem maintains that the starting point has to be knowledge given empirically and it is only through such knowledge that we can arrive at the nature of Reality. The neumenal nature of Reality is suggested and implied by the phenomenal knowledge, but the phenomenal has to be included and transcended before the true nature of Reality can be known. This is neither Cartesian rationalism nor the faith doctrine of St. Anselm. Descartes' theory of metaphysics is based on the rational capacity of man to think and St. Anselm's theory has as its cornerstone the faith man has in his reason to comprehend the scriptures. To the Vedāntin, the starting point is an analysis of knowledge as it is obtained by common sources such as perception and inference. Such an analysis invariably points to a neumena as the source. In such an attempt, it is essential for the philosopher to be completely honest and to start from scratch. The first thing to do is to rid knowledge of all subjectivism. All interpretations of knowledge must be removed and we must then seek in human experience the knowledge of Reality. This method is like the transcendental method of Kant, although the Vedāntin goes much beyond the Kantian position. The Vedāntin holds that we can never get away from knowledge and treat knowledge as an object of criticism. This does not mean that we can never criticise knowledge, but only that while doing so, we nevertheless remain within knowledge itself. Throughout our critical evaluation there is always an element of subjective interpretation. It is only when, by successive levels of criticism, we are forced to see where criticism itself becomes meaningless that we arrive at the truth about Reality. This is the dialectical method of the Vedāntin.

[1] Rudolf Carnap, *Philosophy and Logical Syntax.*

Such an approach to truth is not dogmatic. It is the experimental method. At every step, man must ask "Is this knowledge about the Real or the unreal? Is this the object's true nature or is it only its appearance?" Such a search leads man deeper and deeper into the nature of knowledge and its powers to reveal Reality. In the course of such a search we see that there are various levels of knowledge, but the highest level is that where it merges with the truth about Reality. Thus the Vedāntin is content to start with knowledge as defined by the Naiyāyika as correspondence. This is where empirical experience has to start.

Pramā or valid knowledge is defined by the Nyāya school as presentational knowledge, *yathārthānubhava*. Four factors are involved in this: the knower or the subject, the known or the object, the method by which the knower knows the known, and the resultant knowledge. In Western epistemology it is usual to distinguish between the subject, the object and the resultant knowledge. In Indian thought there is, in addition, what is usually known as the method of knowledge. These four, subject: *pramāta*, object: *pramēya*, method: *pramāna* and the resulting knowledge: *pramā*, mutually constitute the whole truth. Valid knowledge is not possible in the absence of any one of these. Such a four-fold division becomes easy to understand when we examine different ways of acquiring knowledge. In perception, inference, analogy and testimony, the subject, the object and the resultant knowledge are the invariable factors while the method employed is the variable. Thus the operative cause of knowledge is *pramāna*, the method. It is again the efficiency of the method used that ensures the probability of truth for the resulting knowledge. There are four such means, of which perception is the most fundamental. Every other means of knowledge, such as inference and analogy, depend on perception for its starting point. It is the ground on which the knowledge derived from other sources rests. Another reason why the Naiyāyika considers perception fundamental is because it is the final test for all knowledge. We can doubt the results of other methods and verify them by perceptual evidence. But perception itself cannot be so doubted. Hence the most important source of human knowledge is perception.

In Western philosophy perception is given a great deal of importance as a mode of acquiring knowledge. The empiricists starting with Berkeley, raised questions about the validity of perceptual knowledge, and its processes which are still discussed and debated. The school of modern realism led by G. E. Moore is centred almost completely round the primary of perceptual knowledge. Idealistic logicians also accept the primacy of perceptual knowledge. But they maintain that perceptual knowledge cannot be taken for granted to be true. Like any other knowledge it has to be examined and verified. In Western epistemology the whole question of empiricism versus idealism hinges on the value and meaning attached to perceptual knowledge.

Before we go on to give an account of Indian theories of perception it would be profitable to examine broadly at least one of the Western theories of the nature and validity of perception. The arguments run thus. Perception is the result of sensations. Commonsense theories accept the view that the subject has sense titillations derived from objective sources and these in their turn produce ideas which we call knowledge. Thus, granted that there is nothing wrong with our sense-organs, we cannot but arrive at true knowledge about the external world through sense-perception. What we know is reality itself. When a subject encounters the object, knowledge of the object results. Knowledge grasps the object as it were and there can then be no doubt that we have a true knowledge of the object. This explanation of the modern realists does not consider the problems of correspondence between the two separate worlds of ideas on the one hand and objects on the other. This theory, known as epistemological monism, holds that all knowledge is immediate in the sense that it does not depend on the mediation of the idea.[1] In other words, perceiving is "homogeneous with physical or physiological phenomena".[2] E.B. Holt et. al., in *The New Realism* desire to vindicate the independent reality of things and, this can be done only in so far as perception of them is possible.

The Naiyāyika would readily accept this theory. To the Naiyāyika, too, perception involves the perceiving of a thing which is independent of the knowing mind. But we may ask, can such a theory of knowledge lead us to a knowledge of reality? It does so in only one way. It requires that we take the validity of such knowledge on trust. There is no evidence for it. Our knowledge may refer to reality, but there is no evidence that such reference

[1] R. B. Perry, *Present Philosophical Tendencies*, p. 126.

[2] N. V. Banerjee, *Concerning Human Understanding*, p. 106.

is true. To avoid confusing true knowledge with error, we need here an "indubitable criterion within knowledge itself to detect the fact and extent of error".[1] A tree may be a tree at one perceptual moment and may be a ghost at another moment. If there is no such in-built criterion of judging within knowledge itself, our perceptions may be totally untrustworthy. Accepting the validity of any piece of knowledge on trust is neither logical nor justifiable. What is common to all such realistic epistemologies however is their attempt to justify sensible experience and evolve a theory of knowledge based on such experience. The Nyāya school of logic is in the same position.

Perception

Gautama, the founder of the Nyāya school defines perception as "knowledge which arises from the contact of the sense-organ with its object, indubitable, determinate and unerring". The early Nyāya school defines perception as immediate valid cognition of reality arising out of sense and object contact. The Sāṁkhya, Mīmāṁsa and the Vedānta schools also agree that sense and objects in contact (the definition of contact differs from school to school) give rise to knowledge. This is specially true of lower sensations like touch and taste which cannot function unless physical contact is brought about with the object. Though originally perception had this meaning, it slowly came to mean much more than this.[2] The Nyāya school holds that there are four factors involved in perception—the senses, the objects, the contact between these two and the resultant knowledge. When sense-object contact and the resultant rousing of the sense-organ is established, mind (*manas*) takes over and acts as the mediator between the sensation and the Self. This activity of mind is an essential part of perceptual knowledge.

The Naiyāyika argues for this in the following manner. The sense-organs are always coming into contact with objects. When we are attending to one thing, there is no knowledge of other things, even though the sense-organs and the objects are in contact.

[1] G. R. Malkani, *Vedāntic Epistemology*.

[2] Refer to *Tattva Cintāmanī* by Gangeśa; Tr., Vidya Bhusan in ***History of Indian Logic***, p. 13.
Though originally perception meant indubitable knowledge derived through sense activity, later Naiyāyikas like Gangeśa modified this and defined perceptual knowledge as direct awareness with or without sense activity.

Sometimes there is apparently simultaneous knowledge. But this is due to the rapidity of succession of the contacts between mind and Self. The example cited in the *Nyāya Bindu* is: "When we run a pin through a number of sheets it gives the appearance of simultaneity, though really it is only successive." Hence mind, *manas*, is in contact with one sense-organ at a time. Not only this, the same commentary goes on to say: "Remembrance, inference, verbal cognition, doubt, intuition, dream, imagination, as also perception of pleasure and the rest are indicative of the existence of mind."[1] Thus Self and mind are constant invariable factors of perceptual knowledge.

Perception is divided by the Naiyāyika into two broad fields; the ordinary, *laukika*, and the extraordinary, *alaukika*. Ordinary or normal perception is that where the normal sense-object contact persists. The usual channels of sense-perception, such as the sense-organs of sight, hearing, touch, taste and smell, are all acknowledged as means of sensations. However, ordinary perceptions are viewed from two different angles. These are the indeterminate, *nirvikalpaka*, and the determinate, *savikalpaka*. This division is based on the type of the resultant knowledge of the sense-object contact.

Almost all schools of Indian thought accept this division between indeterminate and determinate perceptions, although the meaning and value they give to it differs in the light of their metaphysical predilections. The realistic systems of Mimāṁsa, Sāṁkhya and Nyāya believe that what is given in perception, generally, is the concrete object which exemplifies within it the unity of the universal and the particular. To the Mīmāṁsa and Sāṁkhya schools it is the indeterminate perception, *nirvikalpaka pratyakṣa* which is a whole of the universal and the particular, thus making the individual object indefinite. The object is simply apprehended without being individualised as this or that object. Because it is simple apprehension it cannot be expressed in words. It is like a child's apprehension. Because of sense-perception, the child knows there is an object, but what it is he cannot say. This is not because of his lack of language, but because he does not know definitely. His knowledge is a judgement, but it is non-propositional. This is like the immediate reflex action to a pinprick. What it is we cannot say, but action would be impossible without some sort of an awareness. When definite knowledge,

[1] Tr. from Radhakrishnan's *Indian Philosophy*, Vol. II, p. 51.

savikalpaka pratyakṣa, arises, there is the predicative knowledge asserted of the object. The definite judgement "This is a table" is then made possible. This latter involves an extra-perceptual reference such as recollection and comparison. These are made possible by the prior non-predicative type of perception of the "this" of the object. This is indeterminate perception.

The Naiyāyika agrees in substance, with this view. For him the indeterminate perception is not the knowledge of the bare particular, but the knowledge of the universalised particular. The substantive-predicative relation has not yet emerged. It is an undifferentiable whole, free from the work of analysis and synthesis which later on gives the same perception a determinate aspect. The relations of determination do not emerge all at once. They are first present as an undifferentiated whole in the prior indeterminate perception. It is here that reality is directly and immediately perceived. The distinctions of truth and falsity are not to be used with reference to this knowledge. These belong to the area of determinate perception. In this latter perception, the "this" is present, but it is built up into a concrete object by the mind, possessing a definite name and form and as such may be true or false.

This explanation of indeterminate perception has been criticised by the school of grammarians.[1] They maintain that there cannot be any unverbalised knowledge, since all thinking is done only with words. This may recall the attempts by modern Western behaviourists to define all thinking as "sub-vocal speech". Cognition of an object is possible only when such cognition is denotative, making use of language. Hence there is no indeterminate perception.

The Naiyāyika says that this contention is wrong. There are many experiences which cannot possibly be translated into language. If words and thoughts were equivalent, then children would, without instruction, know the names of objects even as they see them. It is not necessary for cognition to be verbal, and

[1] There was a well-developed school of grammarians in the early days of systematic Indian philosophy. These were linguists who tried to arrive at a philosophy by the analysis of sentences into its grammatical constituents and fixing the meaning of words. Compare Aristotle's development of categories. Also note E. R. Hughes "Centrality of literary analysis as a philosophic method in China" from Charles Moore (ed.), *Essays in East–West Philosophy*.

nirvikalpaka knowledge, which is generalised and unspecific, is really the first stage in acquiring knowledge.

The Vedānta and Buddhist schools of idealism give a different version of indeterminate perception. The Advaita defines indeterminate perception as the perception of pure Being as existent. All determination is characterisation and as such, determinate perception *savikalpaka pratyakṣa* involves affirmations and negations which are brought about by the judging of a discursive mind. The Being of all objects is, finally, one of undifferentiated consciousness. Hence the distinctions and differences seen in determinate perceptions are all appearances. Therefore it is only through *nirvikalpaka pratyakṣa* or indeterminate perception that we get a glimpse of the real nature of things. But even this is expressible in a propositional form. In identity propositions such as "this is that man" we are establishing the identity of "that man" of past experience with the perceptual cognition of "that man" with "this" here and now. On the other hand, there is only an assertion of a non-predicative and unrelated identity of the essential Being here. It is not the result of either memory or recognition but of the perception of identity.

Such perception is the reverse process of what the Naiyāyika believes. To the Nyāya indeterminate perception has to be the first step towards determinate perception. But to the Advaitin, determinate perception as a relational whole of qualities and substance is known first, then comes the realisation of the identity of the object with its aspect of pure Being which is indeterminate perception, *nirvikalpaka pratyakṣa.*

To the Buddhist idealist[1] indeterminate perception, *nirvikalpaka pratyakṣa* is the only true perception. Sense perception as a kind of cognition is fallacious because it does not take many facts into consideration. The Buddhist maintains that every cognition is a new one and not a re-cognition. But this is true only in the first moment of sense-perception. This is the only true cognition by the senses. The next moment, when attention becomes focused on the sensation, it gets transformed by the contributions of the mind. The sense function is to simply signal the presence of the

[1] To distinguish between the different idealistic schools of Buddhism and explain their theories is not possible in a mere outline book such as this. So only basic ideas common to the subjective idealist and the nihilistic idealism are discussed here.

object. Constructing the image of an object so presented, giving it a name, form and meaning is another function which is the work of the mind. What is perceived in the first instance by the senses is *nirvikalpaka pratyakṣa.* This is the perception of the unique individual, *ṣvalakṣana.* Hence the true definition of perception is that it is "a source of knowledge whose function of making the object present in the ken is followed by the construction of its image."[1] This definition means that perception is pure sensation followed by conceptualization. The difference between the Naiyāyika definition and the Buddhist view is that to the latter, *nirvikalpaka* perception gives rise to a sensation of the uniqueness of the particular individual object whereas to the former it is a combination of the universal and the particular, though still at the undifferentiated level.

This whole discussion of the nature of indeterminate and determinate perception is pregnant with a multitude of difficulties. The same difficulties beset Western epistemological theories as well. This only goes to prove that these difficulties are native to the problem which both Indian and Western schools of thought sought to solve. Among eighteenth century European thinkers, Thomas Reid was deeply aware of this problem. To him "sensation" meant a subjective state of feeling without any implication of the external object. When meaning is conveyed by sensation, it has already ceased to be a sensation and has become a perception. Unfortunately Reid did not work out the implication of such a distinction to its far-reaching conclusions. It was left for Immanuel Kant to bring up and emphasize this distinction once again. Speaking of sense-perception and conceptualization of this by the categories of the understanding, Kant says, "By their union only can knowledge be produced."[2] This idea is repeated *ad nauseum* in most ancient Indian texts on logic. Bertrand Russell in his *Analysis of Mind* speaks of a similar theory. "Sensation is a theoretical core in the actual experience, the actual experience is the perception."[3] Indian realists like the Naiyāyikas and Sāṁkhyas would agree with this and say that definite perception is the completed action of sense-perception, revealing the full nature of the object. But the difference between the Kantian view and the Indian views is that to the former, the in-

[1] Th. Stcherbatsky, *Buddhist Logic*, Vol. I, p. 149.
[2] I. Kant, *Critique of Pure Reason*, Tr. Max Mueller, p. 41.
[3] Bertrand Russell, *Analysis of the Mind,* p. 131.

tuitive *a priori* forms of time and space are the original forms of sense-perception, whereas to the latter even these are the result of the imagination and the constructive activity of the mind. This capacity of the mind, known as *vikalpa* in Indian logic, includes everything pertaining to understanding, judgment and reasoning.

But the difficulty of the whole situation of indeterminate perception is that if a moment of sensation is separated from every interpretation and construction, it ceases to be knowledge in the proper linguistic sense of the word. Dharmottara, the Buddhist logician, aptly characterized this situation as "as if non-existent", *asatkalpa*. Therefore the Indian logician was forced to admit that such pure sensations, although caused by sense-object contact, were still beyond the ordinary empirical processes of knowledge. Thus they called this knowledge *atīndriya* or trans-sense knowledge. It is only pure perception derived from the senses, yet going beyond sensations that can give us a glimpse of Reality that is uncognizable, unnameable, and transcendental.

There are certain schools of Indian thought which believe that determinate perception, *savikalpaka pratyakṣa*, is the only perception possible and that there is no such thing as indeterminate perception. This is the view of the materialistic school of Cārvāka, the Jaina school and the Viśiṣtādvaita school of Vedānta. Ramanuja of the Viśiṣtādvaita school while accepting indeterminate perception, says that the difference between this and determinate perception is only one of degree and not of kind. Both of them characterize the object. But the difference lies in the fact that determinate perception is more precise and clear than indeterminate perception.

The Jainās and the Cārvākās reject indeterminate perception altogether. It is their theory that all true knowledge must be a characterization of the object as a "this" and a "what". Otherwise, such knowledge would not be different from doubt and error. The Cārvākas view indeterminate perception as a hypothetical idea which cannot be validated in experience and only determinate perceptions are considered a means of valid knowledge.

Perception, *pratyakṣa*, is a word used both for the resultant valid knowledge as well as the means of acquiring it. We shall here treat it only as a means of valid knowledge. Determinate perception has been defined by various schools in various ways.

We have already stated that the early Nyāya definition of perceptual knowledge was that it is derived from a contact between the sense-organ, *indriya* and the object, *artha*; it has to be "non-descriptive, non-discrepant and definite". A later modification says that perception is immediate knowledge. Such immediacy is possible because, according to Naiyāyika ontology, each sense-organ is capable of perceiving things of its own nature. For example, the eye is capable of seeing colour because it is made up of fire atoms and colour is the peculiar quality of fire atoms. As has already been indicated, the perceptual process involves not only the functioning of the external sense-organs, but also the contact of the mind with the sense-organ and the contact of the mind with the soul. A discussion about the nature of a sense-organ and sensation is necessary here. It must be noted that the later Naiyāyikas do not accept the definition of perception as the true cognition of an object brought about by the activity of sense-organs. The reason for this is the Advaita criticism that in illusory perception, although the sense-organs have become stimulated, the resultant knowledge is not valid knowledge. There are other positive valid perceptions such as the immediate knowledge of our Self and the knowledge of emotions which are direct perceptions without the involvement of the activity of any external sense-organ. The Advaitin calls this *aparokṣa*, non-mediate. Accepting such arguments as valid, the later Naiyāyikas changed their definition of perception to immediate knowledge.

There are two conditions to be satisfied before any knowledge, whether derived through sense-activity or not, can be called immediate knowledge. Firstly, the object of such knowledge should be such that it can be known directly. An ethical concept such as goodness, therefore, cannot be an object of direct knowledge. This is more an indication of the fact that all things are not perceivable. Secondly, the object must be an existent during the time in which it is the object of perception. This would remove all possibility of confusing memory, which is also immediate, with perception. Defined in this manner perceptual knowledge seems to be something that is independent of all sense-activity. This is not so. All that the Advaitins and the later Naiyāyikas maintain is that immediacy is of greater importance for all perceptual knowledge than is sense-object contact, but sense-object contact is not ignored.

It is in this context that the importance of sense activity arises. Even at the outset it must be made clear that the locus of the sensations is never in question for the ancient Indian. The usual question whether the sensation is subjective or objective has no relevance to the classical philosophies. This is because it is assumed that sensations are primarily subjective. There are metaphysical reasons for such an assumption, the most apparent reason being that without the sense-organ there can be no sense-experience at all, whereas sometimes, even in the absence of the object it is possible to have sense-experience as in the case of the illusory perceptions of mirages. This does not mean that the Indian philosopher accepts subjectivism. The sense-organs are those which provide the means of contact between the knowing Self and the external object. It is only when such contact is definite, true and indubitable that a true knowledge of the object can arise in the subject. All this goes to show how, though the sensations are subjective, they are the means of knowing a world of objects which is external to them.

What then is the nature of such a sense-organ which performs the most difficult task of being subjective and yet reveals the objective? The main difficulty in all Western epistemological theories centres round the locus of the sensations. Since a dichotomy is envisaged between the subjective and the objective, the one cannot reach out to the other. Perhaps, realising this difficulty, the Indian philosopher laid a firm foundation against any such dichotomisation in making the subjective and objective a continuous stream. The body is firmly put in the elemental region thus making it share its constitutive aspects with nature. This aspect is variously explained by the different schools depending on their metaphysical loyalties.

The nature of sense-organs and their relation to sense-perception is clearly stated in very few source books, one of them an Advaita treatise, though it is implied in many discussions. The Buddhist maintains that the sense orifices themselves are the senses. To the Mīmāṁsika realist the *indriya* or sense is a peculiar *śakti* or capacity of the physiological organ. To the Nyāya-Vaiśeṣika the sense is a substance residing in the constructive make-up of the same elemental substances the characteristics of which they perceive.[1] For instance, the eye, the organ which perceives colour, is itself made up of the atoms of light whose differentiating quality is the possession of colour. Thus this theory establishes a sort

[1] See the chapter on Metaphysics.

of continuity between the sensation and the object; a similarity of material structure makes it possible for the sense-organ to get in touch with the objects. This is crude physiology, but nevertheless a sincere effort to find some sort of link between the subjective and objective.

One very interesting point about the Nyāya theory of perception is that no cognition can be directly apprehended. The soul's knowledge is always secondary. Cognition is not self-apprehending, although it makes other objects known. Perception relates "the this" with "the that" and to make this relation knowable it is necessary for it to assume the form: "I know that this is a pot". It is the function of the mind to produce this secondary modification of the primary knowledge roused by sense-object contact. That is, the knowledge, "this is a pot", becomes knowledge only when it serves as an object for the knowing Self. Another function of the mind is to act itself as a sense-organ when internal feelings such as pleasure, pain, desire, aversion and volition are made known.

The process of perception is as follows. The impulse that is aroused in the sense-organ by its physical contact with the object is transmitted to the mind which in its turn presents it to the Self which is in contact with it. The contacts between the sense-organ and the object depend on the nature and type of object. They range from conjunction to inherence. For example, a table is a substance and its colour is a quality. The eye has a direct conjunctival relation with the substance of the chair but only an indirect relation with the colour of the chair. And still more remote is the relation with the genus "colourness" which resides in the colour which in its turn resides in the object. In this manner Naiyāyika theory recognizes different types of relations to perceive different types of objects.

The Sāṁkhya, the Mīmāṁsa and the Vedānta systems all accept a mode of perception where there is the contact between the sense-organ and the object before perceptual knowledge can arise.[1] It is only the Buddhist who maintains that the senses need not be in actual contact with the object for sense-perception to arise. The Buddhist argument is that if this were not so, then we would not be hearing or seeing far-off objects. Sounds and sights from

1 Although the different schools mentioned accept basically sense-object contact for perception, still the nature of such contact differs with each school because of metaphysical considerations.

different directions would not be known if the sense-organ had to reach them every time. These objections of the Buddhists are met by the Naiyāyika by citing the rapidity of alternation in the sense-object contact, which gives rise to an illusion of simultaneity. This activity is explained much like the action of the modern cinematograph pictures. Thus while in modern science, perception is understood to be caused by the rays of light striking the sense-organ, the Indian philosopher maintains that it is the light from the eye that goes to the object, and establishing a contact, gives rise to a knowledge of the object.

The Sāṁkhya and the Vedānta systems accept another mode of sense-object contact for perception. Here it is the mind, *manas*, which is a subtle and fine substance, that goes out to the object, making use of the channels of the sense-organs, and establishes an identity of content between the consciousness as limited by itself and consciousness as limited by the object. The Self which is of the nature of pure consciousness cannot become aware of objects unless some sort of identity is established between itself and the objects. This is accomplished when the mind, *manas* which is itself a refined substance, reflects within itself this nature of the Self and when it comes into contact with an object through sense-channels, envelops such objects and takes their form. This is known as *citta vṛtti*, a mental mode. It is thus that these two schools meet the most important question of Indian epistemology: how does the mind which is different from the object not only in nature, but also removed in space, come to know the nature of the object?

These two elements of knowledge, sensation and conception, have always occupied the minds of even very early Indian philosophers. The idea that conceptualization or judgment is an act of the mind arrived at by the synthesis of pure consciousness (the Self) and the semi-unconscious reflex activity of the sense-organs, is well discussed in the early school of Sāṁkhya. The phenomena of trance which is trans-perceptual and trans-sensational is a development of this idea.

If the question of how the mind and the object become related is not satisfactorily answered, there can be no satisfactory epistemological theory. The Indian philosopher, therefore, asks the question: "If the mind (*antaḥkaraṇa*, internal sense-organ) is responsible for knowledge, then of what use are the sense-organs?"

The answer to this is that the mind acts as the generic cause, and the nature of the difference in perceptual knowledge is determined by the nature of the sense-organ through which the mind is functioning. The name used for this type of perception is *antaḥkaraṇa vṛtti* which means the modification of the internal sense-organ or as *citta vṛtti*, a mental mode.

This theory of the Sāṁkhya and the Vedānta that the mind goes out to the object, seems to be a more acceptable theory if we consider the various theories that have been put forward both in India and the West. Movement of the mind is not a metaphysical theory but an actual going forth. Among Western thinkers, the idea that the mind is not merely a passive element in thought has been accepted from the time of Kant. Such activity of the mind as there is, is seen to be limited to the receiving of sensations from the external sense-organs and somehow co-ordinating these into meaningful wholes. The Vedāntic idea is that the mind is active in the collecting of the raw materials in perception. One difficulty with accepting such a position arises from the well-grounded belief that the work of the sensations comes first and then the mind acts if the existence of a mind is accepted. Another difficulty is that sensations are identified with the activity of the physiological organs: when these are impressed, sensations are said to arise for the mind to act on. But actually this is not so.

The fact of attention, often cited with good point by the Naiyāyika, is evidence enough that mere sense perception can never give rise to knowledge. The senses are treated as senses only in so far as they are channels through which the mind knows the objects. If it is said that the senses together with the cerebro-spinal activities explain physical actions fully, then a difficulty arises. It is incomprehensible how, given such a theory, only certain bodies like the human body exhibit mental capacities and other similarly constructed beings do not do so. Even among human bodies the mental capacities are not all identical. Under the same environmental conditions two people do not exhibit the same mental reaction. On seeing a snake one man may be afraid and stand rooted to the spot while another tries to kill it, yet another runs away in fear. Another theory of the Advaitin is that the mind not only goes out to the object, but also assumes the shape of the object.

Let us trace again the process of perception as we have it in realist Western thought. The object has parts and these parts come into contact with the sense-organ. All these sensations of the different parts are co-ordinated, apart from the co-ordination of different sensations that is necessary before knowledge can arise.[1] But such a theory is not accepted both by philosophers and psychologists. Psycho-philosophers like Brentano say that such a function can only be done by the self-conscious mind acting in a teleological manner. Still, the difficulty of co-ordinating these atomic sensations is left without explanation. The Gestalt school of Psychology which views the perceptual process as a synthetic whole closely approaches the Advaitic idea. The form of the object is not perceived atomically, but as a whole structure. The difference between these two is that whereas according to Advaita such a whole view is possible only when mind and senses act together, according to Gestalt theory there is no such action. The point of resemblance is however that in perception the mind knows immediately the whole object.

This view of the Advaitin is open to the criticism that it is nothing more than representationalism, a theory that Advaita itself has severely criticized. The question is raised: how can we know, in the first instance, that it is a likeness at all; for this implies a prior knowledge of the object. These questions, the Advaitin would say, do not arise because in perception there is an identity established between the object-defined-consciousness and the cognition-defined-consciousness. The object is known and understood, not because of any representation involved, but because of the immediacy involved in the identity established between the different constituents of knowledge being limited by the same consciousness. One may compare this to the knowledge gained by a blind man of the form of an object. When the blind man holds the object, a knowledge of the object, as having a particular form, arises from the shape his arms assume on holding it.

There is also the further problem of the nature of the resultant knowledge. This question of the knowledge being true or false is implicit in the whole theory of knowledge. It has been stated right in the beginning that to the Naiyāyika, knowledge, *jñāna*, by itself is neither true nor false. It is only the nature of

[1] Refer Roy Wood Sellars, "The New Materialism" from Virgilius Ferm (ed), *A History of Philosophical Systems*.

determinate perception that gives perceptual knowledge truth or falsity. At the same time it cannot be denied that knowledge is caused by certain conditions.

It is necessary at this stage to state specifically the distinction between the Indian and Western conceptions of the nature of truth and error. In the Western tradition only true perceptions are recognised as knowledge. Erroneous perception, like a mirage, is not knowledge because it is error. But to the Indian logician, knowledge is a wider term. *Jñāna*, which is usually translated as knowledge refers to any awareness that may arise as a result of the mind receiving and codifying sensations. Some of these are true, *pramā*, and some prove to be false, *apramā*. While the experience is at the stage of sense-perception only, all experiences are taken to be true. At this stage, all such knowledge is ego-centric. Some of these experiences are later shown to be false by pragmatic or coherent tests. But such *jñāna* is not merely belief which has a psychological certitude. Whether it is *pramā*, right knowledge, or *apramā*, wrong knowledge, there is belief in such knowledge and it has psychological certainty, which may later be disproved by logical and empirical sublation. This difference between the Western and Indian views of error is basic and all theories of truth and error are here discussed from the Indian point of view.[1]

Granting this fundamental difference, two questions have to be answered. What are truth and falsity? How can we know what is true and what is false? The first question refers to the originating conditions, *utpatti*, of truth and falsity and the second question raises the problems of ascertaining, *jñāpti*, between truth and falsity. These two questions arise because every now and then perceptual processes lead to erroneous knowledge and illusion. The mistake might be in the sense-organ itself, or it might be in the manner a determinate perception is constructed. Sometimes even where there is no physical basis for perception, perception arises. This may be because the mind is diseased as in a state of drunkenness. However the fact of erroneous perception, *viparyaya*, as opposed to valid perception, *pramā*, remains and this has to be explained by logicians.

1 D. E. Trueblood, *The Logic of Belief*, Chapter II, for a slightly similar Western view.

Two answers have been put forward to the question of erroneous perception: the factors or conditions which cause knowledge also give rise to the validity or invalidity of such knowledge, or on the other hand, truth and falsity are brought about by conditions which are external to those which give rise to knowledge itself. This latter statement implies (1) that truth and falsity are not self-evident, but depend on something else for their evidence, or (2) that truth is intrinsic to the conditions which give rise to it and falsity is to be known by external conditions, or (3) that falsity may be self-evident and the truth may depend on external conditions. Thus on the whole these are the alternatives to examine. Each of these alternatives is accepted and defended by some school or other of Indian philosophy, depending on their metaphysical theories.

The Naiyāyika materialist believes that knowledge by itself is neither true nor false. Its truth or falsity depends on its conformity or non-conformity with the object perceived. Correspondence between knowledge and the object makes the latter true or false and truth and falsity are attached to knowledge depending on whether there is correspondence with the object or not. Such correspondence depends on the conditions which make it possible for perceptual knowledge to arise. Though contact of the sense-organ with the object is the generic cause of perceptual knowledge, still the validity or invalidity of such knowledge depends upon the condition of the sense-organ such as disease and the condition of the object such as its distance from the sense-organ, lighting conditions etc. Thus though knowledge by itself is neither true nor false, it becomes so because of the contingent characteristics constituent of perceptual processes. Such truth or falsity must be known. It is one thing for knowledge to become true or false, and it is entirely another thing for us to know it as true or false. Psychological certitude is not the same as knowledge—we may have the one with varying degrees of the other. The Naiyāyika believes that these are known by certain conditions which are external to the whole situation. This school argues that if the conditions which give rise to the validity or invalidity of knowledge also make it evident to the knower, then there would never be any doubt at all about whether a piece of knowledge is true or false. Hence there have to be certain external conditions which make it possible for us to know that knowledge is valid or invalid. The Naiyāyika says that this is known by the capacity of knowledge to produce the results which it promises to produce. This comes close to the view of the pragmatists like Dewey, who maintain that knowledge is to be evaluated in the context of basic human needs and the capacity for knowledge to fulfil these. The Nyāya logician also believes that an idea is true when it leads us to act in the environment successfully.

The Vedāntin criticises this view and says that such workability is only the test of the claims which knowledge makes to truth. It does not constitute the truth of knowledge. This truth of knowledge must be prior to the demonstration of it by workability. For example, a distant perception of water is taken to be true, till we try to go to it and drink it when its being truly water or not is established. Ordinarily, a habitual piece of experience is judged to be true or false at first sight without a pragmatic test. This does not by any means make such validity self-evident. Here the knowledge of the validity of knowledge is conditioned by its familiarity. It only means that instead of testing knowledge every time for validity, we rely on previous verification. The satisfaction derived by a previous similar knowledge extends its verification to the present knowledge because of the similarity of the generic nature of the experience involved. Thus all knowledge claims validity, but is to be proved to be valid or invalid by the pragmatic success of the use of the idea.

Naiyāyika theory says that error arises in knowledge because of wrong subjective interpretation. A piece of shell is judged to be a piece of silver; then later activity proves that the object is only shell and not silver. The first wrong knowledge is thus sublated by a later knowledge, which, in its turn proves to be true under later circumstances. But how does the erroneous knowledge itself arise? The Naiyāyika says that it is caused by wrong construction of the sense impressions by the mind. Error is cognition of an object as other than what it is. The shining of the shell is perceived through sense-object contact and is confused with the recollection of a shining piece of silver. This confusion gives rise to the false knowledge "this is a piece of silver". This falsity of knowledge is exposed and sublated, when, after further experience, it is shown to be invalid. What is denied in the later sublated knowledge is not the existence of the "this" of the judgment but the wrong characterization of the "this". The perception is false because it is devoid of practical efficiency, *arthakriyākāritva*.

This view seems to be quite an attractive and honest exposition of the common-sense view, but it has some important assumptions which have to be brought under the scrutiny of criticism. These ideas are comparable to the ideas of William James, C.S. Pierce and John Dewey, and like these philosophers the Naiyāyikas assume that the knowing subject is sharply distinguishable from the known object. As a result of this, consciousness becomes the result of the interaction between the Self and the non-Self.

Such a theory of epistemology always has to explain how a bridge from the Self to the non-Self and vice-versa is made. If the real is outside thought, and if truth is agreement of thought with the real, then truth-seeking becomes a very difficult thing to achieve, requiring some other field which is neither thought nor reality from where a correspondence between these two can be established. There can be no such field for the Naiyāyika. Hence, he says it is not necessary for truth to be arrived at by correspondence. It is enough if the resultant knowledge is shown to be workable. The content of knowledge may be verifiable by experience and hence shown to be true or false. The Naiyāyika's theory of truth requires that a knowledge of an object be just its meaning in the present experimental situation. For example, water quenches thirst and fire burns for all men. But if such a test is accepted, illusions which can be a common experience of a number of individuals, would be true. The pink elephants seen by drunks are real inasmuch as they serve the purpose of scaring them. Any number of examples of this type, where truth depends on the practicality of the idea, show that the test is not so practical after all.

A far different theory of truth and error is held by the schools of Sāṁkhya, Mīmāṁsa and Advaita Vedānta. Truth according to these schools is a self-evident characteristic of knowledge. Knowledge does not require any external conditions either to make it true or become known as true. The latter two schools maintain that knowledge becomes false because of external conditioning, that is, validity of knowledge is intrinsic whereas invalidity is extrinsic. This position is logical. If we grant that knowledge is not true intrinsically, we then have to have a standard of truth by which we can test knowledge. But this standard of truth suffers from the very deficiencies of thought, since the cognition of such a standard of truth is itself an act of thought. Therefore we can never know truth. Scriptural testimony specially cannot be cited as true or as evidence, as this is the experience based on ideas of people, if we do not accept that knowledge is intrinsically true. As such it is essential that we grant that by nature, all thought is true.

The idealistic Advaita Vedānta school goes a step further. Although knowledge is true intrinsically, empirical prejudices and psychological attitudes vitiate this pure character of knowledge. Empirically speaking truth and falsity have objective reference. Advaita Vedānta accepts the principle of non-contradiction as a test of truth. No knowledge is ever complete as it is always superceded by later knowledge. When complete knowledge of everything is present then the truth that is self-evident is manifested. Till then empirical tests for empirical truths have to be used. According to such a theory, error is caused by insufficient knowledge. Every piece of knowledge is both true and false. It would be true insofar as it is non-contradictory within its sphere and it would be false since it is sublatable and removable by further knowledge. Thus the erroneous perception of silver in a shell is valid perception because the conditions of perception give rise to this knowledge. But at a later state of perception this silver-cognition becomes sublated by the shell-cognition. What is true under certain circumstances is false under other circumstances. But the knowledge judgment "this is silver" remains the same throughout this characterisation of truth and falsity. This cannot be so, for a judgment can only be either true or false. So the Advaitin contends that the nature of the erroneous perception is indeterminable—*anirvacanīya.*

The Buddhist views the whole question from a completely different angle. All knowledge is intrinsically invalid by its very nature. Such knowledge is considered to become valid when it produces successful activity. This is also a pragmatic theory of knowledge but it starts with false knowledge. The validity of such knowledge arises when successful functioning of the idea negates the invalidity that is inherent in knowledge. Dharmakirti, the eminent Buddhist logician maintained that "right knowledge is efficient knowledge". This Buddhist theory is based on their metaphysical beliefs. Buddhism, as we have seen, developed into four different and diverse systems of thought. Inspite of such diversity, all of them adhere to the fundamental tenets of philosophy as supposed to have been taught by the Buddha according to which there is no infinite and eternal Being, but only a flux. Such a flux is referred to by giving it a name and form. Thus the question of valid cognition within empirical limitations would be cognitions of these names and forms. But it is not mere nomination. There is the broad distinction between the flux as characterised by "mental" and the flux as characterised by "physical". The "mental" includes within it perception, conception, volition and emotion. The early Buddhists maintained that perceptual knowledge arises in the consciousness when there is sense-object contact. The contact has to be physical and mechanical since the sensations can only comprehend such objects as are in physical contact with it.[1] But such contact is not absolutely essential. The senses, according to the Buddhists, are generally distant-receptors, *aprāpyakāri*. This is specially the case with the sense-organs of sight and hearing. The eye can see much larger and much smaller objects than itself. The objects of sight and sound are public objects being available on perception to many people at the same time. Thus these two sense-organs do not require physical contact to acquire knowledge.[2]

It has already been stated that to the Buddhist true knowledge is the knowledge of the object as it is perceived for a moment during the first stage of indeterminate perception. All later knowledge derived through determinate perception is nothing but a construction by the mind. Thus there is no guarantee that it is true knowledge. This does not make for subjectivism. The knowledge in indeterminate perception is true because there is the possibility there for both the perception and its object to co-exist at the same moment thus establishing an association between the two. In later perceptions such association is always one step removed from the perceiving object, because by the time determination of perception is built up, the object has already ceased to be. Similarly the knowing entity, the *vijñāna* is also an everchanging series. Since both the series, the object as well as the subject series are always changing, knowing an object as the same object through successive moments might be said to be impossible. The Buddhist gets out of this logical difficulty by maintaining that each instant of existence has, built into it, all the potentialities of its predecessors. (This we have discussed

[1] S. Radhakrishan, *Indian Philosophy*, Vol. I, pp. 402-403.
[2] This argument is not valid scientifically.

more elaborately in the previous chapter). Thus to the Buddhist all determinate knowledge is constructive, being the work of the mind. Perhaps a very meagre parallel could be drawn here between Kant's theory of knowledge and that of the early Buddhists. To both, the object, as it is, is not knowable in a concrete fashion. What is known is that which is built up on the slender basis of sensation into an objective entity. The objectivity is a mental imposition. The psychological aspect of Buddhist theory is echoed by William James when he says: "Things which are known together are known in single pulses of that stream (consciousness) . . . each subject lasts but for a moment. Its place is immediately taken by another which exercises its function, that is, to act as the medium of unity."[1]

In general, early Buddhist philosophy was neither a metaphysical nor an epistemological system. Its emphasis was purely on ethics with a pragmatic approach. Any metaphysical and ontological discussions were treated only as a necessary bulwark to sustain the ethical outlook. It was only later, after the systematisation of Buddhist ideas that a keen controversy over epistemological issues arose. We find all shades of metaphysical approaches, starting from naive realism and going on to a nihilistic idealism; the consequential epistemological theories are also to be found here. The Vaibhāṣikas and the Sountrāntikās exhibit different grades of realism while the Vijñānavādin is a subjectivist and the Mādhyamika is a nihilist. However, all shades of Buddhism agree that true knowledge of the object is possible only in the indeterminate perception and that the determinate perception is always the result of construction.

Jainism, the other non-orthodox system, considers that knowledge is the very essence of the soul. But such a condition of the soul exists only in the realised person. In ordinary human beings this is limited by the functions of the sense-organs and the weightage due to *karma.* The sense-organs and mind, though helpful in attaining knowledge from one standpoint, are impediments from another. Such knowledge is always fragmentary. Insofar as it reveals the true nature of the object as it exists, it is true, but insofar as this is obstructed, it is untrue. Thus there is no judgment that is completely true or completely false. This is known as the *śyādvāda* which means the doctrine of "may be" and it signifies

[1] As quoted by S. Radhakrishnan, *Indian Philosophy*, Vol. I., p. 396.

the basic doctrine of the Jainas that the universe can be looked at from various standpoints. Every proposition is strictly conditional, since absolute affirmation and absolute negation are impossible.

Inspite of such an attitude towards all dogmatisms, whether it be in metaphysics or in logic, we do not find any signs of a systematised logic in the history of Jainism till we come to a later commentator known as Umāsvati. However all the ingredients for the building of a theory of knowledge were all present even before such systematisation took place. For instance, the Jainas believed that the very nature of the soul is consciousness, only such nature is obscured by several encumbrances, the chief of them being that of matter. Immediate or direct knowledge, about which we have spoken earlier with reference to the other systems, is here defined as vivid knowledge. Such knowledge can be gained either through the usage of the sense-organs or without their usage.

As stated before all knowledge is relative to the Jaina and consequently all judgments are relative and interdependent. Each judgment can only describe one aspect of reality. Let us state these in the accepted form. Suppose we are interested in an object A, then "May be" connotes that

1. a thing is — e.g. as A, it exists;
2. it is not — e.g. it is not B;
3. it is and is not—e.g. what is now here A, may become B at a later stage. (Here there is double predication each indicating one aspect of the existence of the object. As matter it is the same no doubt; but the modes in which such matter exists are changeable);
4. that it is inexpressible. The two predications when applied successively can be reconciled. But when they are applied simultaneously, there will be a violation of the law of contradiction. The fact that we do agree that its own nature is present while there is the absence of another's nature in it, makes it difficult to express. Such affirmation and denial are in a single statement. Hence it is inexpressible. Thus Jainism insists that in speaking of an object, it must be done so with reference to its constituent matter, place, time and the state of its existence;

5. it is and is inexpressible. This maintains that while from one aspect an object is A, from another point of view it is not explicable so definitely for the reasons stated before;

6. is not—and is inexpressible;

7. is and is not and is inexpressible. These are merely combinations of the points of view which were mentioned earlier.

Thus the Jaina consciously avoids any dogmatism in his approach to understanding reality. All judgments have only a partial application to reality. Perceptual knowledge can never give us a complete truth for such truth can never be grasped in toto.

Internal Perception

We have so far discussed the nature of knowledge, how perceptual knowledge arises, whether such knowledge is true and the criteria for judging the truth of a knowledge proposition. All this refers to ordinary knowledge involving the knowing Self, the instruments of acquiring such knowledge which are the mind and the sense-organs and the object which is known and which is different from all the above. Western epistemology concerns itself only with the implications of this process of perceptual knowledge. In recent years, with the development of "thinking" machines, a new element of discussion has entered the field. This is the status of a knowledge of internal states such as pleasure, pain, will and other mental states. These experiences are said to be the results of introspection which reveals the existence of a mind-self. But Indian philosophers have devoted much time to a knowledge of these internal states. Instead of saying they are the result of introspection, the Indian logician maintains that these are also objects of normal perception, just like the objects of the external world are. We have already discussed the role of *manas* or mind in the perception of external objects. This *manas* is known, in the context of perception as an internal sense-organ, *antarindriya* or as the cause which is internal, *antaḥkaraṇa.* For normal perception to arise, the mind through the sense-organs reaches out to the object and by establishing some type of a relation with it, gives rise to a knowledge of the object. In the case of the realist schools the relation is one of conjunction and in the case of the idealist schools it is one of identity. This *citta-vṛtti* or mental mode becomes limited to the internal states in the case of perception of pleasure and pain etc. Internal perception is therefore, that perception where the mind does not go out to contact an external object. The object of such perception is already inside the body. To the Naiyāyika the objects of such perception are pleasure, pain, desire, hatred, knowledge and will. These are qualities of the Self which it acquires owing to its association with the mind and the mind therefore, does not have to go outside to unite with the object. Since at the empirical level, the percipient Self, identifies itself with this mental mode, it makes the statements, "I am happy" or "I am suffering". There is a difference between the Nyāya view and the Advaita view in this regard. To the Naiyāyika, pleasure, pain, desire, hatred, cognition and volition which are attributes of the Self, are related to the Self by inherence, *samavāya.* Since the mind and the Self are conjoined (related by conjunction, *saṁyoga*), the latter comes into contact with the mind, which acting as the internal sense-organ, comes to know the qualities which reside in the Self. The pure Self is never perceived. It is the Self as characterised by any one of these six characteristics that is known. Thus knowledge of one's own Self is direct and immediate through a knowledge of its qualities whereas knowledge of other selves is always mediately known by inference from their bodily actions.

To the idealist Advaitin, the *manas* is a combination of these various aspects and it is not an internal sense-organ. When the pure consciousness that is the Self becomes identical with the consciousness that is limited by the *manas*, the mental states become directly known by the Self.[1] An external object may be known or may not be known. This contingency does not arise with internal perception for the mind is always identified with the Self at the empirical level. However, the mind by itself is never known. It is always these characteristics of the mind with which the Self identifies itself and makes the statements "I am happy" or "I am unhappy". This is reasonable, for according to the Advaitin, the mind is nothing else but its states of existence.

This discussion of internal perception leads us to a much debated question in Indian epistemology—how is knowledge known? We have already touched upon this a little when we were discussing determinate perception. A more elaborate discussion is necessary here. Everyone agrees that knowledge manifests an

[1] *Ved. Par.* Chapter I, "Perception".

object. At the same time we know that we have a knowledge of the object. It is this second piece of knowledge that is discussed at length in Indian philosophy. To the Buddhist there is no difference between the object and a knowledge of it. These two are always known together and the one cannot be without the other. "As blue and the consciousness of the 'blue' are invariably known simultaneously 'blue' is not different from the consciousness of 'blue'."[1] Therefore the question of how we know knowledge does not arise. The realist Naiyāyika does not accept this subjectivism, but says that a knowledge of knowledge arises as an act of reflection in a subsequent moment. First we see the object and there is a knowledge of it, but we know we have such a knowledge only on reflection, *anuvyavasāya jñāna*. This is borne out by the fact that we never say we have knowledge unless we attend to our sense-activity. There is always sense-activity, but it is only in certain cases that such activity becomes knowledge.

Another realistic theory, of the Bhatta Mimāṁsika, holds that knowledge is never directly known. It is not known as internal perception, since this school does not recognise any sort of internal perception, though not denying an awareness of knowledge. This school rejects internal perception on the grounds that it leads to *regressus ad infinitum*, for any knowledge of such knowledge of knowledge has to be explained. Therefore knowledge is always known through inference. An object is known because the universal character of "being known" is present in it. Wherever this "knownness" is present that object becomes known. This devious explanation is not generally accepted.

The Advaita absolutist maintains that knowledge is known because of its very nature, it does not require another knowledge to make it known. Knowledge carries with it its own validity and self-revealing nature. This is known as the theory of self-validity of knowledge—*svataḥ-pramāṇya vāda*. We have already seen how, according to the Advaitin, knowledge carries with it its own validity. The second aspect of the theory maintains that not only do the conditions which give rise to knowledge make for the validity of such knowledge, but also that such validity is always accompanied by its manifestation. A knowledge of the object and its manifestation as valid knowledge are simultaneous. This does not mean that the Advaitin accepts the Buddhist theory

1 From *Sar. Sam.*

of the identity of the object and the awareness of it. On the other hand the Advaitin maintains that the awareness of the knowledge of the object and the validity of such knowledge belong to the conscious Self whereas the object is different from it.

This stand of the Advaitin in regard to self-validity of knowledge raises the further question of invalid knowledge or illusory knowledge. We have already devoted much time to the nature and conditions of truth and falsity. Now we shall consider the arising of illusory knowledge. There is no doubt that illusory knowledge is also invalid or erroneous knowledge. Invalid knowledge is a generic knowledge and is applicable to all modes of arriving at knowledge. Illusory knowledge, on the other hand, is limited to sense-perception. Illusion cannot arise where the basis of such illusion is fully known or where the basis is not known at all. Hence it is necessary to understand how an illusion of a perceived object arises. There are some well-known theories explaining illusion known as *khyātivādas* meaning erroneous cognitions.

We shall take the Nyāya-Vaiśeṣika view first. Taking the illusion of silver in a shell, the Nyāya thinker accounts for it as follows. Owing to some defect in the sense-organ or the nature of light or some other cause a person fails to cognise a shell as shell but perceives only its brightness. The brightness is recognised to be the same brightness that is a characteristic of silver and recalls a vivid memory of silver. The perception of silver has been in some other time and at some other place. Yet that perception, because of its association with brightness becomes imposed on the present "this" of the shell, and silver is perceived in its place. The character of brightness is common to both and the knowledge that brightness is a quality of silver is recollected and silver is perceived as present. This type of perception is possible because of the extraordinary relation established between a perceived quality in its universal aspect and an object which does not exist then and there, known as *jñānalakṣaṇa sannikarṣa* (we will have occasion to discuss this and other modes of extraordinary perception in the next section). That is, the same silver which is perceived before elsewhere is now perceived in the shell. What is not here is seen to be here. Thus the shell is seen as silver. Neither the shell nor the silver are unreal. It is only a transference of a perceived object from its locus to another locus where it does not really exist. Erroneous perception arises due to the determination of the nature of one presentation by another derived through association and memory. Thus it is *anyatākhyāti* or wrong judgment due to the "other" perception. This is also known as *viparītakhyāti* meaning error due to distortion of the presented with the remembered.

A form of this theory known as *sat-khyāti* is put forward by Ramanuja's Viśiṣṭādvaita. This is based on the cosmology of this school which maintains that things are real and are composed of the five elements, thus similar objects have similar constituents. Shell and silver are similar with regard to their shining character. So shell contains elements of silver in it. What is perceived in illusion is the silver element instead of the shell element. It is the apprehension of the real object, *sat-khyāti.* But this is subject to criticism. If the silver perceived is real, it can never be sublated by further knowledge of shell-perception. Another difficulty with this theory is that illusions are not common experiences to all people. A tree in the twilight may look to one like a thief, to another, like a policeman, in which case this justification of illusory knowledge will not hold good.

The Prabhākara Mīmāṁsa school of realism advocates a theory known as *akhyāti.* Here error is explained simply as want of discrimination between perception and memory. As in the Nyāya theory, there is a perception of brightness which is common to both the shell and the silver. Silver is a remembered fact. But not discriminating it as memory of it is imposed on the perceived object. When a distinction between what is perceived and what is remembered in the perceptual context is made, then illusion vanishes. So error is due to non-discrimination between the perceived object and the remembered object. This view of illusory perception is the theory accepted by Western philosophers. Illusory experience is a subjective interpretation of objective stimuli. The subjective interpretation may be due to diseased sense-organs or lack of proper conditions in the environment.

The Mīmāṁsika view is not a happy one and has not found favour with other Indian systems of philosophy for it deliberately considers perception itself as producing valid knowledge at one time and invalid knowledge at another. In the first place how can subjective factors such as ideas or memory images be actually felt as perceived out there in space? Even if they are so perceived, how can we say they are illusory for in this case they would be as much objects of perception as normal objects are?

The next theory we have to examine is the one postulated by the dualist Sāṁkhya philosophers. They explain that illusion is a perception of something unreal in a "this" which is real. Taking the usual example of perceiving silver in a shell, the Sāṁkhya philosophers maintain that the silver that is perceived is real elsewhere but unreal in this perceptual context. The unreal silver is seen to be present in the shell which is real, so illusion is perception of the unreal in the real. This is *sadāsatkhyāti.*

It remains now for us to examine the Buddhist and the Advaita views. The Vijñānavādin gives an explanation which is in consonance with his subjective idealism. It will be remembered that according to this school, all cognitions are subjective as there is no extra-mental reality. Reality is made up of a subjective stream of ideas which is called the subject and an objective stream which is called the object. All cognition is the objectification of what is subjective and is thus wrong. This is also the case with illusory perception. It is merely an apprehension of a subjective cognition, *ātmakhyāti.* But this position of the Yogacāra is not tenable for their basic position of subjectivism itself is not acceptable.

The nihilistic theory of the Mādhyamika is known as *asatkhyāti*, apprehension of the non-existent. In illusory perception what is non-existent is perceived as existent. Both the object of illusion and the locus or substratum of it are unreal. Taking the shell-silver illusion as example, one is apt to ask: Why should one contradict the other when illusion is removed? Why should there be any contradiction of the non-existent shell? Then again how can there be cognition of a non-existing thing? How can that which is experienced be unreal? Because of all these questions, this extreme position of the Mādhyamika is not acceptable.

The Advaita criterion of truth being non-contradictoriness and non-sublatability, the perception of silver in the shell is illusory for it is sublated by the later shell perception. However, the illusory knowledge is not characterised as false knowledge while it lasts. Whatever is experienced cannot be false, so as long as the illusory object is perceived it is considered to be real. But actually it is not and cannot be real for its knowledge is sublated. Therefore it is called the indefinable knowledge, *anirvacanīya-khyāti.* This is in conformity with the fundamental tenet of

Advaita that what is experienced cannot be unreal and that there are levels of existence and that each level appears to be true as long as it is not sublated.

Śaṁkara does not say that there can be knowledge without an object. In the process of knowledge, the terminii, the subject and object are essential. Both in illusion and in waking experience there is always an object which is experienced. Both are real in their own respective spheres. The difference between these lies in their difference in character. The illusory object is seen by only one person, whereas the object of empirical perception is common to all. These two may be characterised as "private" and "public". The latter is more enduring than the former. Each is real in its own sphere and becomes unreal or illusory with reference to a higher knowledge. Thus the status of each knowledge, though determinable within its own parameters becomes indeterminable fundamentally.

Extra-Sensory Perception

All schools of Indian philosophy, except the Cārvāka and the Mīmāṁsa schools, believe that ordinary modes of perception do not set the limit to human cognition. The mind of man is capable of soaring up to higher levels of understanding which are not impeded by sense perceptions. But all the schools give only a description of these supernormal perceptions without explaining them. These supernormal perceptions transcend all known limits of time, space and causality. The Mīmāṁsa school rejects the possibility of any such extraordinary cognition for knowledge of all the past, the present and the future is to be derived from the Vedas. In addition, sense-organs as such, can only perceive sensuous objects which are brought into contact with them and by their very nature they cannot go beyond them.

According to Nyāya there are three kinds of supernormal perceptions. The first is the perception of the universal that is inherent in the particular. This is called *samānyalakṣaṇa sannikarṣa.* The perception of the universal *jāti* along with the particular *vyakti* is not omniscience. If such a perception of the *jāti* is not admitted, then a knowledge of the universal becomes impossible. Just as J. S. Mill contends, so also the Indian logician accepts that a universal can never be revealed by a mere counting of instances. Instead the known as well as the unknown instances are perceived in their generic nature by *samānyalakṣaṇa sannikarṣa.* Merely to have a conceptual knowledge of the *jāti* is not enough to identify a particular. The universal also must be perceived. Such a cognitive knowledge of the universal is a supernormal cognition. It is not perceived ordinarily in the instances which are counted.

The *ñānalakṣaṇa* is the second type of extraordinary perception accepted by the Nyāya-Vaiśeṣika system. Where a memory of past experience intervenes with the sense of sight and a perception of that object is produced we have the above-named perception. For example: when we see a sandalwood tree far away and make the judgment "I see a fragrant sandalwood in the distance", the fragrance of the sandalwood is not given to sense-contact although it is capable of being perceived sensuously. The present perception works through the medium of another knowledge. It is the memory of past experience which leads to the perception of its object in the present.

There is still another type of extraordinary cognition recognised by the Nyāya school known as *yogaja* which means born of yogic practices. By constant meditation on supersensibles such as the Self, a knowledge of these can be gained by the *yogin.* Living beings possess various degrees of perceptual capacity. A cat can see in the dark, a vulture transcends normal barriers of distance. It is contended that a human being can attain these capacities with regard to perceptual attainments. Just as gold reaches a high state of purity by constant heating so too, by constant meditation, the *buddhi* of each individual receives better and better impressions and thus reaches the highest point from where, independent of the limitations of sense-organs, perception of things in their real nature is possible.

The discipline of the mind and the consequent powers acquired by the mind given by the Yoga system is the most famous in all Indian thought and almost all other schools accept the psychological principles given by this school. The forms of mental activity have been very broadly divided into five types by yoga. They are: *kṣipta* or restless, wandering; *mūḍha* or infatuated or forgetful; *vikṣipta* or distracted; *ekāgra* or one-pointed, and *niruddha* or restricted or restrained. It is only in the last two mental modes, *ekāgra* and *niruddha,* that contemplation is possible. *Ekāgra* is that state where by the steady following of one path of concentration on one thing, the mind attains knowledge of the nature of Reality. This in turn removes ignorance, making the mind ready for the next change where even this concentration on any one thing becomes restricted and the mind is turned inwards towards its own nature and thus realises *mokṣa.* It is these two types of yogic concentrations that are known as *samprajñatā* and *asamprajñatā samādhi.* Depending on the objects of concentration, several extraordinary mental powers result.[1] By concentrating on the nature of time, as represented by the past, the present and the future, and also as responsible for all change, the seer comes to have a knowledge of the past and the future. When the mind is steady and *one-pointed* on time, it is able to move with ease into both the past and the future or, to use modern terminology, to have precognition. The experiment with time carried out and recorded by Dunne[2] produced results almost akin to this. Similarly the *yogin* due to his concentration on sound is able to hear and understand the sounds produced by various animals. We shall see, while discussing *śabda pramāṇa*, how the Indian philosopher explains perception of the meaning of language. In short, while the vocal organs produce individual sounds, it is the *buddhi* or intellect which puts them together and gives them a meaning and a content based on experience and memory. The capacity of attribution of meaning to words had been handed down to man from his forefathers and the analysis of words into syllables and sounds is a later capacity based on man's memory of the meaning of words. By concentrated meditation on the distinction between word, meaning and idea, the *yogin* becomes capable of hearing and understanding the sounds of animals, insects etc.

When ideas as presented, or concepts as they are formed are meditated upon, a capacity for acquiring a knowledge of other minds is cultivated. But the knowledge here is only limited to the mental states of the other's mind and not the objects of such mental states. What the *yogin* perceives is only the impressions left in the other's mind by the other's acts of perception. These impressions in the mind-matter of the percipient Self are known as *saṁskāras.* The mind of the *yogin*, being of the nature of fine matter is capable of entering into a relation of identity with the

1 *Y. Su.*, Book III, 16 & 17.
2 Dunne, *An Experiment with Time*, pp. 119-120.

percipient's mind. This we have already said is known as *citta vṛtti*, mental mode. It is thus that the *yogin* knows the mental modes of the other man's mind. Referring to this the *Yoga Bhāṣya* says, "He knows the mental emotion of love, but does not know the object of love, because that which has been the object of the other man's mind has not been the object of the yogi's mind."[1]

A great deal of research is being done today on these extraordinary or extrasensory capacities of the human mind. Wheatly Carrington showed, by various experiments, that the capacity of the mind to know other minds does not diminish with distance, as would be the case if it had been the result of some mechanical force like wireless or radiation.[2] This capacity can be explained in two ways. It may mean that this type of knowledge is the result of another extraordinary power of the mind or sense-organ, not yet discovered, or it may mean that this type of perception is completely independent of sense-activities. Both these explanations are not acceptable to the Yoga thinkers. In such perceptions it is the mind itself which is considered as a sense-organ, though a subtle one. It follows that it is due to an intense activity of this *citta* in the state of concentration that brings about a knowledge of other minds. The mind, if it is properly trained, goes beyond the present limits of time and space. The difference between the views established by scholars like J. B. Rhine in this field and the Yoga view lies in two very important aspects. The knowledge of the mind of the other person is limited only to the other person's mental states and not to the objects of such mental states according to Yoga. Despite this, time and again, experiments in telepathy have been designed to find out if the objects seen by one person are reported exactly by another person who has the capacity for telepathy. For instance Carrington says, "Some subjects appear to pick up an impression of the linear form of the original without succeeding in interpreting it directly...."[3] This is explained by the *yogin* on the basis that every cognition leaves its mark on the mind and what is perceived in telepathy are these impressions of the cognitions and not the objects of such cognitive impressions. That is why with inexperienced and untrained persons these telepathic perceptions are either hazy or meagre.

[1] Wood's translation, Book. III, 19.

[2] W. Carrington, *Telepathy*.

[3] *Ibid*, p. 66. *Op. cit. p.* 66.

A second difference between the modern conception of such powers and the Yogic conception is that while the latter holds that these can be attained by every person who is willing to undergo the necessary training in concentration, the former maintains that these are just sporadic capacities present by chance in some people. To the *yogin*, every individual who wishes to have such knowledge which would lead him to attain salvation must undergo the necessary practice in concentration when the mind can be emptied of all thoughts, both good and bad. In the process of attaining this final stage, the mind becomes so pure and sharp that it develops the extraordinary powers of precognition, telepathy etc.

There is still another point of difference between the Western view of mind during these mental states and the Yoga view. According to the former, there is a suggested dissociation of mental faculties during telepathic activity. For example, more often than not people who experience telepathy do so under hypnosis or a state of voluntary trance, but it is just the opposite with Yoga. The mind is more integral, more whole during these experiences. Such experiences do not weaken the person; they leave the mind and the personality of the individual stronger and brighter than before. There are many other types of extraordinary powers which the person acquires, such as controlling of the muscles of the heart and stopping its action for certain periods, controlling the breathing, blood-pressure, becoming small in size, becoming young, etc. All these are considered not ends in themselves but accidental capacities which should not lure the person from the path he has set for himself which is the attainment of *mokṣa.*

Inference or Anumāna

The most important method of knowledge is *anumāna* or inference. Its nature, form and content have been discussed by all schools leading to the development of an elaborate literature, unequalled for its precise expression and analysis. The basic document, for all these discussions was the Nyāya theory of inference. The Naiyāyikās naturally influenced to a considerable extent the thought of many schools and many of their theories regarding inference were accepted almost *in toto* by some of the other schools.

The Saṁskrit word *anumāna* is usually translated as inference. Scholars like Prof. D. M. Datta[1] object to such translation on

[1] D. M. Datta, *Six Ways of Knowing*, p. 203.

the ground that the scope of the Saṁskrit word is much wider than that of the English word. However, for want of a better word, it is usually agreed to retain the word inference. *Anumāna* itself means a type of knowledge which follows from other knowledge. The Nyāya view is that *anumāna* is a type of secondary knowledge deduced from a prior knowledge. A knowledge of the invariability of concomitance between two things helps to deduce the existence of one of them when the other is perceived.

That inference is a complex process of knowledge is accepted by all schools of Indian thought except the empiricist Cārvāka who denies it altogether. To the Jain philosopher *anumāna* is the method by which an unknown object becomes known through a perception of its sign and its invariable relation to the object itself. The Bauddhas consider *anumāna* to be a perception of an object which is known to be invariably related to another thing. Such an invariable relation, according to them is either a causal relation or a relation of identity. Therefore the knowledge that is derived from such relational knowledge is inferential knowledge. To the Vaiśeṣika inference of a thing takes place when there is a perceived knowledge of a sign which is always related to something else. To the other systems, Sāṁkhya, Mīmāṁsa and Vedānta, inference is the knowledge of one of the terms of an invariable relation through a knowledge of the term and the invariable relation. Thus it can be seen that the basic pattern of inferential knowledge is a knowledge derived through another knowledge. It is always, therefore, mediate knowledge. There is no specific mention in Indian philosophical treatises of the variety of inference known as immediate inference. Perhaps the reason lies in the fact that the Indian inferential argument is always conceived to be knowledge derived through the mediation of another knowledge. Immediate inference is an expression of the relations that can exist between the subject and the predicate of a given proposition expressed by the various forms the copula can take and the distribution of the terms. It is very formal in nature. The meaning and the import of the original proposition is kept without violation in the subsequent immediate inferences. In the Indian form of inference, importance is not given to the form of the syllogism, so much as to the relational knowledge it implies. Moreover there is no such thing as a proposition involving a subject and predicate and their relation expressed through a copula in

Indian logic. The proposition is always a direct predication without the use of any copula. This is a language peculiarity. Thus a formalisation of the syllogistic pattern of inferential argument based on the copula is not appropriate to Indian inference. The division of inference into inductive and deductive does not also arise with reference to Indian inference. The purpose of inference, according to Indian logicians is not universalisation, but arriving at new knowledge based upon and deduced from a prior knowledge. All inference should invariably give rise to new knowledge. Inference is also the instrument of argumentation, and for providing of proof. As such the question of inductive logic as a separate form of inferential thought does not arise in Indian inference. However the problem of induction—how we arrive at a universal—is discussed in detail because it is the universal relation that forms the ground of inference even for the Indian logicians. The conclusion of the syllogism is implied by the known universal relation of either concomitance or causation and follows from it. The purpose of inferential thinking is the demonstration of an already known knowledge or the discovery of a new piece of knowledge made possible by a subsumptive relation. This forms the core of the Indian syllogism which will be discussed later. It is essential that we point out at this stage that one fundamental classification of inference postulated by the Nyāya and the Mīmāṁsa schools is based on the idea that inference is used in both discovery and demonstration. When a person argues and infers so that he demonstrates something for himself, it is called technically "inference-for one's self" or *svārthānumāna.* This type of inferential form need not be as elaborate and analytical as the one where a known truth is demonstrated for the purpose of convincing another. This is known as "inference-for-others" or *parārthānumāna.* Whatever the form, inferential argument depends upon certain factors. As already stated the simple function of inference, as the Indian logicians view it, is to arrive at the knowledge of some unperceived factor through the perception of a sign, *liñga*, which in turn is known to be universally concomitant with that factor which is to be inferred. The first step in this inferential process is the perception of the sign, *liñga*, or *hetu* in any particular locus. Such a locus is termed a *pakṣa.* This perception is called *liñga darśana.* The second step is a memory judgment, involving a recollection, based on past experience that the sign or *liñga* is invariably concomitant with another character which is the subject of inferential argument. This is called *sādhya*, the existence of which in the *pakṣa* is to be established. This invariable concomitance is technically known as pervasion, *vyāpti*. Thus the above two steps together involve perception of a *liñga* or *hetu* in a *pakṣa*, and recollection of the *vyāpti* relation between the *liñga* or *hetu* and the *sādhya*. From these two follow the conclusion of the inferential argument where an assertion is made that the *sādhya* is also present in the *pakṣa*. Let us illustrate this with the help of the Indian logicians' classic example.

"The hill is perceived to be smoky." Here the hill is the *pakṣa* or the subject and smokiness is the *liñga* or *hetu*. This is the sign or the cause which helps in deducing a further characteristic residing in the hill. But such deduction is possible only on the experienced and recollected fact that wherever there is smoke there is fire. This invariable concomitance of smoke and fire is the *vyāpti*. From the subsumption of the particular case of smoke perceived on the hill under the universal recollected knowledge of the *vyāpti* relation, the conclusion "therefore this hill also must be fiery" arises. The whole syllogism may now be presented in different steps as follows:

1. This hill is fiery—*pratijñā*, challenge
2. Because it has smoke—*hetu*, reason
3. Wherever there is smoke there is fire as in the kitchen—*udāharaṇa*, example
4. So is this hill smoky—*upanaya*, application
5. Therefore, this hill is fiery—*nigamana*, conclusion

These five members constitute a *vākya* or syllogism according to the Nyāya philosophers. Let us examine each step in detail.

1. *Pratijña, the challenge:* The first proposition of the syllogism is called the challenge. We must remember that the purpose of the syllogism is not only to discover but also to demonstrate. In fact according to Indian logicians the primary function is demonstration of a truth to a person who is to be shown that the conclusion is true. Hence the first proposition states what it is that is in doubt and has to be proved; this is the challenge. The quality or characteristic sought to be established may be either positively or negatively related to the subject. The *pratijña* consists of a subject, *pakṣa* to which a predicate is sought to be

established. This may be said to be equivalent to the major term in Aristotelian syllogism. But no copula or verb relates these two words, e.g., *parvato vahniman.*[1] (This is an important point to be remembered for formalisation of Indian syllogism becomes impossible because of the lack of the copula.)

2. *Hetu, the reason:* This is the second member of the five-membered syllogism. This is important because here a statement of the perceived mark, *liñga*, is made and is said to be the reason for predicating the *sādhya* in the subject. Here the hill is perceived to have smoke, which makes it possible for us to predicate the existence of another character, fire, on the hill. The second proposition is a one-word proposition and is the reason. It is equivalent to the middle term in Aristotelian syllogism.

3. *Udāharaṇa, the example:* This member of the syllogism is known as the example, because it is based on the knowledge of the example. It consists of a proposition which asserts a universal relation or concomitance, *vyāpti*, between the *sādhya*, the major term, and the *hetu*, the middle term, based on the remembered experience of their concomitance in some particular instance. In the example here the presence of smoke is observed to be co-existent with the presence of fire in the kitchen. Recollection of this, combined with the perception of the smoke on the hill makes us draw the conclusion that wherever there is smoke, there fire must also be present. This *vyāpti* is a very essential member of the syllogistic argument, for without this, one can never establish the major term in the subject. The meaning of the term *vyāpti* is pervasion and it means that in all the loci where smoke is present there fire must also be present. Such a *vyāpti* can be either a positive or negative relation. In the negative form it takes the form "wherever there is no fire, there is also no smoke, as in a lake." Thus this third member, since it states the universal relation, may be said to be similar to the major premise in Aristotelian syllogism.

Scholars like Prof. D. M. Datta, have stated that this major premise is both inductive and deductive in nature. It is inductive because the universal premise is derived from an observation of particular instances. The whole syllogism is deductive in nature because the particular conclusion sought to be established is dependent on the truth of the universal premise given as the third

[1] It is difficult to translate this without using the copula "is". The best equivalent is "the hill possesses fire."

member of the five-membered syllogism. We shall discuss later how this inductive generalisation is arrived at. For the present it is enough if the idea that a syllogism is both inductive and deductive is stressed. The need for the two forms of inference did not arise in Indian logic for both are blended together in the five-membered syllogism itself. The syllogism has not only to be formally valid but also materially sound. This is possible in the Nyāya view of the syllogism.

4. *Upanaya, the application:* The purpose of this member of the syllogism is to subsume the perceived particular under the major universal premise. This is done by asserting that the middle term is present in the subject or minor term and is thus liable to be judged as belonging to the universal class indicated in the third member. To use the example, smoke which is the *hetu* or middle term is asserted to be present in the *pakṣa*, the minor term. This is not merely a repetition of the second member of the syllogism which states that because there is smoke perceived in the hill, the conclusion is possible. On the other hand the purpose of the fourth member is to establish an identity between the middle term, "smoke", mentioned in the second proposition, and that of "smoke" which is universally related to the major term, "fire", mentioned in the third proposition. Thus it synthesizes by means of subsumption the second and third members of the syllogism.

5. *Nigamana, the conclusion:* In this proposition, the truth that was categorically stated in the first proposition is shown to be demonstrated as true. It restates the *pratijña* as a demonstrated and proved statement. The first proposition is a mere hypothesis and the last statement is a truth established by an inferential process and free of fallacies.

These five members of the syllogism may be represented symbolically as follows:

1. *Pratijña:* S is P
2. *Hetu:* because S is M
3. *Udāharaṇa:* M is P as in the example
4. *Upanaya:* S is M
5. *Nigamāna:* therefore S is P

The Mīmāṁsikas and the Advaitins do not accept this five-membered syllogism of the Naiyāyikas. They agree that the function of the syllogism is demonstration but they contend that for such a demonstration the five members of the Naiyāyika syllogism are unnecessary. Either the first three premises or the last three premises are enough. That is, the first form expressed symbolically would be:

1. *Pratijña:* S is P
2. *Hetu:* because S is M
3. *Udāharaṇa:* M is P as observed in the example

The second form of the syllogism would be:

1. *Udāharaṇa:* All M is P as observed
2. *Upanaya:* S is M
3. *Nigamana:* therefore S is P

It is to be observed that in both these forms the universal proposition indicating the *vyāpti* relation is included. These philosophers hold that in actual life we are not presented with premises first from which we draw a conclusion as the Naiyāyika presumes. On the other hand, we are aware of the conclusion already and we try to find a universal premise which will support the conclusion and justify it. While the Naiyāyika chooses a more elaborate and scrupulous manner of demonstration, the Mīmāṁsika and the Advaitin formulate a psychologically more acceptable method of demonstration. As soon as the universal *vyāpti* relation is established, this knowledge together with the perceived presence of the *hetu* on the *pakṣa,* makes it possible to establish the conclusion which is sought to be proved.

This method of syllogistic argument, irrespective of the number of premises, is generally accepted by all Indian logicians. This is similar to the method of demonstration that Bradley had in mind when he stated: "Man is mortal, and Caesar is a man, and therefore Caesar is mortal, there is first a construction as Caesar—man—mortal, and then by inspection we get Caesar—mortal."[1]

There is yet another point of difference between the Nyāya and the Advaita view of syllogism. The Nyāya school classifies all inference into three types based on the nature of the invariable concomitance, *vyāpti,* used. We have said that the *vyāpti* is the result of observation of two instances which occur concomitantly

[1] Bradley, *Logic,* Vol. I., p. 259.

in any particular locus. When the *vyāpti* is established based purely on positive occurrences, the syllogism is known as *kevalānvayi*, purely affirmative syllogism. For example, when it is said "wherever there is smoke there is fire" it is a *vyāpti* based on "agreement in presence" and it is a pure affirmative syllogism. When the *vyāpti* is established on agreement in absence, it takes the form "wherever there is no fire, there is no smoke" and the syllogism is called *kevalavyatireki*, agreement in absence. The third type of syllogism uses both these methods of establishing the *vyāpti*, namely agreement in presence and agreement in absence and it is known as *anvayavyatireki.* The examples are as follows:

1. *Kevalānvayi*, agreement in presence:
   Wherever there is smoke there is fire as in the kitchen.
   There is smoke on this hill.
   Therefore there is fire on this hill.

2. *Kevalavyatireki*, agreement in absence:
   Wherever there is no fire there is also no smoke, as in a lake.
   There is smoke on this hill.
   Therefore there is fire on this hill.

3. *Anvayavyatireki*, affirmative-negative presence:
   The major premise "wherever there is smoke, there is fire" is established by an examination and observation of both the positive and negative instances.

While this is the general position in regard to these syllogisms, the Naiyāyika lays down certain conditions for its use. The *kevalānvayi* is to be used only when no negative instances are possible. For example, in "Whatever is knowable is nameable" it is not possible to have any negative example at all. One cannot find nameability in the absence of knowability. In such cases only *kevalānvayī* syllogism is possible. Similarly in *kevalavyatirekī* inference it should be impossible to find a positive instance. In other words a co-presence of the two terms is impossible in any other place except in the one cited. Everything else is only a negative example. "God is omniscient, because he is the creator" involves the universal relation between omniscience and being a creator. There is no positive knowledge of the co-existence of these two. We can only observe their agreement in absence and state a negative concomitance: "Whoever is not omniscient is not also a creator". The *anvayavyatirekī* is the common form where the universal relation can be established based on either agreement in presence or agreement in absence and sometimes for the sake of emphasis, on both.

Later Advaitins[1] do not accept this threefold classification of inference. They accept only the "affirmative" inference which means that the *vyāpti* is based on affirmative instance. They reject the negative type because they state no inference is possible if a negative relation is stated in the *vyāpti.* The purpose of inference is a subsumptive correlation of the particular observed under a known universal. This becomes impossible if such a universal expresses only a negative concomitance. This is not inference although it may give rise to valid knowledge. The Advaitins give it another name and call it *arthāpatti.* Following from this the third variety of inference also becomes impossible since it is a combination of the first two types.

We have already stated in the beginning that Indian logicians did not classify inference into deductive and inductive inference, but classified it as that which is useful for one's own self and that which is useful for others. The division of syllogistic inference into categorical, hypothetical and disjunctive forms also does not arise. Since the syllogism requires both formal and material validity, there was no need for any formal division of the syllogism. The hypothetical form being reducible to the categorical form can claim only formal validity. Thus like Aristotle, the Indian logician believed that a syllogism must necessarily be a categorical statement. The disjunctive form of inference is not altogether absent. But we find it under the name *arthāpatti* which we will be discussing later on.

Before we come to the end of this discussion one important and controversial aspect of inference, namely, its universal premise, must be examined once more. The soul of inferential argument is the *vyāpti* relation. How is this *vyāpti* arrived at? We have stated that it is arrived at by an examination and observation of either a positive example or a negative example. But as J. S. Mill points out, how is an inductive generalisation possible by merely counting instances? Like Mill, the Cārvāka philosopher maintains that inference from a universal to a particular is impossible, since no universal can be arrived at by a counting of instances. (In fact this is the reason why the Cārvāka denies the validity

[1] The author of *Ved. Par.* and his school of thinking.

of inferential reasoning altogether and asserts that immediate, perceptible knowledge alone can be valid.) On the other hand the Buddhists believe that inference is possible since the universal relation exhibits a causal relation between two instances and a causal relation is a universal relation. The Buddhist joins issue with the Cārvāka position and says that if causality is not admitted as universal then there is bound to be self-contradiction in our thought. We will be forced to accept that an effect can exist and be perceived without having a cause. The Buddhist follows the same method as was advocated by Mill for the establishment of causal relation. He maintains that if all conditions remaining the same, the appearance of one event is immediately followed by the appearance of another, then we have to assume that these are causally related. Similarly the Buddhists assert that identity is also another factor based on which a universal relation between two things can be established. The definition of identity given by the Buddhists is rather interesting. Since they believe that no object exists for more than one moment, actual identity between two things is impossible. So identity means only co-existence in the same locus, *samānādhikaraṇyam*. For example: "a tiger is feline" is an identical proposition for the thing cannot be a tiger if it is not also feline. A thing is always related to what is identical with it in this sense, and this leads to a generalisation. Thus a *vyāpti* is always based on causality, *tadutpatti*, or identity, *tadātmya*. These two are presuppositions of all experience and thus are universal truths.

The Naiyāyika, who is primarily a logician, maintains that even if it is granted that the *vyāpti* can be established based on these two principles, they are not the only possible principles which lead to a universal. There are many cases of *vyāpti* which are neither causally related nor exhibit the relation of identity. Even in these relations it is not always possible to have a *vyāpti*. We know that fire is the cause of smoke. So we can establish a *vyāpti* like "wherever there is smoke there is also fire". But the opposite of this *vyāpti* "wherever there is fire there is also smoke" cannot be established based on causality for it is against experience. We do perceive a red-hot ball of iron but there is no concurrence of smoke here. Hence merely causal concomitance is not enough for the *vyāpti*. The Naiyāyika maintains that the *vyāpti* can be ascertained based on any invariable, unconditional, universal relation. The *vyāpti* is the result of the invariable and non-contradicted experience of concomitance between two things. This is arrived at by simple enumeration. First a uniform co-presence is perceived and observed. Second, a uniform co-absence is also perceived and observed. Then a conclusion regarding their universal concomitance is arrived at. This is like Mill's methods where he tries to establish causality based on agreement and difference. But the Naiyāyika like Mill is not yet out of the woods. The problem remains, of generalisation from simple enumeration. There can be no evidence for such passage from "some" to "all". It is here that the ingenious Naiyāyika calls upon the extraordinary perception that he has already enumerated. He maintains that while the particular is perceived, its universal *sāmānya* is also perceived. Hence we have the universal proposition which maintains not merely a universal relation between particulars but a universal relation between qualities. We have thus the *vyāpti* in the form "wherever there is smokiness there is also fireness". Thus the problem of the *vyāpti* is not merely a discovery of a universal, but a discovery of class-essences or universals which are exemplified in particular. Thus although it is simple enumeration that leads to a *vyāpti* relation, it is not merely simple enumeration but a supersensuous perception of the particulars that leads to *vyāpti*.

The Advaitin accepts generally the Nyāya method of obtaining a *vyāpti*. That is, they also accept that it is simple enumeration that leads to the generation of a *vyāpti* relation. But there ends the similarity. The Advaitin maintains that the number of times an event is observed is inessential. It may be just once or it may be many times. Along with the Bhāṭṭa Mīmāṁsikas, the Advaitins also believe that a universal proposition is derived deductively from a universal concomitance between the qualities of the facts observed. To the Naiyāyika, a universal is the generic quality of the object inhering not only in one particular, but in all particulars of that group. To the Advaitin a universal is the common attribute, *anugatadharma*, of the many particular objects. If we take a table for example, the perception of the universal "tableness" is the perception of such qualities of the table which are common to all tables and by means of which there is a connotation of "table" to such objects. It is the perception of the object itself along with its qualities. This view enables the

Advaitin to arrive at a *vyāpti* relation. But such a *vyāpti* must not be doubted. For the *vyāpti* to function in an inference, it must be a valid one. Therefore, in cases of doubt, the Advaitin recommends a canon for establishing the soundness of the *vyāpti.* This is the *anvaya* method where the agreement in presence is tested by taking a random sample.

The classic criticism of Mill that all inductive inference involves a *petitio principii* is anticipated by the Indian logician and answered as follows. The answer is based on the relation between the particular and the universal. Both the realist Naiyāyika and the idealist Vedāntin agree that the universal is perceived along with the particular as characteristic of the particular. Thus a *vyāpti* can be arrived at by the perception of only one event of smoke and fire co-existing. But then the *vyāpti* so derived is only connotative and not denotative. It will not tell us anything about any actual particular instance. When we know the *vyāpti*, "all cases of smoke are cases of fire", we have no knowledge about the particular case of fire on the hill. This is yet to be studied and brought under the connotative universal. Thus it is new knowledge which is not involved in the knowledge of the premises. Thus the charge of *petitio principii* against inference does not hold good in the case of the Indian syllogism.

Fallacies of Inference

The usual division of fallacies into inductive and deductive, into formal and material does not arise in Indian logic. The reason is that the form of inference must always be sound and the soundness of the form depends not on the formal position of the terms, but on their validity. Therefore, the fallaciousness of the inference is due to its material conditions. All these material conditions turn round the *hetu*[1] as the primary factor. It is based on a valid *hetu* that a conclusion is drawn. It is because of a valid *hetu* that a *vyāpti* relation between the *hetu* and *sādhya* is possible. Therefore a vitiated *hetu* leads to fallacious reasoning. So all fallacies are known as *hetvābhāsa*, fallacious reason, or middle term. The *hetu* or the middle term appears to be valid, but on closer scrutiny, become invalid. We have therefore to find out how this comes to be. For this we should know actually the various conditions which are necessary to make a *hetu* reason, a good reason. Five conditions are listed by Nyāya logicians.

[1] This is known variously as *liṅga*, *sādhana* and *hetu.*

First, the *hetu* (reason or middle term) must be found in the subject (minor term or the *pakṣa*). It will not and cannot function as a reason to draw a conclusion if it is found elsewhere. For example: unless smoke, the *hetu* is found in the hill, the *pakṣa*, there cannot be any further argument about the existence of fire on the hill. This condition is said to be *pakṣadharmatā*. Secondly, to establish a *vyāpti* relation between the *hetu* and the *sādhya* (the middle and the major terms) the major term must be found wherever the middle term is found. For example: wherever we have smoke there fire must also be present. If this is not a valid relation there can be no inference. The third condition for a good *hetu* follows from this, that is, the middle term or hetu must be absent in all places where the major or the *sādhya* is also absent. These two are known as *sapakṣasattva* and *vipakṣasattva*. The fourth condition goes a step further and maintains that a good reason must not be present if the *sādhya* is absent, and it must not be found in contradictory or contrary cases. For example: smoke must not be found in things which are contradictory to fire such as "coolness" etc. This is known as *abhādhitaviṣayatva*. Last, but not least, is the condition which lays down that no known cause should supersede or contradict the function of this *hetu*. It should not be possible to prove the opposite of the *sādhya* by using any other valid reason. This is known as *asatpratipakṣatva*. If one or any of these five conditions of a good *hetu* are vitiated, there is a *hetvābhāsa*, which either leads to a wrong conclusion or which makes it impossible to arrive at any conclusion. There are five kinds of fallacies which we shall now consider.

1. *Savyābhicāra or the inconclusive reason:* This type of reason leads to more conclusions than the one desired. This is because the pervasion of the middle term, the *hetu*, by the major term, the *sādhya*, is not there. Thus the second condition of a good *hetu* is violated. The *hetu* is seen to be concomitant not only with the *sādhya* but with the non-existence of the *sādhya* as well. This fallacy is also known as *anaikāntika* for it leads to many conclusions. It is distinguished in three forms. The first is *sādhāraṇa savyābhicāra*, common inconclusive. This occurs where the reason is so wide that it embraces not only the cases where *sādhya* is present but also where it is not present. For example, the syllogistic argument: "This hill is fiery because it is knowable" commits this fallacy. Knowability pervades not only

cases of fire, but also instances where there is no fire. So it is not possible to draw any conclusion from the given reason.

The second one is *asādhāraṇa savyābhicāra* or the uncommon inconclusiveness. Here the reason given is too narrow for it is found only in the one instance cited. This is illustrated by the argument: "Sound is eternal because it has soundness".[1] Since "soundness" is to be found only in the one subject "sound" it is impossible to argue about its eternality.

The third type of inconclusive reason is the indefinite or *anupasamhārin.* Here the reason is not only pervasive of the major term, but in all other things as well. In the example: "The jar is nameable, because it is knowable", knowability is the reason given to infer the nameability of the jar. But knowability is not the characteristic of the jar only. It exists even where the jar does not exist. In general the *savyabhicara* fallacy can be represented by the following example, "John is a scholar because he is a man". Being a man cannot merely be the reason for being a scholar. It can be given as a reason to prove other things also of John such as his anger, his eating habits etc.

2. *Viruddha or the contradictory:* This closely follows the above and sometimes even becomes confused with it. The reason here is not merely too wide or too narrow or indefinite as in the above, but it is capable of proving exactly the opposite of what is sought to be proved. The reason given acts as an obstacle to the conclusion required to be arrived at. For example: "The hill has fire, because it has water". The reason given, "because it has water", proves the non-existence of fire rather than the existence of fire. Another example would be "Water is cool because it is heated". While the *savyābhicāra* fails to prove because it is irregular in concomitance with the *sādhya,* the *viruddha* fails to prove because the contradictory *hetu* disproves (or proves the contradictory) of what is required.

3. *Prakaraṇasama or the equivalent to the proposition:* The fallacy literally means a reason which is similar to the point under discussion. When there are two possible views in regard to the same subject so that they give rise to a state of indeterminacy and vacillation in the mind and when the reason given does not help in resolving such vacillation, we have a case of *prakaraṇasama.*

1 Almost all examples are taken from classical texts like *Tar–sam,* and *Bhā-Par.*

When two reasons oppose one another and neither can sublate the other, the syllogism which uses either of them is counterbalanced and opposed by the other. Hence the fallacy is known as *sat-pratipakṣa,* the counterbalanced subject. An example for this would be the two statements: "Sound is eternal because it is audible", and "Sound is non-eternal because it is produced". Both these inferences are fallacious for the one cancels out the other. When the reason given is the only one which is available to prove the opposite then the fallacy is *savyābhicāra.* For a *satpratipakṣa* fallacy, there must be two different reasons each proving contradictory things with reference to the same subject.

4. *Asiddha or the unproved:* In this fallacy the *hetu* requires as much to be proved to exist as the *sādhya.* The middle term is only an assumption and is thus unproved, *asiddha.* There are three forms of this fallacy. Firstly the *hetu* is unproved with reference to its locus. The *hetu* must be present in the minor term or *pakṣa.* If the *pakṣa* itself is fictitious then the presence of the hetu in *pakṣa* (*pakṣadharmatā*) is violated. For example: "The sky-lotus is fragrant because it is a lotus", is a fallacious syllogism since the *pakṣa* "sky-lotus" is fictitious. This fallacy is called *āsrayāsiddha,* unproved locus.

The second form of *asiddha* is that where the middle term is not found in the minor. This being so, the minor premise which relates the middle to the minor becomes false. For example: "Sound is eternal because it is visible", is false because visibility as the *hetu* can never be found in sound which is the *pakṣa.*

The third form of *asiddha* is that where the invariable concomitant between the *hetu* and *sādhya* is not possible because the *hetu* can never be so related to the *sādhya.* This is known as *vyāpyatvā-siddha,* unproved with reference to the *vyāpti* relation. For example: "All that which is real is momentary. Sound is real, therefore sound is momentary", is invalid because a thing that is momentary is not real according to Nyāya metaphysics.

5. *Bhādita or the vitiated reason:* This is a simple fallacy where the reason or *hetu* given to prove something is no reason at all since the contradictory has already been proved. For example: "Fire is cool because it is a substance" is a wrong argument as the hotness of fire is already known through another *pramāṇa* or means of knowledge. In the *satpratipakṣa* or

prakaraṇasama fallacy one inference is actually contradicted by another. In *bhādita* the inference is contradicted by a knowledge acquired through another *pramāṇa* which is non-inferential.

We have merely stated and explained here the major forms of fallacious arguments accepted by the older Naiyāyikas. A number of other fallacies are mentioned by later Nyāya philosophers who discussed the subject in great detail. We also find other forms of fallacious arguments discussed in Nyāya literature. These are used mainly in discussion and debate and are thus not fallacies really, but sophistications in argumentation. Most of the other schools of Indian thought accept the five-fold division of fallacies of the syllogism. There are some minor differences of opinion but these need not concern us here.

Upamāna or Comparison

All schools of Indian philosophy except Saṁkhya accept *upamāna* as a valid source of knowledge. But the manner of explanation of this *pramāṇa* by the Nyāya school differs slightly from that of the Advaita.

The Nyāya explains comparison as mediate knowledge by which we gain knowledge of a thing from its similarity to another. Usually the example given in the classical Nyāya texts is this. A man is told by his friend, a forester, that there is a *gavaya*[1] in the forest which resembles a cow. The man goes to the forest and comes across an animal which is like a cow. He recollects the words of his friend on perceiving the similarity, and comes to the conclusion that the animal before him is a *gavaya.* Two factors are involved here in this argument. First there is a knowledge of the nature of the object; this knowledge was obtained by hearing what the forester had said. That is, language or words are used as symbols to carry knowledge of the object. Secondly there is the perception of similarity. A combination of these two steps leads to the resultant knowledge: "This is a *gavaya.*" Thus the Naiyāyikas maintain that *upamāna* is a process where we come to know that a certain word denotes a certain object.[2] The Advaitins and the Bhaṭṭa Mimāṁsikas are the other two schools which accept *upamāna* as a valid means of knowledge. The Sāṁkhya does not accept *upamāna* as an independent *pramāṇa*

[1] A wild cow.

[2] "Samjñā-samjñī sambandha"—*Tar–Sam.*

on the grounds that it is merely a combination of verbal testimony, *śabdapramāṇa* and perception. Dinnāga, the Buddhist idealist maintains that *upamāna* is a case of perception and so he does not accord it a separate status.

The Advaitins and the Bhaṭṭa Mimāṁsikas accept *upamāna* as a separate means of valid knowledge but explain it in a different way from the Naiyāyikas.

A man goes to the forest and perceives an animal and forms the judgment: "This is a *gavaya* which is like my cow." From this he goes on to another consequent judgment: "My cow is like this *gavaya*." The first judgment is the result of perception while the second is got through the mediation of the perceptual knowledge and is the result of *upamāna*. The mental processes involved here are: first, there is a perception of similarity, secondly there is the remembrance of the cow at home and lastly there is the judgment that the cow seen in the past is like the *gavaya* seen here. The Nyāya judgment of *upamāna* is: "This is a *gavaya* for it is like my cow". The Vedantins concluding judgment is: "My cow is like this *gavaya*". The Vedantin argues that it is natural to make the statement: "This *gavaya* is like my cow" based on a perception of similarity, but from this alone we can never arrive at the conclusion that "My cow is like this animal, so it is a *gavaya*." This judgment is one which is derived by the perception of similarity applied through memory to what has already been perceived in the past.

The other schools of Indian philosophy which do not accept *upamāna* maintain that it is merely a combination of perception and memory and thus does not deserve separate status. This is felt to be unjustified. While perception and memory are components of the judgment by *upamāna*, they do not explain the judgment itself. That these two components are combined together in a peculiar manner is the strength of the argument by *upamāna*. We may know the cow through memory, we may know the points of similarity by perception but the combination of these two to produce the resultant knowledge is neither perceptual nor inferential as there is no universal proposition involved. Hence *upamāna* as a separate *pramāṇa* is justified.

Of the Nyāya and the Vedānta views, the former seems to be more sound. The implication that knowledge is derived through language used denotatively is something that is used in educating children, or illiterates in the initial stages of learning. Then again, the denotation of a word is normally gained from a description of the objects denoted by it. A definition is either a spoken or a written word. Again objects possess attributes included in the definition or description. Thus the learning process is a combination of perception, memory and the resulting *upamāna*.

Arthapātti or Postulation

The Naiyāyikas accept only four *prāmāṇas* which are perception, inference, comparison and verbal testimony. The Mīmāṁsikas and the Advaitins add two more to the list which are *arthāpatti*, postulation, and *anupalabdhi*, non-cognition.

Arthāpatti is a combination of two words—*artha* meaning fact, and *apatti*, meaning supposition or assumption. When the explanation of one fact leads to the knowledge of the fact that explains it, we have *arthāpatti.* When a fact is inexplicable by ordinary means, another fact is postulated which is found finally to explain it. The classic example given is of a man, known to be alive, but not seen anywhere. This is the given fact. To explain this it is presumed that he must be out of town. The presumed fact explains the known facts. Similarly, a person is known to be fasting, yet he continues to be fat. To explain this contradiction it is assumed that the person must be eating surreptitiously. In other words, *arthāpatti* is the postulation or assumption of a fact to resolve a contradiction that is present in perceived facts.

This method of obtaining knowledge is like the method of hypothesis used in Western logic but with this difference. In Western logic it is understood that a hypothesis need not be the explanation. Before it is accepted as such, it has to be proved. But in *arthāpatti* the supposition or postulation is the only possible explanation and is absolutely certain. The method used by Kant in giving his transcendental proofs approximates *arthāpatti*, when arguing from consequent to its possible antecedent, which alone can explain the consequent. He argues from the apparent conflict found between the necessity which is *a priori*, and novelty which is *a posteriori* in physics and mathematics which are based on the concepts of time and space. So he postulated the idea that these are *a priori intuitions*. These are both *intuitions* as well as *a priori* and thus resolve the conflict in judgments of mathematics and physics.

Anupalabdhi or Non-cognition

This is a *pramāṇa* accepted only by the Bhāṭṭa Mīmāṁsika and Advaita schools. All the other schools reject it and explain its function in other ways. *Anupalabdhi* or *abhāva*, as it is also known, is a means of knowledge where the non-existence of something is made known. We come to know such non-existence by other means as well. For example: by watching and reading a spectroscope we can infer the non-existence of a particular chemical. This is purely inferential knowledge. We may also come to know the non-existence of a thing when someone tells us about it. For example: someone who had been to New York may come back to India and tell his friends that there are no bullock-carts in America. Depending on the trustworthiness of the person we accept this as true and acquire this knowledge. But there is one type of knowledge of negation which does not come under all this. When a person misses a familiar object in the room and says: "I do not see such and such an object here", how can we account for the perception of such non-existence? It appears to be perceptual knowledge for it seems to be immediate, yet it is not so. How can there be any sense-grasping of something that does not exist? The problem is solved by the Naiyāyika when he maintains that all non-existence of a thing is an adjunctive to the locus of the thing. It is the ground which is characterised by the *non-existence* of the jar. There is no dispute about sense-organs not grasping this characteristic. So granting this, the Naiyāyika maintains that the non-existence of the object on the ground which is a quality of the ground is perceived by a special sense-object contact known as *viśeṣaṇatā* or adjectivity. Therefore it is also a case of perception and no separate *pramāṇa* is necessary.

The Prābhākara Mīmāṁsikas and the Sāṁkhyas also reject this *pramāṇa* for they say it is absurd to talk of non-existence separately from its locus. When the bare locus is perceived we get the knowledge of the non-existence of the object on it. The existence of an object is one aspect, the non-existence of it is the other aspect. Non-existence has no basis apart from that of the thing's existence. When the bare locus is perceived then the non-existence of the thing becomes known.

The Advaitins and the Bhāṭṭa Mīmāṁsikas whom they follow in almost all these matters maintain that knowing non-existence is not so easy. They say non-existence of a thing is not identical with the bare locus. When the pen is not there on the table, it does not mean that the absence of the pen is known because it is identical with the bare table. There may be other objects like books, papers, etc. on the table. Still the absence or the non-existence of the pen is noted. The non-existence and existence of a thing are two different things not reducible to each other. Thus non-existence can neither be perceived nor inferred. The Bhāṭṭa Mīmāṁsikas maintain that if a thing exists it must be known by the other *pramāṇas* of perception, inference, comparison, etc. If the object does not come to be known through these *pramāṇas* then this non-cognition of the thing is the means of knowing the non-existence of the thing. For example, if a jar is known to have its existence in some place at some time, then it is known by means of perception, inference, etc. But if even after such means of knowledge are used, the object is not known, then through such absence of knowledge it is judged to be non-existent in that place at that time.[1]

There is a further question to be answered in this context. Do all cases of non-cognition of objects lead to the non-existence of the objects in that locus at that particular time? Evidently, this is not so. When the conditions required for acquiring cognition of the object are not favourable, even if the object were to be present, there may not be a knowledge of it. For example, a man may be deaf and thus not be capable of hearing sounds. This does not mean there are no sounds present. Therefore the Advaitin maintains a conditional non-cognition as a source for the non-existence of the object.[2] The condition is that whether the object not known would have been known under the same circumstances, had it been present there.

The most important point to be noted in the above discussion is that while perception of an object as existent is a positive act dependent on a sense-perception of the object leading to a cognition or knowledge of its existence, the non-existence of an object is just a state of ideation referred to its locus secondarily and from which the judgment of its non-existence is drawn. The judgment:

1 *Śa. di.*, p. 83.
2 *Ved. Par.*

"This is a red rose", is a direct judgment based on perception and a resultant knowledge. But the judgment: "There is no red rose", is not so easy to explain. Bradley maintains that "the basis of negation is really the assertion of a quality that excludes".[1] For example: when we say that the traffic lights are not green it can only mean they are some other colour like red or amber. But this assertion of Bradley's is not as simple as it looks. To be able to assert on the basis of negation is not the same as straight assertion on the basis of perception. The former assertion is the result of two mental stages—one, the ideal recollection of the residuum to negation and the second, the fact that what is recollected is not the same and even opposed to what is perceived. It is only then that an affirmation is possible based on negation. This is what the Bhaṭṭa Mīmāṁsika explains when he says that the cognition of non-existence leads to a perception of non-existence. The idea is first and then the application of it to the locus of the object. That is, negative judgments are primarily subjective insofar as they arise from subjective knowledge. This is admitted by both Bradley[2] and Bosanquet.[3]

Śabda Pramāṇa or Verbal Testimony

The word *śabda* literally means sound. *Pramāṇa* means a method of acquiring valid knowledge. So the words *śabda pramāṇa* literally mean sound as a means of acquiring valid knowledge. Sounds are of various kinds. There is the spoken word which can also be perceived as the written word. Sounds, therefore, are to be considered as objects of perceptual knowledge since we get to know them through sense perception. But there is a snag in such consideration. Merely having heard a sound or seen a written word does not constitute a means of valid knowledge. If anything is to be considered as a means to valid knowledge, then it must serve as an instrumental cause for a resultant knowledge which should be valid knowledge. The definition of a *pramāṇa* is *pramā kāraṇam pramāṇam.* A *pramāṇa* is an instrumental cause, *kāraṇa*, for valid knowledge, *pramā.* It will be readily granted that all sounds do not fall into this category. All perceivable sounds cannot produce any meaningful knowledge. Therefore the Indian philosophers divide all sound into mere

[1] Bradley, *Logic*, Vol. 1, pp. 116-117.
[2] Bradley, *Logic*, Vol. I., p. 120.
[3] Bosanquet, *Morphology of Knowledge*, Vol. I., p. 280.

sound, *dhvani*, and meaningful sound, *varna*. The former are sounds of nature and sounds which are repetitive and whose meaning is not fixed. For example: the ringing of a bell. It has no fixed nature of its own although there is some duration. There is no order or arrangement of its parts. Its meaning, if any, is not fixed by its own nature. Such sounds are *dhvani*. *Varna* is a sound that is articulated and usually refers to the alphabet of any language as pronounced by the human vocal chords. Thus *varna* is a sound which is organised, with definite symbolic connotations which have a definite form and order. The symbolic fixation of the sound order is derived from the fixity of the meaning which it symbolises. Thus words like "name" and "mane" although constituted by similar sounds are different symbols. Thus symbolic sounds stand for elements of thought. Indian philosophers have discussed very exhaustively the problem of how a knowledge of the meaning of words and word-combinations arises, while all that is perceived is discrete sounds. The different sounds arise independently and discretely. Yet the meaning that arises is that of a whole. The meaning arises only after the word is heard completely. To say that the different syllables together express the meaning is to beg the question, for our enquiry here is, how is such meaning expressed. It will be seen here that it is the same problem as that which arises out of the perception of a temporal and spatial series so much discussed today by Western epistemological theories. Indian philosophy gives some significant answers to this question. We shall now consider these.

The Nyāya system maintains that memory is responsible for the perception of the whole. The syllables are heard one after the other in succession. But each syllable that is perceived leaves behind an impression in the form of its memory. As the word is completed, all the impressions left in the mind conjointly produce the meaning. This theory does not solve the problem, but pushes it back one step to impressions and memories. One can still ask the question, how do the impressions come together when they are also discrete entities being produced by discrete entities.

Śaṁkara, the Advaitin, avoids the question altogether, but maintains that it is due to a specific quality of the intellect, *buddhi*, that we are able to put together the whole. The word as a whole with its structural components are "grasped in memory through the synthetic activity of the intellect".[1] This is something like Kant's synthetic unity of apperception and also reflects the Gestalt theory of modern psychology.

The next question that is usually discussed is the meaning of the word. The essential nature of a word does not lie in its syllables, but in its meaning which is symbolic and symbolises something which is other than itself. A word may have different meanings according to the different relations it establishes with the external object. In spite of all such explanations the word must have a primary meaning whatever may be the forms of secondary meanings it enjoys. Almost all schools of Indian thought have discussed this problem fully. Usually the discussion centres round the question: does a word mean primarily an individual, *vyakti*, or does it refer to a universal or *jāti*? The importance of this question becomes evident if we pose the question in a different manner: which is known first, the particular or the universal? Logicians starting from the schoolmen up to the positivists have not been able to give a satisfactory answer. In Indian philosophy the question does not arise with reference to both the Cārvāka and the Bauddha schools for they reject verbal testimony as a valid means of knowledge. The Jaina school is definite that the word can only mean the universal. They maintain that we do not mean one object alone when we use a word, but all objects which have the same generic form. Since the form is to be understood only with its realisation in the particular, knowledge of the particular arises. Thus a word, the primary meaning of which is a universal, still refers to a particular indirectly through the generic form. This position is criticised by other schools. They maintain that even when the form changes as in a growing man or animal, the name sticks. Therefore the particular is not the meaning of the word but the universal only. The Naiyāyika criticises this latter view and maintains that the meaning of a term cannot be a mere universal. For example: a toy man possesses all the universal characteristics of a real man including the generic form, but we never call it a man. Therefore the Naiyāyika says that the primary meaning of a word is neither the particular nor the mere universal but the class character of the object. In fact the word *jāti* means this. It is the class-characteristics which help in the identification of an object either as a particular or as a universal. Therefore the primary meaning of a word is this *jāti*.

[1] D. M. Datta, *Six Ways of Knowing*, p. 261.

The Advaitins hold the view that the primary meaning of the word which is a symbol, is the universal alone. They argue that it is in virtue of the knowledge of the universal that we can apply the word to the particular and the individual. It is maintained by the Advaitin that a knowledge of the particular meaning of the word is always subsumed under the knowledge of the universal meaning of the word. In experience there is no question of a priority either for the particular or for the universal. Our perception reveals the individual as possessed of the universal characteristics. So the primary meaning of the word is also the universal.

A word has a meaning. Such meaning is a concept, a universal connotation. As such it also becomes an idea. An idea, says Bradley, stands not only for a psychical existent, a content, but also for a meaning. The first two are particulars while meaning is universal. The content may vary and with it the nature of the psychical existent may also vary, but the meaning remains the same.

Indian logicians were not satisfied with fixing the primary meaning of the word. They considered the fact that words are not often used in their primary meaning. When we refer to a wise man as a Solomon and to a beautiful woman as a Cleopatra, we are using these names in their secondary senses. When the primary meaning of a word does not serve the context of discourse then the secondary meaning is used. There is yet another suggestion by Indian logicians that sometimes words are used neither in their primary or secondary meanings but in a third manner which is a suggested meaning. Such meanings are indirectly suggested and insinuated. Inspite of these varied possibilities for the meaning of a word, it is the primary meaning that is important from a logical point of view.

If language is to be considered as a mode of presenting valid knowledge, then we cannot rest by merely fixing the primary meaning of words. Words form sentences and it is these sentences that give rise to coherent valid knowledge. Now it is our concern to examine the theories of the Indian logicians with regard to the nature of a sentence and what constitutes a meaningful sentence. There are three requirements for this. First there must be aroused a feeling of incompleteness when a word is pronounced. When this happens such incompleteness is fulfilled by putting it together with another word to form a sentence. For example: if I merely say the word "president" one is bound to raise further questions like "Which president?" "What about the president?" So to satisfy the incompleteness we have to finish the word-meaning by attaching it to other words such as "The president is on tour". This hankering after fulfilment left by hearing or reading a meaningful word is known as *ākāṃkṣa.* At the same time not every word can satisfy the hankering left in us by the given word; if I say "the president" and then add the words "the wall" to it, there is no resulting satisfaction. So the words used must be such that they are capable of fulfilling the meaning of the prior word. The words "is on tour" do this. They are, therefore, said to have the capacity or *yogyatā* which is the second condition. The first condition says that the word must arouse in us a curiosity for further understanding and the second condition says that the words used must be capable of fulfilling the desire so roused. These two, *ākāṃkṣa* and *yogyatā* are the material conditions. There is yet another formal condition for this fulfilment of meaning. This is *āsati* translated as spatial and temporal proximity. If one word is spoken now and here and the rest after a lapse of time and in another space, the meaning of a sentence is utterly lost.

So far we have been discussing the meaning and structure of a sentence. A few words regarding the relation between a sentence and a proposition are necessary at this point. It should be clear by now that a *vākya* or a sentence is not merely a grammatical combination of words. It is something which establishes some thought relations. As Johnson says, "The understanding of the grammatical structure of a sentence...requires us to penetrate below the mere verbal construction and to consider the formal structure of thought."[1] In Indian logic, no special name was allotted to a proposition as distinct from a sentence; both were referred to as a *vākya.* This contained the subject and the predicate. But as regards the copula—which is a form of the verb "to be"—there is no mention. Saṁskrit idiom is such that it does not require the use of this verb "to be". So there is no discussion about its function. This copula is responsible for the formalisation of all Western logic. Indeed, the name "formal logic" is evolved out of the formal manner of dealing with a proposition bearing in view the functions of a copula. This whole vexing problem is non-existent in Indian logic. In recent times there have been some efforts by some American Indologists to introduce formalism into Indian

Johnson, *Logic,* Part I, p. 8.

logic via the different modes of inferential reasoning.[1] While this may be so, the fundamental objection to any formalisation of Indian logic is the complete non-existence and non-recognition of the copula as the connecting link between the subject and the predicate.[2] In his book *Ways of Knowing*, Montague says, "We accept on trust nine-tenths of what we are told as true."[3] Now we have to discuss what constitutes the validity of verbal knowledge. That it has a meaning and reference we have shown. Some Indian philosophers like the Vaiśeṣikās and the Buddhists reject words and sentences as sources of valid knowledge. They maintain that knowledge derived from language has to be validated later either by inference or by using perception. So they maintain that *śabda* by itself cannot be a means of valid knowledge. But this objection can be raised against all means of knowledge. For a piece of knowledge to become valid, it has to depend on other considerations such as non-contradiction and non-sublatability. If this is not accepted then knowledge must be inherently valid. This applies to knowledge conveyed through language.

It is the Nyāya system which explicitly states the conditions of validity of the spoken and written word. It is the virtue of the source that makes knowledge dependable and valid. It is defined as the testimony of a trustworthy person, *āptavacanam śabdaṃ*. A trustworthy person is one who knows the truth and is capable of communicating it correctly. He is trustworthy for he is truthful and unselfish. It is the spoken word of such a person, whether he be God or man, whether he speaks of scripture or science, that constitutes *śabda pramāṇa*.

1 Ingalls, *Materials for Navya Nyāya Logic*.
2 Refer to the idealist thinkers like Bradley on this matter.
3 Refer the chapter on Authoritarianism.

CHAPTER IV[1]

PRINCIPLES OF MORALITY

Farquhar, the well-known Indologist remarks: "There is practically no ethical philosophy within the frontiers of Hindu thinking."[2] This is the normal attitude of many Western philosophers. Taking their impressions from mythologies, many Western theologians and moralists maintain that Indian philosophy as a whole has no theory or ideals of morals. Such an opinion about moral principles which govern Indian thought is ill-conceived. While judging the ethical predilections of a people, we should always judge their ideals rather than their practices, for practices depend on human frailties and environmental conditions and do not always conform or even remotely approach the ideal. Similarly in India also there is a wealth of moral philosophising which bears testimony to the ethical ideals of the people.

While talking of ethical ideals, I wish to emphasise that ethical theories such as hedonism, utilitarianism etc., do not find a place in Indian thought. The reason for this is that the ideal of life for all Indian philosophy is to attain freedom from sorrow and suffering. That man who seeks pleasure and economic well-being is accepted as a fact and is fitted into a scheme of values whose apex is the attainment of *mokṣa.* Except for the extreme hedonist, Cārvāka, all schools of Indian thought accept this scheme of values and the need to cultivate them is conceded as a *sine qua non* for all philosophising. This will become clear in the ensuing discussion.

There have been many solutions to the question "Why should I do good?" from both the philosophical and the theological points of view. It is maintained that when these two points of view come together we can find a justification for the moral code. Is faith in God necessary for a man to behave morally? Or putting the same question in negative language: is it possible to lead a moral life while not subscribing to a belief in God? This question leads us to others like: "What is the source from which morality springs?" "Does such a source of morality lend support to the view that the moral law is inviolable?"

1 Part of this chapter, in a modified form, forms a part of my book *A Critical Study of Hinduism.*

2 *Hibbert Journal,* Oct. 1921, p. 24.

We have to find answers to these questions from a study of Indian ethics. There are two distinct theories regarding the ethical code in Hindu thought. One equates the moral ideal to a universal law, a law which operates not only in the human behavioural context as the moral, but also as the operative supreme universal law of nature, *ṛta* of the *Ṛg Veda*. *Ṛta* is understood as the principle which was not only in charge of the changing seasons but also of the affairs of man and was considered as the guiding principle for all his actions. The importance of this law for the Vedic man becomes clear when we find that in the Vedas the gods were looked upon as the keepers of this moral order. They were *ṛtajāta* (born within the moral law), *ṛtajñā* (knowing the moral law), *ṛtapa* (protecting the moral law), *ṛtasyagōpa* (guardians of *ṛta*). Thus, the gods were there to see that man did not break the moral order to which they themselves were subject. He was considered the good man who adhered to the law and he the evil one, who either opposed it or disobeyed it. This moral order was considered a law, because it was obeyed by the whole universe. If the law was so stringent, then why did man disobey it? This question seems to have agitated the minds of the Vedic seers a great deal. Slowly, the term "evil" came to be associated with that which was in opposition to this moral order. It was *anṛta*. Gradually by the time we come to the *Brāhmaṇas*, *ṛta* had become identified with the performance of ritual sacrifices. A ritual sacrifice was considered as a means of attaining not only worldy goods and happiness, but also happiness and joy in the hereafter. Thus it became obligatory for a man to perform sacrifices. Each ritual act has its own reward prescribed and according to the moral law, *ṛta*, suffering and pain would result if and when the law was broken. Thus welfare and pleasurable life became associated with the moral life.

Along with this impersonal interpretation of the moral law, there was also another belief that the sanctions for morality rested on the will of God. Generally speaking, the ordinary Hindu is satisfied when the origin of the rules of conduct is traced to some scripture or the other. He is not interested in reasoning about it, for his faith in the bonafides of the scriptures is strong. Scriptures to him are the revelations of God and they cannot be wrong. We have already had occasion, in the first chapter, to discuss the nature of revelation with reference to the Vedas and we have pointed out that the word "revelation" could be used only in a restrictive sense in this context. Yet, the Vedas are generally accepted as infallible, because they are eternal. It is interesting to note that the different Indian philosophical systems which accept the Vedas as authoritative, attribute different reasons for such authority. The Vedas prescribe the moral code. So the authority for the moral code is dependent upon the authority attributed to the Vedic word. Some schools like Nyāya, and certain schools of Vedānta and Mīmāṁsa say that God or Iśvara utters the Veda at the beginning of each *kalpa* (cycle of time) and this makes the Vedas revealed scriptures. But there is a snag here. Iśvara does not reveal the Vedas. He only recollects them as they existed in a previous *kalpa* (cycle) and gives them to mankind afresh. He is only the carrier and not the producer of the Vedas. Hence, in the last resort, the Vedas are immemorial tradition, preserved and handed down by God during each *kalpa.* The other atheistic school of Mīmāṁsa maintains that the authority of the Veda cannot be derived from its being uttered by an omnicient God but that its authority is intrinsic. For the omnicience of such a God, they hold, is something that is not established by reason but which is derived from the Vedas themselves. When omniscience of the Gods themselves is to be established by the Vedas, then such a God cannot be prior to the Vedas. Gods, who are the creatures of the Vedas cannot be chronologically "before" such Vedas. Whatever may be the starting point, it cannot be denied that all shades of opinion agree that the Vedas are eternal and their authority is based on this characteristic only and not because they are revelations. Thus we have to come to the conclusion that as far as the moral order is concerned, its source lies in the Vedas and along with the Vedas the moral order is also eternal.

But such a conclusion should not lead us to believe that just because the sources of the moral ideals are eternal the moral code itself has been static through the ages. The traditionalists believe that the moral order is not only ancient but also inviolable and unchangeable. This implies that there can be no progress in moral concepts. Such a belief is not in accordance with the actual history of the moral ideals as depicted by the various historical phases of the development of Indian ethics. The question of the progress of morality is a moot one and is very closely tied up with the source of such moral ideals. It can be easily shown that in

India the moral code has been changing in some form or other. At this stage I would like to differentiate between a moral ideal and a moral code—the ideal is the perfect principle and the code is the imperfect approximation. The moral ideal in Indian thought is closely linked up with its philosophy while the moral code has changed with changing times.

Indian philosophy is not merely a set of beliefs and articles of faith. It is a way of life. The faith and belief which form the background permeate the social organisation. As the needs of the society change, its articles of faith are reinterpreted to suit the changing conditions. This does not mean that morals in Indian thought are opportunistic in nature. It only means that although the moral code has been changing from time to time, such changes have not violated the fundamental principle of the continuity of the *dharma* as the highest ideal. We should remember, in this context, that right from the earliest times, the Indian has enjoyed a very great latitude in speculations in the field of religion and ethics as evidenced by the variety and diversity of beliefs and faiths which flourished side by side.

We have stated earlier that the earliest notion of a moral order was known as *ṛta* and how in the course of Vedic development and system formations, this *ṛta* came to be identified with the performance of sacrifices. But as man attained maturity of stature, he was not prepared merely to obey the law. He started asking why he should obey the law. In the realm of physical nature the answer is self-evident. Violating laws of nature brings about physical illnesses. But nothing like this immediate retribution is to be found in the moral realm. Even then, threats and rewards are never going to provide incentives for a thinking man to behave morally. The "oughtness" of a moral judgment, according to Indian thinkers, cannot be enforced by an external sanction. Hence we find a scheme of human ideals were evolved. The whole code of such ethical ideals presupposes the notion that the soul survives after death and that it is eternal. Whether such a theory of the eternality of the soul is metaphysically justifiable, or not, the usefulness of the concept as a tool for ethical discipline cannot be denied. If man thinks that his efforts at leading a moral life have no other goal than the life here and now, there may not be much incentive for moral behaviour. It is this on the one hand and on the other the idea that no action can be done without its effect being felt either immediately or later on, that has given rise to the doctrine of *karma* leading to the doctrine of rebirth. We shall discuss this in detail later.

Ancient Indian thinkers laid down four factors which govern a moral life—*dharma, artha, kāma* and *mokṣa.* These are known as *puruṣārthas* or human values. The term literally means the "motives of man". These values took a crystallised form in a species of literature known as the *Kalpa Sūtras.* These have three sub-divisions, each dealing with one particular aspect of human activity, and these were known as *Śrouta*, *Gṛhya* and *Dharma Sūtras.* Of these, the first two systematise the rituals to be carried out by people while the third deals with customs, morals and laws that must be followed by people in various walks of life. That is, the *Dharma Sūtras* lay down the norms of the social and legal life of the people. These *sūtras* claim their sources as the Vedas and the Upaniṣads. Another source for these moral norms is the *Mahābhārata.* The most famous of the *Dharma Sūtras* is the *Manu Dharma Śāstra.* This is a commentary by an ancient seer named Manu on the *Dharma Sūtra.* It is from this commentary that we derive the meaning of the term *dharma* as duty. Such duties include both the duties towards oneself as well as towards others. The nature of *dharma* and its definition has been exercising the minds of Indian thinkers for quite a long time, for this word *dharma*, is one which has been used in Saṁskrit literature in a very comprehensive manner. It is used to mean law, justice, virtue, duty, innate nature, morality, social obligations and also the acts which result from all these. In some places it is used to mean a particular type of spiritual merit which secures for man, welfare, not only in this world, but also in a world which the soul goes to after death. After laying down that *dharma* is based on the *śruti* or the Vedas, this theory maintains that *dharma* is eternal and immutable both in its content and as an ideal. But this is only a theory. The rules of conduct laid down by the *Dharma Śāstras* have not remained constant nor can they be eternal. It is wrong to say that the content of the ideal *dharma* is eternal. It is the principle of *dharma,* as a code of conduct necessary for the well-being of man, that is eternal. Otherwise the claim that *dharma* is eternal has no meaning in the light of its changing contents. By this it must not be understood that moral principles are not universal. For, if so, then they cease to be moral principles. The moral code has undergone subtle changes to suit the changing conditions of life of the people through the ages. The saints called such codes of life *yuga dharma* which means laws and codes of conduct suitable to the peculiar conditions of life in each *yuga* or period of time. The divergences between what was taught in the Vedas, which are claimed as the source for the *Dharma Śāstras*, and the *Dharma Śāstras* themselves are said to be considerable by scholars. This constitutes another evidence to show that the code is changing. Yudhiṣṭira, the eldest of the Pāndavas in the *Mahābhārata*, said to be an expert in the *Dharma Śāstra*, says that where the sources of the *Dharma Śāstra* cannot be traced to the Vedas, it is safe to follow the path trodden by learned people, thus indicating that not all of the *Dharma Śastra* can be traced to the Vedas and also that the content of *dharma* is not eternal. The changing position of women in Hindu society indicates the changing of concepts generally. It has been established beyond doubt that in the Vedic society women were considered on an equal footing with men. Women were married only after they had come of age and were in a position to choose their partners in life. The *mantras* chanted at a marriage ceremony bear ample evidence to this. Spinsterhood was not looked down upon. Women were free to study anything they liked, including the Vedas. They were invested with the sacred thread and were entitled to carry on daily oblations in the same manner as were men. Some of the hymns in the *Ṛg Veda* were composed by women saints. Conflicting with this, we have definite statements in the *Dharma Śāstras* which maintain that girls should be married before puberty. They were not permitted to study the Vedas and were unfit to chant the Vedas. Women were considered equivalent to *śūdras* or the lowest caste since they had no right to the sacred thread. They had to be dependent on man at all stages of their life. Thus we find that a girl was declared to be dependent on the father before marriage, on the husband after marriage and on the good-will of men relations on both sides if she happened to become a widow without a son. If she had a son, then she was dependent on him. This subjugation of woman was perhaps due to economic and sociological factors, but it became a part of the moral code. Today, there is a swing back to equality in all realms except the religious and ritual. Examples of such changes in the notion of what is *dharma* can be seen in many walks of life. The central thesis is that *dharma* as a principle may be unchanging. But its content has always changed.

Thus *dharma*, if we mean by it the moral code, is a relative concept and is dependent on the conditions of society. It is a bond which keeps the society together. This meaning of *dharma* is derived from its etymological source as well. The Sanskrit word *dharma* is from the root *dhṛ* which means to bear, to carry, that which supports or upholds.[1] Hence *dharma*, in one sense is the cause of the maintenance of a society within law and order; in another sense it means the essential nature of the individual, his character which determines his duty to society. Thus moral standards became working principles. It is this latter idea that is stressed in the *Gīta*. *Dharma* is that which maintains the society and is the *dharma śāstra* of the period, and by virtue of this becomes the legal code and customary morality.

How is man to determine what that duty is, fulfilling which, there might be harmony and progress in society. According to Manu there are four ways of determining this. These are *Veda*, *smṛti*, *ācāra* or custom and most important of all, conscience. *Ācāra* is for the majority of the people who neither have the time nor the inclination to devote some thought to such matters. Such customary morality is always in the form of restrictive commands. But for the few, whose conscience is active and is regulated, not only by a veneration of the Vedas and *ācāra*, but also by deep meditation and logical reasoning, it is the dictates of such conscience that becomes the guiding law. It is not selfish decisions and self-maintaining principles only that are usually covered by conscience which are emphasised here; the dictates of such a conscience should not be against *loka saṁgraha* or the welfare of the whole society. Thus one determines what is good conduct and what is bad. Hinduism today owes much of its reformation including the reforms sought to be introduced by Mahatma Gandhi to this principle.

Once such broad outlines are fixed, the ancient moralist has gone on to lay down such particular aspects of life which have to be so governed and bound together by *dharma*. These aspects are *artha*, economic well-being; and *kāma*, physical desires and satisfactions. To a man who does not have the means of livelihood, all talk of *dharma*, duty, and *mokṣa*, liberation, becomes meaningless. It is only when a person is economically comfortable

[1] It is this meaning which is predominant when the earth is called *dharā* or as *dhātrī*.

that he begins to think of the welfare of his soul. This fact was recognised very early by the Indians. Fulfilling the obligations of social life and a gratification of sensuous enjoyment become impossible without possession of the means for such actions. Thus the word *artha* has come to mean material possessions. But in the acquiring of such possessions man has to be careful. He must not resort to any anti-social practices to acquire wealth. Ruthless rivalry, and heedless competition are not countenanced. One must always have the general principle of the greatest happiness of the greatest number as the aim in acquiring money or property. A great treatise called *Arthaśastra* by Kautilya is the recognised authority for the rules and legal codes of these days for the acquisition of wealth by either an individual or a government.

The next sphere of life where *dharma* offers the basic guidelines is the sphere of pleasure. Happiness can be achieved in many ways. But that happiness which tends to make man more large-hearted, more understanding, is always preferable to that which makes man narrow-minded and selfish. All pleasures, *kāma*, are to be oriented towards this. Man is always striving for pleasure and happiness. When this striving is not channelled into proper paths, it becomes license. Control is, therefore, advocated. *Kāma* is very often used to mean only sexual love but actually this word means all physical and sensual pleasures. In ethical treatises it is used in both the senses. A person who leads his life according to *dharma* has to regulate and discipline all sensuous pleasures, including his sex life. This is so because any undue attachment or desire always leads to unhappiness and dissatisfaction. One should never forget that sensual pleasure cannot be an end in itself but is only a means to other things. It is emphasised that pleasure always involves pain. They are like two sides of a coin. So if a man wants to enjoy life he must never forget that he should be prepared to suffer too. If such enjoyment is carried out according to set rules and regulations then the corresponding pain can be borne with some equanimity. So if the Indian ethical code enjoins *kāma* as one of the aims of a good life, it is because it envisages the need to make man lead a composite life taking into account all his requirements. But such a total life must always be governed by the welfare of not only the total man, but also the whole of the society of which, as a member, he is an organic part. Pleasures and riches remain mainly human ends. They can be considered as such only when they make a man a good man in the sense that he becomes a worthy member of the society and does not neglect his own final welfare.

To attain salvation, man must first desire it. The ancient seers attained *mokṣa* because they desired it with a burning intensity. Whether it be material success or spiritual success, desire is the springboard that takes man to it. Hence these three, *dharma*, *artha* and *kāma* are known as the *trivarga*, the three-fold aims which have to be practised by man assiduously. That man is to be considered superior "who rejoices in all the three" say the scriptures.

Thus this three-fold aim provides the necessary goals to make the life of man a full and rich one. As to why one should lead a moral life this question is answered by the assumption that it is only by leading such a life that man can be happy and comfortable in this world. Attaining wealth illegally and indulging in enjoyments that have no social sanction invariably make man unhappy. It is only when his actions are based on *dharma* or the laws of the society that man can find happiness. This is stressed over and over again in the two important *itihāsas Rāmāyana* and *Mahābhārata.* Both Rāma and Dharmarāja exhort the people to lead a life of *dharma.* This discussion could mislead the reader into thinking that according to Indian philosophy, the good man is he who obeys the laws of the society in which he lives. While this is generally true of any society there is also a higher ideal for determining what constitutes the welfare of a society. Like Kant, Indian thought stresses two principles. First the guiding motives of any action must be capable of universal application. Secondly since God is to be found in every man, no man must be used as a tool for the furtherance of another's selfish purposes. Laws and customs of any prevailing society must always be judged in the light of such considerations and followed.

The fourth value *mokṣa* is the ultimate aim of all religious endeavour. It is always the final aim of man to acquire release or *mokṣa* from the bondage of life in this world. The immediate purpose of a moral life is the attainment of a balanced and contented life in this world; the ultimate purpose is the attainment of *mokṣa.* The nature and content of the idea of *mokṣa* differs with different persuasions. But that *mokṣa* is the most desirable goal towards the achievement of which, all other activities must be aimed, constitutes a basic doctrine for the Indian. The very fact that traditional thinkers put *dharma* first and *mokṣa* last in the scheme of the *puruṣārthas* is not to degrade the one and upgrade the other, but to show that all actions must be rooted in *dharma* and aimed at *mokṣa*. In other words, the life of man is sandwiched between the moral ideal, *dharma*, and the ideal of freedom from all sorrow and suffering, *mokṣa*. Since *mokṣa* is the final goal, there is nothing much to be discussed about it as such. But we have to examine the various methods prescribed and suggested for the attainment of *mokṣa*. Before doing this we shall first of all concentrate on the moral principles and then proceed to the socio-ethical order of society accepted by the traditional thinker and then finally discuss the prescribed ways of attaining *mokṣa*.

The answer to the question why man should lead a moral life is based as much on the content of what we mean by moral as well as the purpose for which it is prescribed. The purpose for which it is prescribed would, in a way, define its content. In Indian philosophy the purpose of moral life is not so much to fulfil the will of God, as to seek one's own salvation. Salvation is attaining freedom from sorrow and suffering. This can happen within the span of this life or in a life after death. Salvation is the final aim, but there is another intermediary purpose to be served by a moral life—to make a just society. By his voluntary actions, a man must not cause sorrow and suffering to others. Thus, that which provides a sanction for moral life is the pressing need for man to live in a happy and contented society. The two aspects of social life, namely the economic and the emotional, must be controlled and directed by such motivations which would make the life of man in society, not only just, but also free from misery. To facilitate the development of this attitude two ways of life are prescribed. One way, known as the way of negation, *nivṛtti mārga*, requires man to cease all involvement in activities and lead the life of a recluse. The other way is the positive way, *pravṛtti mārga*, where man is required to participate in all activities but with moderation and detachment. All men cannot become *sanyāsins* or recluses, nor is it desirable. So, for most men it is renunciation in action that is suggested as a way of life. This is the famous *karma mārga* of the *Bhagavad Gītā*. It says that man should not shirk his responsibilities as a member of the society. Yet, he should not become attached to his role in society. It is because of this attachment that man commits the atrocities that cause suffering not only to himself but also to all others. The *Gītā* describes the man who is excessively attached to the objects of this world thus:

> When a man dwells in his mind on the objects of sense, attachment to them is produced. From attachment springs desire and from desire comes anger. (II. 62)

> From anger arises bewilderment, from bewilderment, loss of memory; and from loss of memory, the destruction of intelligence and from destruction of intelligence he perishes. (II. 63)

Thus, it is strictly enjoined that man should act but without attachment. But is this possible? The achievement of a goal is the motive force behind all actions. When this motive is nullified by the withdrawing of attachment to the goal of action, how can there be any action at all? Can man act in a motiveless fashion? To this the Hindu answers that it is by transubstantiation of the lesser goal by the larger that such actions are made possible. Instead of aiming to achieve selfish motives, man could aim to achieve the greatest happiness of the greatest number. Such transference of motivations is a very slow and arduous process. It is towards this end that certain ways of life are prescribed. These are practical accessories which help in the attaining of discriminative knowledge. These are eight in number known as *yamas* and *niyamas*. *Yama* is restraint. *Niyamas* are daily observances which have the purpose of clearing the body and mind of obstructions. In *āsana* and *prāṇāyāma*, through certain body postures and control of breath, the mind is purified and made fit for further steps which lead it to enter into a trance-like state. Let us take these one by one. The *yamas* are five in number. These must be deliberately and consciously cultivated. These are *ahimsa* (abstinence from doing injury to others), *satya* (speaking and living truth), *āsteya* (non-stealing), *brahmacarya* (continence in things of sense-enjoyment), *aparigraha* (abstinence from avarice). Of all these, *ahimsa* ranks the highest. *Ahimsa* is defined as "the not causing of pain to any living creature in any way, at any time".[1] In other words positively speaking, *ahimsa* demands friendliness towards all creatures. One has to

[1] *Y. Bh.*, Book II, 30.

give up all hatred, selfishness and jealousy which are the root causes for all injurious behaviour towards others. *Satya* or truth is defined as conformity of word and thought to facts. The other *yamas* are meant to discipline the mind and body and set it in a state of equanimity.

The *niyamas* are *sauca* (cleanliness), *santoṣa* (contentment), *tapas* (purificatory actions), *svādhyāya* (study) and *Iśvara praṇidhāna* (devotion to God). All these along with *āsana* and *prāṇāyāma* are meant to help man to lead a good and controlled life and are prescriptions which must be followed by every man, every day. One can easily grasp the importance of the above scheme of prescriptions. The former are psychological and the latter are physiological controls. They are prescribed to help man lead a peaceful life. All these can be summed up into the one basic principle of *dharma* namely that an action whose results are disagreeable to us would also be disagreeable to others and as such must not be done. As aids to the development of such a mental attitude the two-fold physical control known as *āsana* (proper posture) and *prāṇayāma* (breath control) are prescribed. Once the mind is prepared to view life with equanimity, that is, when all the motives of greed and hatred are conquered, man can, not only lead a happy life here, but also divert his efforts towards his own personal problem of attaining salvation. However much a man may be free from greed and jealousy, still he cannot escape from sorrow and suffering which are consequences of the very nature of the physical life he leads. He may achieve a sort of enforced contentment by practising non-attachment to the fruits of action. But it is not enough. There has to be a permanent relief for the soul from all such suffering. This release is the state of *mokṣa.*

Mokṣa is not merely a negative concept of attaining release from sorrow and suffering. There is also a positive side to it. While on its negative side it means freedom from sorrow, on its positive side it stands for plenary happiness. For some, it is that state which indicates the true nature of the soul as existence and bliss and is to be realised here and now, while for others it is a post-mortem stage to be attained on the strength of a good and devoted life here in this world. Some schools believe that there are many souls, all of them eternal, while others believe that the soul is only one and eternal and the experienced plurality of souls is a mere figment of the imagination. But all schools believe that the soul of man is bound by ignorance of one variety or another and that there is an imperative need to get freedom from such bondage. Man is bound by his own ignorance of the true state of affairs and has a capacity for a passionate desire to get rid of such bondage. But all men are not alike either in their spiritual, physical or physiological attainments. Depending on these differences their capacity to attain perfection also would differ. Hence the ancient seers have laid down certain pre-requisites for the quest for perfection. These have been classified under four headings and they are known as *sādhana catuṣṭaya.* These are:

1. The discrimination between that which is permanent and that which is ephemeral is called *nityānitya vastu viveka. Nityā* here would mean that which is fundamentally true. In our experience of both the subjective and the objective, what is true is to be sought after and what is untrue must be rejected. This requires a general sense of discrimination calling upon the person to distinguish progressively between things of greater and lesser value. This in turn leads to the discarding of that which is less permanent in favour of that which is more so. This attitude is well established in the Upaniṣadic story where Maitreyi, the wife of Yājnavalkya, asks her husband, "Sir, if this whole earth filled with wealth were mine, would I be immortal thereby."[1]

2. The feeling of rejection created by the ephemeral nature of an object is renunciation or *vairāgya.* This can take place only after a firm conviction that the object we seek after is not going to provide either permanent satisfaction or enjoyment. Such a conviction should start with an empirical evaluation of the object leading to a trans-empirical attitude of renunciation.

3. The next pre-requisites are the six-fold attitudes. These are *śama* (equanimity), *dama*, (restraint), *uparati* (renunciation of formalism), *titikṣa* (endurance), *śraddhā* (faith) and *samādhi* (concentration).

4. Once such a character has been built up by the conscious effort of man, then he must prepare himself to receive a knowledge about *mokṣa* and think about it. This again is to be carried out in three ways. First there is *śravaṇa*, hearing what is stated in the scriptures and lcarning about it from a competent master.

[1] *Br. Up.*, II 4-2.

Secondly, one must cogitate upon what has been learnt and find out if the teaching is satisfactory from all points of view. This is *manana*. Next comes *nidhidhyāsana* or contemplation on the truth so gained. During this stage, what remained merely theoretical knowledge till then, becomes a part of one's experience. When man is thus prepared, both physically and mentally, he is firmly set on the path to achieve *mokṣa*.

We started out by saying that all men are not alike either physically or psychologically. What is most suitable for one man's mental attainments may not be suitable for the other man at all. Here the ancient seers have said that each man can follow the method that is most suitable to him for the attainment of *mokṣa*. We may roughly classify all men into the active, the emotional and the contemplative types. Suitable to each of these natures we have *karma mārga*, the path of action, *bhakti mārga*, the path of devotion and *jñāna mārga*, the path of knowledge. All Indian philosophers, both classical and modern, do not agree on the relative merits of these pathways to *mokṣa*. But it cannot be denied that since each man differs in the gradation of the manifestation of these characteristics, these three ways must be suitable to different types of men. Of these *jñana mārga* or the path of knowledge is the most difficult one though the most desirable one. Man is a rational being. Rationality has been defined in various ways. The most important definition, as far as I can see, is that it is the capacity to distinguish between the worthwhile and the useless in any context. When this capacity is exercised, man has to differentiate between that which will help him to attain *mokṣa* and that which will hinder him. It is the recognition of this fact that is the basic requirement of *jñāna mārga*. Man has to learn about empirical matters. Things are not what they seem. When such knowledge is absent or when there is ignorance, there can be no discrimination. Hence removal of ignorance is the first and last step. Things of this world appear to be one thing but in reality are entirely different. To a jaundiced man, everything looks yellow though the objects are really multi-coloured. So it is ignorance of the true nature of things that makes man cling to the ephemeral, bringing suffering to himself. The discipline required for acquiring knowledge of the real nature of this world has already been outlined above. After learning and meditating, man makes such knowledge his own by living it. When this is done he is said to have attained *mokṣa*. According to those who believe that *mokṣa* can be attained only through knowledge or wisdom, such *mokṣa* need not be a postmortem state. The real nature of things including the soul of man and the relation between *Brahman*, the Ultimate Reality and the world of empirical experience is known and realised in this world itself. Such a realised soul is known as a *jīvanmukta* (one who has realised *mokṣa* while living). The religious history of India bears witness to the existence of such realised souls. In the *Bhagavad Gītā* there are many passages which praise the path of knowledge, and generally it is considered a most difficult though worthwhile method of attaining *mokṣa*.

But all people either do not have the integral grit to pursue the path of knowledge or are not by nature equipped for it. So, another path, more suitable for the emotional type is recognised. This is *bhakti mārga*, the path of devotion. Love of God and offering of devotional prayers are the most commonly accepted forms of worship according to all religions. Love is the response of the human being to beauty. When this beauty is of the things of this world the person becomes enamoured and entangled in it, this entanglement brings sorrow and suffering. But when such love of beauty is directed towards God, the man is well on the way to achieving his heart's desire, namely *mokṣa*. Such a purging of emotions and directing them to the love of a personal God is the crux of *bhakti mārga*. One important difference between *jñāna mārga* and *bhakti mārga* is that while the former does not require God to be limited to personality, the latter does so. A God with a form is necessary, for only then can the devotee use it as a focus for his devotion, grasp the nature of the Lord with his mind and adore him with his heart. In such an adoration no personal satisfaction or gain is involved. The devotee loves God for His own sake, because God is lovable. There is no motive attached to such love. A form of such love is *prapatti* or complete surrender to the will of God, as taught by Rāmānujāchārya. In this, the *bhakta* or devotee has no personal predilections at all. Come well or ill, it is God's will. In both these forms of worship, the worshipper loses his identity and considers himself one with God himself. While *bhakti* requires certain qualifications such as knowledge, good works, *prapatti* is above all these things. It is a full and complete surrender to God without either requirements or reservations.

Often, in the *bhakti* literature, the love of God is compared to many human loves. The attitude of the *bhakta* to God depends on the intimacy which he is able to achieve with God. Such relations are known as *bhāvas*. Six of these attitudes are recognised as most essential and to be successively experienced. Amongst them the first is *dāsya bhāva*, the servant-master attitude. This attitude is a mixture of respect, fear and devotion. While the servant adores the master, such adoration is not free from either fear of punishment or a feeling of inferiority. The second one is *sakhya bhāva*, the love that exists between friends. There is no fear here and there is no sense of inferiority. There is an equality of affection, a relationship of give and take. But the separateness between God and man persists and the possibility of affection and love failing to fulfil its function of binding, is always there. The third is the *vātsalya bhāva*, the love of a parent for its child. Here the Lord is loved and treated like a child. The protective and corrective elements are predominant. The mother is prepared to do anything for her child without going into the reasons. It is the happiness of the child that is the ruling motive. Similarly God is the eternal child and man must be prepared to do anything for him without asking for reasons. *Śānta bhāva* is the attitude of the child to the parent and it is the reciprocal attitude to *vātsalya bhava*. The child looks to the parent in love and trust. So also the *bhakta* loves and trusts God, leaving everything in His hands. The last two attitudes are the *kānta bhāva*, the love between husband and wife and the *madhura bhāva*, the love between the beloved and the lover. These are the most intimate kinds of love known to man. The devotee calls upon God to grant him the same place that mortals would grant to their beloved. Here the language used is erotic language, the sentiments expressed are sensual, but the content is neither erotic nor sensual. Words are but poor vehicles of the inner delight and bliss that the *bhakta* realises in the immediate presence of God. He cannot be separated from God. For him there is no life in separation. It is such outpourings of love that characterise all mystical experiences. The *Gīta Govinda*, a collection of mystic poems and songs, the songs of Mīra Bai, the Ālvars, the devotional lyrics of the Saivaite saints—all these are expressions of this attitude to God.

Jñāna marga, the path of knowledge requires intellectual detachment while *bhakti mārga* the path of devotion requires intense disinterested love of God. Both become difficult, unless fired by a consuming zeal for the achievement of *mokṣa.* In the light of such difficulty still another method of achieving *mokṣa* has been laid down. This is the *karma mārga* or the path of action. This emphasises how actions performed without attachment to their fruits can lead a man to *mokṣa.* This is the central theme of the teaching of the *Gītā.* Man cannot live without acting. The very breathing which sustains life is an action. But all actions do not involve a desire for their result. While not considering such involuntary actions such as breathing and blinking of the eyes as actions in the real sense of the term, all other actions of man are divided into two groups. These are actions which are obligatory and actions which are desired because of the results they bring about. Obligatory action or *nitya karma* includes certain routine actions which are carried out daily. These are the daily oblations to gods, eating food etc. It is the desired actions or *kāmya karma* that have a possibility of leading to *mokṣa.* When the personal motive for gain is substituted by the motive for universal happiness the first step in desireless action has already been taken. Every action binds in two ways. It not only carries its own reward but also moulds the mind to itself and leaves its impression, thus facilitating a repetition of the action. When there is a selfish motive the successful achievement of the goal invites the person to repeat the action for further gains and thus involves him in a chain of action and reaction. But when the selfish desire is replaced by a desire for universal happiness, the repetition of the action leads to universal good. The constant doing of such good actions removes all selfish traces from man and he becomes able to perform any action without a desire for its result. It is the lofty ideals of dedication and detachment that constitute the motive force for all actions. As we have already seen, this leads man to sunder that which binds him to the objects of this world and realise the true nature of his soul.

There is one important aspect of this doctrine of *niskāma karma* (desireless activity) that has to be discussed at this stage. The *Bhagavad Gītā,* which expounds this doctrine, maintains that desireless action is possible for all men when each man does his duty. This is called the doctrine of *svadharma* and this idea is given in one single verse in the *Bhagavad Gītā.*[1] Man is exhorted

[1] III. 35. "Better is one's own law though imperfectly carried out than the law of another carried out perfectly. Better is death in (the fulfilment of one's own law, for to follow another's law is perilous"—S. Radhakrishnan's translation.

to perform that type of work which is incumbent on his own status rather than desire to perform that for which he is not fit. One's own duty is better than another's. The word *svadharma*, one's own duty, has been interpreted in various ways. One interpretation is that it means the duty which devolves on a man because of his birth in a particular caste. It is also that which refers to the predominant quality with which a man is born and which is developed to fruition by environmental factors. Both these interpretations are not satisfactory. The difficulty involved in determining duties based on caste is a very great one. Whatever might have been its origin, the idea that particular castes have particular vocations is no more tenable in the present day. Similarly no man can act merely as his inclination directs him for it is not feasible for anyone to obey his elemental nature. On the other hand the idea of *svadharma* can be equated to include both these ideas and go beyond them. Each person has some position to occupy in society. Society itself can function fruitfully and peacefully only when all its members perform their respective functions. The choice of the station a man occupies in society depends upon his nature and training. So doing one's duty in accordance with the station one occupies in life, as a member of the society, is the highest duty one can perform. Doing such duty without attaching importance to its consequences naturally leads man to the desireless performance of duty. It may be that a man derives satisfaction from doing his allotted work with a sense of devotion. But this satisfaction is a desirable one for it is the result acquired in the course of discharging a duty selflessly.

The word *dharma* when used in the context of one's self does not make for a distinction between the "ought" and the "can" of moral life. What a man "ought" to do is a prescription based on the ideals of the good of society and the need for the attainment of *mokṣa* or freedom. When man, as a member of society and as a person seeking freedom from bondage, acts from such motivations he is converting these external prescriptions into the law of his being. Thus the "ought" becomes the "can".

All the three pathways discussed above for the realisation of *mokṣa* are usually termed *yogas*. The word *yoga* means "to bind". These pathways bind man to God on the one hand and on the other release him from the bondage of the world. We also find that these paths, though each is difficult in itself, can be viewed as forming a gradient. *Karma yoga* is the ethical path where man cultivates the ideal of the greatest happiness of the greatest number and achieves selflessness, to such a degrce as to be able to renounce the entangling activities and understand the true nature of freedom. *Bhakti yoga* requires that man not only act selflessly, but also forgets himself in complete dependence on God. It is very difficult to say, "Oh God! let thy will prevail and not mine." The presence of even the slightest egoism would obstruct such complete surrender. Man being what he is, it can be said that to be a true *bhakta* or a devotee is almost impossible. *Jñāna yoga* or the path of knowledge requires that man devote himself to true knowledge and concentrate on realising such knowledge in this life. A true knowledge of things reveals the impermanence and ineffectualness of the things of this world, and the permanency of the Ultimate Reality. In the other two paths, man has the solace of either doing his duty or depending on the grace of God. But in *Jñāna mārga* he stands by himself and, using his discriminative knowledge, finds out that there is nothing real and worthwhile outside *Brahman*. This is perhaps the most difficult path of all.

While thus grading the paths, it is also important that we notice that each path includes the other as a pre-requisite to a certain extent. To act, one must know the situation and be engrossed in the act. To love one must know through and through the object of love and be willing to dedicate all one's actions to that one object of love. To know, the life of a person must be purified, which involves ethical behaviour. Thus each pathway involves the other to a greater or lesser degree.

So far we have been discussing the ways to attain *mokṣa* and the preliminary training for this. We have studied the ideals of *dharma*, *artha*, *kāma* and *mokṣa* as accepted by the ancient seers. Now we have to digress somewhat and study two other types of auxiliary theories accepted in Indian thought. One is the socio-ethical-metaphysical principle of the doctrine of *karma* and rebirth and the other is the socio-ethical-economic doctrine of theories of caste and the stages of life. We shall consider the latter first.

The institution of caste occupies an important place in the life of the traditional Hindu. Not only does it colour his social practices, it also pervades his very outlook on life, its purposes and values. The system was originally meant to provide a basis of division of labour. It was meant to provide a harmonious social set-up in which each man had a place and a task and discharged his obligations. But later this deteriorated into a hereditary principle.

> "The original designers built the edifice of caste on the secure foundations of obligations; the lesser men who came after them produced a caricature on the shifting sands of right with the result that what we have today—the labyrinth of castes and sub-castes—resembles the original only in the sense in which the cartoon can be said to resemble its subject."[1]

It is indeed very difficult to formulate a single principle which would apply to all the castes as they are found in the India of the twentieth century. However, to be able to at least get a modicum of understanding, it is necessary to trace the idea through its various stages of development. The earliest reference to caste is shrouded in mystery and it is first expounded in the *Puruṣa Sūkta*.[2] This is obviously allegorical and mythical. The exact nature of the functions of each caste and the nature of their inter-relations is not well defined at this stage. But from a passage in the *Aitareya Brāhmaṇa* we gather that an upward or a downward change of caste could occur in a family in two or three generations. A *kṣatriya* family could produce "one like a *brāhmaṇa* in the second or third generation" if the *kṣatriya* committed a particular kind of mistake. Similarly for another type of mistake he might have a son with *vaisya* or *śudra* propensities.[3] There is evidence to show that, in the beginning, there were only the two contrasting groups namely the Aryans who were the aliens and the Dāsas who were the indigenous people. The former were fair-complexioned while the latter were dark-complexioned. Scholars are of opinion that the word "varna"[4] was not originally applied to caste but to the colour differences between the aliens and the indigenous people. But in the course of time the term acquired a different meaning. From colour-connotation it changed into a group-connotation. The idea of the castes and their duties became, in later Hinduism, so fixed in the minds of the people that Hinduism

[1] T. M. P. Mahadevan, *Outlines of Hinduism*, p. 69.

[2] Part of the *Ṛg Veda*, referred to in the first chapter.

[3] Quoted from G. S. Ghurye, *Caste, Class and Occupation*, p. 44.

[4] Very often the word *varna* is used to mean the four castes, *caturvarna*.

itself came to be denoted as *varnāśrama dharma* (the duties of castes and stages of life). But from this it cannot be argued that caste took its origin from differences in colour or *varna*, for the people of one caste do not all have the same colour or even shades of the same colour. Various other theories are forthcoming from a perusal of the extant literature of the times. One account is that the four important castes, *brāhmaṇa, kṣatriya, vaisya* and *śudra* had four different saintly proginators. Another account is that Manu was the primordial proginator of all the castes. Still another account was the division of the people into castes based on their character (*guṇa*) and occupations. Whatever may be the origins, actually the priest-class *brahmaṇa* was already a well-established functioning caste by *Ṛg Vedic* times. The function of this caste was to officiate at sacrifices, teach, and generally act as the custodian of all spiritual knowledge. The profession must have been hereditary, although in the course of literary history we come across *kṣatriyas* also officiating as priests. Endogamous marriages do not seem to have been a rule of the day, for sages like Chyavana are said to have married *kṣatriya* girls. *Kṣatriyas* who were known as *rājanyas* emerged as a distinct group later. We have the names of such saintly kings as Janaka, Ajātaśatru, Asvapati Kaikeya occurring in the Upaniṣads. It is interesting to note that there were other occupational groups mentioned in the *Ṛg Veda* over and above the four classes.[1] Some of these group, like the builders of chariots (*rathakāra*) seem to have enjoyed high religious and social positions. Generally, all these castes were hereditary more by common custom than any regulated law. As we have stated already it was possible for a man to change his caste.

The divine origin of the four castes is stressed repeatedly in the post-Vedic period. But an emphasis was laid on the idea that the fourth caste, *śūdra*, was created to serve the other three castes known as the *dvija* or the twice-born castes, the second birth taking place at the time of initiation into the sacred lore by the donning of the sacred thread. In the *Bhagavad Gītā*, God is said to have created man and apportioned duties and functions to him according to his capacities and character. This theory tries to rationalise the rigid caste ideas that were in existence and thus marks a change in the attitudes of at least some men. What was hitherto considered as hereditary and consequently not to be

1 *Ibid.*, p. 50.

tampered with was now sought to be explained on a rational basis. A man must perform such duties as are incumbent on his social status. But God is pleased and salvation is attainable not merely because work is done, but because such work is done with devotion and without an eye on the consequences. Thus we find a persistent effort to remove the inequalities inherent in caste or to rationalise them by transforming caste into a functional theory of society. The story of Nahusa in the *Mahābhārata* illustrates this fact very well. In this, Yudhiṣṭira, the eldest of the Pāndavas answering a question about who is a *bṛahmaṇa*, answers that a *śudra* possessing the character of a *brāhmaṇa* should be considered as a *brāhmaṇa* and that a *brāhmaṇa* who possessed the character of a *śūdra* must be considered as *śūdra* without any doubt. Thus caste was determined by the character and conduct of a person and not his parentage.

Simultaneous with this struggle to give a rational interpretation to the caste organisation was going on a process of very rigid stratification. Internal solidarity within each caste also developed around this time. The main principle which cemented the caste system was the prohibition of inter-caste commensality and marriage. Although these were strictly enforced by the leaders of each community, still, right through the ages, we find these principles being violated. Certain types of inter-caste marriages were allowed—a *brāhmaṇa* could marry a woman of any of the three lower castes, a *kṣātriya*, of the next two castes and so on, provided he had first married within his own caste. This meant that hypergamous marriages were permitted and men could marry women of a lower caste, and children born of such marriages were accepted within the caste. But the opposite was not countenanced. However hypogamous marriages did take place, and the offspring of such marriages formed a different caste. Gautama, a law-giver of the middle ages says that if girls from five or six successive generations belonging to the mixed stock married *brāhmaṇa* men, then the progeny would eventually revert back to being *brāhmaṇas*. The epics give us some examples of inter-caste marriages. Daśaratha, the father of Sri Rāmā, had a *śūdra* wife. Śantanu, a *kṣatriya* married Satyavati, the daughter of a fisherman. The famous Bāṇa, the Saṁskrit playwright and poet had two step-brothers born of a *śūdra* mother to his *brāhmaṇa* father. Inspite of such instances, the institution of caste became rigid.

During the period when the *Dharma Śastras* developed, two important features of *dharma* were forged which have a very great bearing on the caste system even today. First, the practice of giving gifts to the priest which was referred to in some hymns of the *Ṛg Veda*, took fresh root and became an obligatory function for the rest of the castes. Manu, for instance says that giving gifts to the *brāhmaṇa* is the highest duty of all men.[1] Secondly the notion of suffering in a hell became more pronounced and a gradation of hells was described. The fear of suffering in such hells made men conform to caste rules. Closely following this was an increased and skilful use of the idea of rebirth. The person who committed certain offences, was told that he would be degraded to a much lower status in his next birth as a punishment. For example : it was stated that a *śūdra* who violated his caste rules would be reborn as something whose main food was moths.[2] The result of all this was to give the *brāhmaṇa* an exalted position and to make him almost the equivalent of the gods. It is said that on account of the excellence of his origin a *brāhmaṇa* was entitled to the whole of this world.[3] But at the same time, a *brāhmaṇa* is defined as a *brāhmaṇa* only when he followed the rules of conduct laid down for him such as learning and expounding the Vedas, following his profession of being a priest at sacrifices and other such religious duties. The *brāhmaṇa* was prohibited from eating food prepared or offered by any other caste. He could not even live in the same locality as that in which the *śudras* and *vaisyas* lived.

However, in outlining this development of the caste system, we should not forget that side by side there have always been movements protesting against such treatment of fellow human beings. This attitude in a very pronounced form, was repugnant to religious leaders. Ramānujācharya preached religious equality of all men. One of his apostolic disciples, Rāmānanda was not a *brāhmaṇa*. There were many *śūdra* saints, both Vaishnavite and Saivaite. Namdev, Tukāram and Mīrābai in the North, Kaṇṇappar, Tirujñāna Sambhandar, Tiruvalluvar and many other saints in the South were non-*brāhmaṇas*. In addition to this, the special functions of the *brāhmaṇa* as a sacrificial priest and custodian of the Vedas was gradually lost and the *brāhmaṇa*, under

1 *M. Dh. Sa.*, 1, 86.
2 *Ibid.*, VII, 54-80.
3 *Ibid.*, I, 100.

such special circumstances, was permitted to take to other occupations. This led to a general relaxation of the occupational functions of the caste, thus leaving only the form without the content. In a way, the only inherent principle of the caste system that has survived through the ages to some extent, is the hereditary function of the *brāhmaṇa* to act as a priest to all other Hindus. Even here the connotation of the word priest has changed. With the disappearance of Vedic sacrifices and all its paraphernalia, the term "priest" has come to mean one who officiates at temples and at special religious functions such as marriages[1] and funerals.

The fundamental characteristic of Hinduism is the belief that man should attain freedom from sorrow and suffering incident in life in this world, and attain *mokṣa.* Since the scriptures have not anywhere laid down caste membership as a prerequisite for the attainment of *mokṣa,* giving up caste does not adversely affect a Hindu in the practice of his religion. The description of the perfect man given in the *Bhagavad Gīta* tells us of the characteristics he must cultivate. Such a man must be above the dualities of this life and be unfettered by attachments. From this it is clear that the caste into which a man is born has nothing to do with the final state of release to which all men must aspire. So to the real Hindu, caste is more a hindrance than a help in realising *mokṣa.* This truth that it is not birth that makes a man pure is repeatedly given to us in the various *purāṇas.* The story of the *brāhmaṇa* who was sent to a butcher by a *brāhmaṇa* housewife to learn the truth about *dharma* is given to us in the *Mahābhārata.* The caste system has changed over the centuries and will continue to change to suit changing conditions.

A much more tenacious aspect of Hinduism is its belief in the doctrine of *karma* and its corollary, rebirth. This involves not only the metaphysical belief about the eternality of a soul, but also that such a soul is involved in a causal chain which is responsible for its birth again and again in this world. Such a cycle of births and deaths is the root cause of all misery, and the soul is forever trying to get rid of this entanglement in the wheel of *saṁsāra.*

1 Even this is disappearing today as many people are resorting to a form of civil marriāge.

There are two aspects of this theory. First there is the law of *karma*. This theory maintains that the law of causation is applicable not only in the physical realm, but also in the moral realm. Just as the physical universe obeys the law that cause produces an effect, so also in the moral realm, every action must have an effect. There is no action, whether good or bad, which does not give rise to a reaction. The seeds of this idea are to be found in the concept of the *ṛta* enlarged upon in the *Ṛg Veda*. *Ṛta* is the inexorable law, obedience to which ensures the existence of nature. It is also the law which man has to obey in his moral life. If a man does a good deed, he reaps the benefits of such an act. When he acts otherwise, he cannot escape the consequences. Thus *ṛta* is a law which is applicable to both the physical and the moral world. Such a *ṛta* was believed to be operative here and now and it did not extend its tentacles into a future life as well. But in later times when the notion of a sacrifice yielding its results in another world developed, the idea of *ṛta* changed gradually into the doctrine of *karma*. But the law of *karma*, as envisaged by later systematisers of Hindu thought, is not merely an expression of the law of *karma*. Some actions produce their reactions immediately following upon the performance of the action. Some others have delayed reactions. The question which bothered the ancient Hindu was how such a reaction, as a fruit of the action performed, could be said to be preserved during a considerable time lag. In the absence of a physical evidence for the occurrence of the effect the ancient Hindu conceived of *adṛsta* or unseen potency which served as a repository of all such unfulfilled effects providing a bridge to cover the time lag. Each man has his own *adṛsta*. Here we come across the second aspect of the *karma* theory, namely the theory of reincarnation of the same soul in different bodies. From the above account of the functioning of the law of *karma*, it is evident that one life-time may not be enough to enjoy the fruits of actions stored up in the form of *adṛṣta*. Thus many births became necessary for the soul. The nature of the embodiment depends on the nature of the fruits of actions performed by the person. If a person has always done good, then the fruits would be naturally good and the resultant embodiment for the soul would be such that he would be born in benevolent circumstances; if his actions have been evil the soul is reborn in more trying circumstances. The final purpose of man is to get rid of this bondage to action and its results. So man should strive towards the achievement of salvation. But the situation is unsatisfactory. If the whole process of birth, death and rebirth is strictly controlled by such a law of causation, where is the opportunity for the individual to strive for *mokṣa* and get rid of the cycle of birth, death and rebirth known as *saṁsāra*? The law of *karma* and the consequent theory of rebirth spells determinism in the affairs of men. If this is so, we deny the freedom of the human will. How are we to reconcile the possibility of a release from *saṁsāra* for the human being with the absolute determinacy advocated by the *karma* theory?

Two ingenious loopholes are provided for this. One is the very nature of *karma* itself. *Karma* is action in time. So there are past actions, present actions and there will be future actions. That portion of the fruits of the actions performed in the past which have become fructified and therefore are to be experienced in the present life are known as *prārabdha karma.* This is something that cannot be interfered with but must be suffered. There is a portion of the fruits of actions which is still suspended in *adṛṣta.* These are the *sañcita karma.* To prevent the fructification of these actions, the grace of God is invoked. If God so wills man can become free from the burden of *sañcita.* But man must surrender himself to God completely. The theory exonerates God from the charge of cruelty or partiality. A man reaps as he sows. God only dispenses justice as man deserves it. But when man pleads for mercy he gets it. In addition to this, a second way is also provided for escape from *saṁsāra.* When man acquires true knowledge of the nature of his soul and its relation to body and mind, he ceases to act from any selfish or avaricious motive. When this motive is removed, the fruits of such actions cease to bind man. When this bondage is not present the cause for rebirth is removed. The mode of the transference of the results of action may differ from system to system. But all traditional views except that of the Cārvāka school accept that such a transference does take place and that as a result there is a repeated reincarnation of the soul.

There is an opinion prevalent that the principle of such a theory of rebirth and the theory that the nature and status of such a reborn person depends on previous actions and their results was developed and reinforced when there was an urgent need to glorify the caste system and uphold the supremacy of the *brāhmaṇa* caste.

During the *Ṛg Vedic* age a practice of giving gifts to the priest was prevalent. But this practice remained on the fringes of the sacrificial religion and was lost sight of during the Upaniṣadic period. The glorification of the gifts to *brāhmaṇas* took a new impetus during the days of the *Dharma Śāstras.* Manu was almost mandatory in saying that giving gifts to the *brāhmaṇas* was the supreme duty of man in the *Kali* age.[1] Since no mandatory principle can be effective without a scheme of punishments and rewards, a schematic postulation of imaginary hells as places of punishment for offenders, and a strengthening of the doctrine of rebirth developed. Thus the theory of rebirth was very skilfully used as a sanction for certain rules of conduct. For example: the murderer of a *brāhmaṇa* was reborn, not as a human being, but as a beast or an insect,[2] whereas one who pleased the *brāhmaṇa* with gifts and services deserved rebirth in a higher status than that which he had occupied in this life. Naturally such attitudes, spoken authoritatively by the *brāhmaṇa* teachers of those times, strengthened belief in rebirth and a fundamental place was given to it in later Hinduism.

Let us now examine this theory more closely. The word *karma* which is basic in the context, has various meanings. Depending on the context it could mean any act, whatever its nature may be; secondly it could mean only a moral act specifically in the accepted ritualistic sense; thirdly it also means the accumulated, unfructified fruits of all actions, whether moral or immoral or non-moral; fourthly, it could mean a fate which shapes the destiny of man. There is an underlying unitary idea in all these four meanings. It is that a man by his very actions, shapes his own future in the form of, preferably, rebirth.

Karma or moral action, the philosophers tell us, can be of three kinds: *nitya karma* or daily actions of worship, *naimittika karma* or obligatory actions of worship such as offering oblations to the manes and teachers, and *kāmya karma* or optional rites performed with a view to enjoying their benefits. The last type of actions alone produce a result. But here the meaning of the word *karma* is restricted to ritual performances. Does it mean that other *karma* has no reward or punishment? Is an action judged good

1 *M. Dh. S.*, 1. 86. The cycle of the universe is divided into four ages. First is the *Treta Yuga* and the last which we are living through is *Kali Yuga.*

2 *Ibid.*, 1. 87.

or bad only in a ritual context? If we are not to be involved in this interpretation, then it is necessary to interpret the word *karma* not in this narrow sense of ritualistic worship, but in the wider sense of any good or bad action. Here lies the crux of the problem. An action is a good action if it achieves two results. One, it must be instrumental for the harmony and happiness of all beings in this world, second it must be instrumental in bringing about *mokṣa* or self-realisation for the individual. The first aspect is the social aspect and the second is the religious aspect. Each may be dependent on the other. But still it is possible to view them as separate activities to some extent. A combination of these two is what is meant by *karma* in the *Bhagavad Gītā*. To do one's duty, religious or otherwise, with a sense of detachment to the fruits of its action, takes away any involvement in such results. Inspite of this generous interpretation of *karma*, we are still left with a vagueness regarding what is meant by the fruits of action, *karma phala*. Let us take an ordinary action like giving charity. The person to whom charity is given benefits from that charity and normally this is the meaning considered as the result of that action. But in this context the fruit of the action is two-fold. Firstly it accrues to the receiver of charity, and secondly the giver of charity derives a pleasurable satisfaction from achieving something or doing an action well. However *karma phala* is not these two results, for the results of such actions are immediate and do not require the postulation of a reincarnation. Therefore, in addition to such immediate results, all actions are supposed to yield merit, *puṇya* or demerit, *pāpa*. It is these that cause rebirth. As such to interpret *karma* theory as one where every action which brings about a reaction and that fulfilment of such reactions require a series of births and deaths seems to be far-fetched.

Rather than holding that rebirth is the result of all accumulated unfulfilled fruits of actions, it would be better to say that rebirth is the result of hankering after the pleasures of *kāmya karma*.

The doctrine of rebirth is traditionally explained in another manner by saying that the inequalities and unmerited sorrows and joys of this world can only be explained if we go beyond one life-span. A man who continuously does good suffers whereas a man of evil deeds flourishes and prospers. A learned man begets an idiot and an illiterate man begets a genius. It is said that such occurrences can only be explained by referring to the accumulated *karma* of past lives which are now bearing fruit. As we had sowed earlier, we now reap.

There are certain lacunae in the above argument. It is a well-known fact that the law of causality is applicable within the empirical sphere of activity. If the effect is empirical, the cause must necessarily be empirical. Attribution of transcendental causes to empirical events is a mistake. Things belonging to one category cannot be explained by reference to another category. Even if it were possible, it becomes difficult to state, while arguing from effect to cause, which transcendental cause is to be cited for which empirical effect. In addition to this, there is not one single cause for one single effect and vice-versa. Unless this is possible the linking up of rebirth, as an effect, with the fruits of *karma*, as cause, becomes difficult.

Whatever might have been the utility of the *karma* theory in the past, it has lost its disciplinary hold amongst Hindus. With the spread of scientific and technological knowledge, an explanation for the physiological and mental inequalities so far-fetched as the *karma* theory has become unacceptable. Facts of sociological economics and social psychology combined with anthropology are able to explain inequalities that so puzzled our ancestors.

In the earlier portions of this chapter, we have pointed out how the ultimate goal of all human endeavour is the attainment of liberation for the soul. We have already explained the nature of the bondage from which the person is trying for release. The pure soul is bound to this world of appearance and the soul is forever striving to rid itself of this bondage. To the questions, why a soul which is pure should be bound in the first instance, and what is the need for the creation of this world, the Hindu has given a two-level reply. To the man of faith, the activity of creation is a play, a *līlā*. To question further is not right, for who knows the ways of God? To the man of limited faith and a questioning mind, Hinduism provides the doctrine of *māyā* which says that this world-creation is inexplicable. It is neither ultimately real nor unreal. To those who are in the world, the processes of creation and destruction seem to be real. But to one who has attained true knowledge all this appears to be illusory. So from one level it is true and from another it is not true. But this is inexplicable, because a thing cannot be both. It is only true knowledge that can remove the blinkers from our eyes and lead us to salvation.

The paths to salvation, as we have already explained are two-fold, each leading to the other. The first is the path of *pravṛtti* or involvement in the affairs of the world and the other is the path of *nivṛtti* or renunciation. For a man who cannot renounce, the former way is prescribed. Accordingly, his actions are all for the welfare of the society in which he is a member. Since man is a member of a society, his life in society is to be governed by progressive stages of involvement and renunciation. These are known as the *āśrama dharma* or the duties of the stages in life.

The first stage is that of the student. A student is known as a *brahmacāri,* one who walks in the path of *Brahman* or Reality. He has to live with his teacher, usually a man of profound learning, and lead a very austere life. His sole aim is to learn and study, and thus acquire the quality of a discriminative intelligence. Once he attains such a knowledge theoretically, he enters the life of a *gṛhasta*, a family man. Here he is required to discharge his duties to his family, to his ancestors and to the society of which he is a member. After this comes the stage of *vānaprastha*, where the man with a satisfaction of having discharged his duties, feels free to devote his time to a further and deeper study of the scriptures, and to meditation. The last stage is that of *sanyāsa* where a man renounces everything seeking only a means to his salvation.

These four-fold stages of life are the ideal prescribed by the Hindu scriptures. They must have been the ideal division of the life-span of a person suitable for the various requirements of the time. But, as it must be evident, even from a casual glance of present day Hindu society, none of these divisions exist today. This is because of the changing conditions of life and the changing ideas about the aims of life. Thus the *āśrama dharma* can only serve as a reminder to the present Hindu society of what the ideals of life in a bygone society were. Its value, other than this is nil. The only order that still persists is that of the *sanyāsin*. But even there, there are changes in the concepts. It is more a mental *sanyāsa* of desires, rather than a physical isolation that is recognised as *sanyāsa* today.

In the account of ethics that has been presented it should be evident at a first glance that ethical theories as prevalent in Western philosophy are absent here. Even the Buddhist who does not subscribe to a permanent soul believes and accepts the necessity for a moral life in the social context. Of the four values set down, *artha* and *kāma* take care of the economic and social aspects of moral life. *Mokṣa* is a strictly personal ideal wherein each man has to strive for himself to attain it. *Dharma* provides the general guiding principle. A man can become an aspirant for *mokṣa* only when he fulfills the requirement of having led a worthy and blameless life. Thus Indian philosophy and religion require man to be moral, not because of any extraneous compulsion, but because all these experiences help a man to realize his nature. Since the whole approach is different, it is very difficult to draw parallels with any other moral theory from the West. It is incorrect to say that this approximates the Christian belief that man should be good, for only then will God give him salvation. Even this amount of externalisation of the sanctions of morality is not acceptable to Indian philosophy. Man is moral because he and he alone desires to be so in the interest of his own salvation.

CHAPTER V

PHILOSOPHIES OF RELIGION

In the first chapter of this book it was stated that there were three important commentators on the *Braḥma Sūtras* of Bādarāyana. Of these, Śaṁkara was the chief architect of the Advaita philosophy of Absolutistic non-dualism. The various aspects of this philosophy we have already studied in the previous chapters. Rāmānuja and Mādhvā are the other two commentators who have given distinctive philosophies of religion implied in the *Brahma Sūtras.* The main currents of modern theology in India stem from the writings of these two great savants and from another indigenous theological development known as Śaivism. The sources for the former are the Vedas, the Upaniṣads and the *Gītā.* For the latter it is the *Śaiva Âgama* literature, hymns of the Śaiva saints and the works of later theologians that form the sources. The philosophical aspect of Śaivism is known as *Śaiva Siddhānta.* The Viśiṣṭādvaita of Ramānuja, the Dvaita school of Mādhvā and the Śaiva Siddhānta form the major religious persuasions in India today. We shall present each of these separately, stressing on the philosophical aspects of their theologies.

Before we do this, it is necessary first to try and dispel one common erroneous view of Indian philosophy. It is usually maintained that all Indian philosophy is spiritual in nature, the word spiritual being interpreted to mean concerned with God and the eternal soul. It should be evident to the intelligent reader after a perusal of the previous chapters how very misleading such an interpretation of Indian philosophy is. Indian philosophy is not merely the Vedāntic schools. It consists, as we have seen, of the non-Vedic rebellious systems of the Cārvāka, Bauddha, Jaina and the six Vedic systems. The different schools represent materialism, pluralistic realism, dualistic realism, idealistic monism in addition to the philosophies of religion which we are now going to study.

Viśiṣṭādvaita of Rāmānuja

Viśiṣṭādvaita is translated as qualified non-dualism. The name itself is suggestive. Rāmānuja made a very striking contribution to religion and to a philosophy of religion by his strenuous efforts to reconcile the non-dual Absolutism of the Upaniṣads with the prevailing religious faith. These two lines of thought, namely, philosophical Absolutism and personal theism can be traced far back into antiquity. But a concerted reconciliation between them was successfully attempted by Rāmānuja and his followers. Rāmānuja totally rejected the abstract non-dualism of the Advaita school; especially the theory of *māyā*, which reduces all empirical existence to an illusory existence, was anathema to Rāmānuja. Rāmānuja wished to show that there was some kind of distinction between the individual Self, *jīva* and the Ultimate Reality, *Brahman*. That it is not identity is a foregone conclusion, for Rāmānuja argues that the limited sinful self cannot by any length of imagination be identical with the pure eternal Self, *Brahman*. At the same time propagating a complete difference between the two is also not acceptable. Rāmānuja says that such difference would contradict the great Upaniṣadic sayings like "That thou art"—*Tat tvam asi*. Therefore Rāmānuja's theory envisages a situation where while the three entities, matter, soul and God are seen to be distinct from one another, yet they exist together in some kind of unity. Rāmānuja replaced the absolute idealism of Śaṁkara with a realism of his own brand and in the process provided for a *Brahman* with qualities as the Ultimate Reality.

Rāmānuja recognises three ultimate factors, (*tattva-traya*)—matter (*acit*), soul (*cit*) and God (*Īśvara*). Though they are all equally ultimate and fundamental the first two are dependent reals while the last is an independent real. The nature of dependence is not external, but is like the dependency of the body upon the soul. The whole of the material reality, *acit*, and all the souls of the world, *cit*, constitute the body of which the immortal indweller is *Īśvara*. The relation is one of inseparability and dependence. While God as the supreme soul can exist by Himself, the world and the souls lose all their meaning if separated from God. In fact their very existence is dependent on being related in this manner to God. This dependent and yet inseparable relation is called *apṛṭhak siddhi*. The body is defined by Rāmānuja as that which a soul controls, supports and utilizes for its own ends.[1] This soul is in its turn something which constitutes the body of God and thus

1 Rāmānuja's commentary on *Su. Bh.*, Tr. Thibaut, II. 1. 9.

is subservient to God's control. God is thus the central pivot round which revolve the souls and matter. This God is the Absolute and is an organic unity of parts. The subordinate parts are the *viśeṣanas* while the predominent one is the *viśeṣya.* This unity is usually explained with the help of the example of the blue lotus. While the blue is quite distinct from the lotus, yet it cannot exist without the substance, lotus. It is not a relation of identity nor of complete difference. It is not even a relationship of identity-in-difference, for then we would be conceding some identity. The unity that is affirmed is an organic unity which is the unity of a complex whole. *Brahman*, the Ultimate Reality is a unity of this type. The world and the souls exist along with *Brahman* as an organic whole. The distinction between matter, souls and God is not denied, but an organic unity is affirmed. *Prakṛti* as material reality is recognised. But it is the dwelling-place of the soul and through the soul of God Himself. So there is nothing which is not God-permeated. This matter has two forms. While it is fine or potential it remains in its uncreated form. In its gross or actualised form it constitutes the things of this world. The creative activity of the Lord is only to make what is potential actual. With reference to human beings God makes this actualisation in conformity with their own *karma.* Apart from bringing about such fruition of man's *karma*, God's creative activity is not activity performed from any motive, but pure *līla* or play.

In this context we should be careful to note that the term *Īśvara* is used in a double sense. In this sense God is the entire universe both material and spiritual. Here the existence of *Īśvara* may again be viewed in two stages as cause and as effect. But God is self-determining and does not create from anything other than Himself. He *grows* into this cosmos. Thus He is *Bṛahman.* The changeless one changes and becomes the universe. The change is not in Himself, but only in His inseparable attributes which are the world and the souls. It is this which constitutes the second sense of *Īśvara.* In the first sense He is the *Bṛahman*, the Ultimate Reality; in the second sense He is the *antaryāmin*, the indweller-immortal who dwells in everything, whether matter or soul.

Rāmānujā's conception of God is not one of ascending series of self-conscious personalities. It is also not the purely transcendental *Brahman.* God is the ground of this universe, its *ratio essendi.* Yet He is not the mere immanent ground. He is both transcendent and immanent. When the Upaniṣads say that *Brahman* cannot be comprehended, Ramānuja argues that its meaning is that the glory of God is great, his qualities so pure, that we cannot know them. This God is given many names, the most important of them being *Viṣnu*, *Nārāyaṇa* and *Vāsudeva.* These names are purānic names indicating the fact that the prevalent religion of Vaiṣnavism, was sought to be made into a philosophy by Rāmānuja and his followers.

A few words are necessary here about the nature of the soul or *jīva.* The soul is the possessor of *jñāna* or knowledge. But unlike other schools of Indian thought where *jñāna* is either a quality or the essence of the *jīva,* Rāmānuja treats *jñāna* as a separate existent which is neither matter nor spirit. It is of an intermediate nature. It is not matter for it can not only manifest itself but also other material objects. But unlike spirit, it is never aware of its manifestation nor does it manifest for itself but always for another. Such *jñāna* pertains to both the *jīvas* and *Īśvara* and constitutes the basis of similarity between them. Thus *jñāna* is said to be *dharmabhūta-jñāna* or attributive knowledge. In the *jīva,* in its natural condition of *mokṣa,* the *jñāna* expands to its maximum. Thus there is complete knowledge for the *jīva* at this stage. However in the embodied stage there is a contraction of knowledge owing to various factors. In its original state, the *jīva* is also of the nature of bliss which again is present in a diminutive form while in the embodied condition. There are two types of *jīvas*; those who are bound and are seeking release and, those who have already achieved release—the *baddha* and the *mukta.* The *jīva* with its physical body derived from *Prakṛti* and God as the indweller is considered as a sort of meeting point between *jada,* matter, and *Īśvara,* God.

Jīvas that are bound must be released from the shackles of their bondage. The soul is bound because of its past deeds, or *karma.* Each soul has the freedom to act according to its own will, but bears responsibility for the burden of its actions. When the *jīva* forgets that it is a dependent reality and tries to act independently, it commits the mortal sin of turning its face away from God. But even to such a sinner salvation is possible. Salvation is realising one's own dependence on God. This is possible not by acquiring knowledge. Knowledge is always there. But it is through surrender to God in worship, *bhakti,* that one can attain one's true nature. Even then mere *bhakti* or worship is not enough. God also, on His part, grants His *prasāda* or grace to man. Only then can man attain *mokṣa.* Offering devotion to God is an arduous task and requires preparation. Thus it requires *viveka,* discrimination about sensual pleasures such as eating; *vimoka,* freedom to long for God; *abhyāsa,* continuous thinking about God; *kriya,* doing good to others; *kalyāna,* wishing well to all; *satyam,* being truthful; *ārjavam,* integrity; *dayā,* compassion; *ahimsa,* non-violence; *dāna,* charity; and *anavasada,* cheerful hope—these are essential pre-requisites before a man can offer worship to God.

Such worship according to Rāmānuja is very difficult. So he said that there is another way, the way of complete self-surrender, *prapatti,* which everyone can adopt.

The Dvaita of Mādhvā

The protest and reaction against the monism of Śaṁkara was carried much farther by Mādhvā than by Rāmānuja. Mādhvā gave up all pretence of believing in a monism and expounded a purely theistic philosophy based on the reality and plurality of the universe. There are three entities existing eternally. These are God, the soul and the world. These are all fundamentally different from one another and all of them are real. The soul and the world are separate from God, though dependent on Him. The only independent reality is God or *Brahman.* God is described in the Vedās which are revelations and as such God is not only knowable but also describable. God is perfect and is known as Viṣṇu. He controls, directs and protects this world by His will. Lakśmi, his consort, is the personification of God's creative energy. God creates this world out of already existing matter which is *Prakṛti.* He is only an efficient cause and not a material cause.

The souls, according to Mādhvā are many. Everything, every object is endowed with a soul. The soul, being a dependent agent, cannot act as it likes. Though its true nature is bliss and complete knowledge, while in the embodied state, it is subject to many limitations which are the result of *karma.* Matter is the substance which is inanimate and forms bodies of all beings. The unmanifested *Prakṛti* is its original form. God moulds forms out of *Prakṛti.* Thus while God is the efficient cause, matter is the material cause of this universe.

The world and the soul are not mere emanations of God, but are entirely different things. It is the supremacy of God which introduces order and unity into the world. When man as a soul has knowledge of God it makes him absolutely dependent on Him and develop an intense love for Him. So *jñāna* or knowledge is a means of attaining to a full love of God. Salvation means attaining the feet of the Lord and staying there eternally immersed in the act of adoring Him. To attain this it is necessary to lead a virtuous life and also to meditate on the qualities of God. But this aspiration alone is not enough to lead a man to God-realisation. God must bestow on him His grace before he can attain salvation. No man can be saved on grounds of merit alone. It is only God's grace that can save a man.

Śaīva Śīddhānta

While the two foregoing paths are based on the supremacy of Viṣnu as God, the Ultimate Reality, Śaiva Siddhānta gives that place to Śiva. Śaivism and Vaiṣnavism have been rival sects from time immemorial as evidenced from their recorded clashes and conflicts. Śaivism is the popular religion of South India. While Viśiṣtādvaita and Dvaita owe their codification and popularisation to Rāmānuja and Mādhvā, Śaiva Siddhānta does not owe its allegiance to any one saint. On the other hand there has been a galaxy of mystics and saints who have sung the glories of Śiva, among them, poet-philosophers like Manikkavasagar, Sundarar, Thirujñāna Sambandhar and others. This doctrine owes its inspiration to the *Rudra-Śiva* cult of the *Brāhmaṇas,* to the theological portions of the *Śvetāśvatara Upaniṣad* and to the twenty-eight *Śaiva Āgamas.* Commentaries have been written on these *Āgamas* which form the source books for modern studies on the subject.

According to Śaiva Śiddhānta, the Supreme Reality is Śiva who is eternal, pure, uncaused, the all-knower who helps man to free himself from the bonds of *samsāra.* Śiva is the cause of this universe, but not its material cause. The material cause is *Prakṛti* which is transformed by Śiva through his *Śakti* or energy into this world. This *Śakti* is mythologically hypostatised into a female principle, considered to be the consort of Śiva. *Sakti* is considered the instrumental cause of the universe. Thus we have here a three-fold causation. Śiva is the first and final cause, *Śakti* the instrumental cause and *Prakṛti* the material cause. God works through the instrument of His *Śakti* which is conscious energy and not unconscious matter. *Śiva* and *Śakti* together are responsible for five functions which are creation, sustenance, destruction, embodiment and liberation of souls. *Śakti* is the link between pure consciousness which is *Śiva* and *Prakṛti* which is matter and utterly unconscious. Thus *Śakti* is conscious but not in the same manner in which *Śiva* is consciousness. But *Śiva* and *Śakti* are not two separate entities. They are different aspects of the same reality. The Absolute is *Śiva* and the Absolute in relation to the world of objects is *Śakti*.

Śiva is known as *Pati*, the Lord. To him belong all the souls which are called *paśu*. *Pati* does not create these souls for they are eternal and hence are neither created nor are they destroyable. That the soul is distinct from the body which it occupies is evidenced by experience, the factors of memory and recognition. Such souls are obscured by their association with *āṇava*. *Āṇava* is a word derived from *aṇu*, the atom. By implication then the word means that which restricts and makes small what is big. Because of such restriction the souls become incapable of knowing either their own nature or that of the Lord. While *āṇava* is the cause for the limitation, the actual ignorance itself is the result of tainting factors being present in the soul. These are generally known as *mala* or impurities. Lord Śiva in His grace helps mankind to get rid of both *mala*, the impurity, and the *āṇava*, the restrictions. It is then that the soul reaches salvation. For man, release is possible only if he treads the path of worshipful adoration and self-abasement before God. Even in the state of salvation the dualism between God and the soul persists.

An account of the Vaiṣṇava and Śaiva sects outlined above does not exhaust the religious philosophies of India. Even the account given here does not do justice to the variation of the doctrines and the wealth of thought embodied in these systems.

CHAPTER VI

SOME STRAY THOUGHTS

We have in the last five chapters outlined in a very brief manner most of the important philosophical concepts dealt within Indian philosophy. The method I have adopted in presenting these concepts has been one of dialectical development from plural explanations to monistic explanations in metaphysical concepts and from perception to verbal testimony in epistemology. However I found an innate difficulty in presenting concepts thus. To begin with, this method of presentation differs in many significant ways from that usually adopted by Indian philosophers. Almost all of them present one school after another, each with its own final message, and in each we have the metaphysical ideas entwined with the epistemological. Such a presentation no doubt gives a complete picture of each school, but it leaves the student with a feeling that since the task is accomplished there is nothing more to be done except review each school and write footnotes to it. If this is philosophy, then indeed, philosophy is dead in our country. Secondly, the common man's attitude to philosophy in India as something that is invariably non-separable from religious mysticism and that all one can do is only to study carefully what has already been said and clarify the ideas and ideals for himself with the aid of a competent guru, has tended to stifle any true philosophical thinking. The idea persists that philosophical thinking is not only mystical but also that it is esoteric. Hence my first objective has been to separate philosophy from religion in the Indian philosophical context. There is no doubt at all that there are many common areas between the two and a hard and fast separation cannot always be achieved. But this does not mean that the method of tackling the subject matter is common for both religion and philosophy nor does it mean that the conclusions arrived at are also common. A major difference, according to me, is that while religion requires understanding based on faith and depend on the grace of God for the achievement of targets which it has set up for itself, philosophy abhors dogmatism and requires an understanding based on logical arguments and rational inferences. The starting point for philosophising may be either mystical experience or empirical analysis. It cannot rest at this starting point. It has to go further and substantiate and justify itself at the bar of reason. Such justification is neither called for nor is it acceptable in religion. The peculiar situation under which philosophy has developed in India has been responsible for much of the difficulty in separating philosophy from religion. The *brāhmaṇa* community which was the custodian of all knowledge in ancient days, was also the priestly class performing all religious functions and acting as mediator between God and man. This dual capacity made the *brāhmaṇas* identify their religious activities with their philosophical enquiries. Thus philosophising as an intellectual enquiry was subordinated to religiosity as a social and communal activity. This was further emphasised by the fact that religion and philosophy deal with much the same thing. Notwithstanding results produced by this situation, we do find a clear and distinct development which can be designated philosophical, in contradiction to the religious quest.

We have said much about philosophy and philosophising. But then we have not defined what philosophy is. That it is not religion has been made clear already. Philosophy is providing answers to a number of important and meaningful questions. The answers to such questions depend upon the person who raises the questions and seeks answers to them. In this sense, questions have been raised and answers provided by the ancient seers and saints right from Vedic times. The philosophers of ancient India sought to clarify their mystical intuitions regarding fundamental questions and to reinforce them with a rational understanding. That is why philosophy is called a *darśana*, "that which is seen". But a *darśana* has a claim to be a *darśana*, only when it becomes a *tarkaśāstra*, a science of dialectics as well. It is necessary to point out here that while the word *darśana* smacks of the theological and the religious, it is not actually so. The arguments given in support of metaphysical theories are both rigorous and authentically logical. In the course of the development of Indian philosophy, the oft-proclaimed catholicism and tolerance are not much in evidence. The desire to make an intellectual conquest of the opponent and expose the weaknesses of his logical arguments has been the ruling passion of the later philosophers, each system claiming logical perfection for itself. Thus the task of philosophy in India became the task of establishing certain metaphysical theories by a series of dialectical arguments starting with a given *prima facie* view and ending with the established and accepted view for that particular philosopher. Hence we may define philosophy in India as the defending of one's own views on reality by the use of the logical canons of reasoning.

It is now necessary to go deeper into the problem of philosophy. It is usually said that philosophy in India is spiritual for the fundamental tenets are both "given" as well as of the nature of the transcendental. Whatever meaning we may attribute to the word spiritual, we have first to enquire which aspect of philosophy can be considered spiritual. Evidently it does not apply to the logical or the epistemological portions, because these are modes of thinking and argumentation to establish a view-point. Arguments are either logical or illogical and are instruments of achievement or not. As such the question of attributing any spirituality to them does not arise. If Indian philosophy is to claim any spiritual characteristic, it is the metaphysical aspect of Indian philosophy that is to be considered as spiritual. In this context what do we mean by spiritual? The word today has been used with many connotations. Let us examine some of them.

In its most common usage "spiritualism" refers to anything that deals with "spirits" or disembodied souls including God as the highest soul. This is a religious notion. In another meaning the same word is used to refer to the alleged activity of souls or spirits which have become disembodied and which though not perceptible, still take part in and influence the activities of men. This meaning cannot be used to characterise a metaphysical quest. However the former meaning can be accepted but only, if a system of philosophy is theologically oriented and maintains that the whole universe is created and maintained by the will of God who is the Supreme Soul or Personality. The religious philosophies of India, the schools of Viśiṣtadvaita, Dvaita and Śaivism, are all "spiritual" in this sense. But these do not exhaust Indian philosophy, and it is illogical if we use a term which is applicable only to these systems to describe the whole gamut of Indian philosophy. Therefore, we have to further examine and analyse the meaning of the term "spiritual".

Since the word is used with reference to Indian metaphysics we should be aware of what the word means. In Saṁskrit, it means "non-material", or more precisely it means "without form" or "formless". An elaboration and analysis of this idea would give us that the ultimate ground of this universe is a sort of formless and non-material spirit which exists as its over-lord. It can also mean that the souls and not matter are the Ultimate Reality. This interpretation again has religious overtones. If we limit the meaning to merely "non-material" then we have the theory that the world of reality is an idealistic world where sense and sense-perception are not really valid, though useful. In this sense the use of the word spiritual would apply only to Advaita which considers the whole of the universe as an appearance of an ultimate and eternal Reality which is formless, distinctionless and nameless. What, however, is applicable only to a part cannot be said to describe the whole. There are other systems like the Nyāya and the Vaiśeṣika which are materialistic and pluralistic; the Mīmāṁsa system embodies thorough-going materialism and empiricism denying even the existence of God; the dualism of Sāṁkhya which while acknowledging the difference between spirit and matter stresses the need for both in reality. We also have the non-orthodox systems which are as much Indian philosophy as the orthodox systems. Of these we have the thorough-going empiricism of the Cārvāka, the multi-faceted dualist Jaina, and the Buddhistic system, the dominant metaphysics of which is nihilism. To ignore these systems saying they are not active today and thus omit them from any serious consideration of Indian philosophy is indeed to shut our eyes to the obvious. So even this meaning of the word spiritual is not applicable to the whole of Indian philosophy.

There is one suggested and implied meaning of the word spiritual which we should consider now. This meaning is not apparent at first glance, but has to be drawn out from the value implications of the various systems. There is one common element in the metaphysics of all systems, religious or philosophical. This is the primary importance which all systems give to the ideal of *mokṣa* or freedom. This ideal presupposes the existence of a soul or *Ātman* which is capable of existing in an isolated manner without being related to the empirical world. In other words, the soul is that which can exist unrelated to anything else. In the empirical world the soul is found fettered by the empirical life and its requirements, and it seeks to rid itself of such fetters. When this is achieved, it attains freedom or *mokṣa*. As we have seen already, the conceptualisation of the nature of *Ātman* or soul is different in different schools. For some it is non-material and ideal; consciousness constitutes its very nature. Here consciousness is not a cognitive factor but is the innate quality of the soul. For others, like the Nyāya, the Vaiśeṣika and the Mīmāṁsa systems the soul acquires the characteristic of consciousness as an inseparable quality owing to its cognitive activities at the empirical level. With the death of the physical body, when all cognitive activities cease, the soul becomes free and attains its original status of being without any experience of empirical factors leading either to pleasure or to pain. From all this we gather that for all schools of Indian philosophy the reality of consciousness as an existent is of vital importance. Consciousness whether at the embodied stage or at the disembodied stage or existing as both is that which makes the ultimate value of *mokṣa* viable.

This *mokṣa* is a trans-empirical concept involving the notion of consciousness on the one hand, and on the other, the notion of freedom. In this manner it is both an ontic concept as well as a moral concept. As an ontic concept it characterises the soul as consciousness; as a moral concept it upholds the ideal of freedom. Freedom is freedom "from" something; here freedom as a value means attaining freedom "from" such conditions and factors which hide or veil the essential nature of man from himself. This essential nature is either to be consciousness or to possess consciousness. Thus *mokṣa* as a value passes over into the ontic realm. The soul of man as consciousness is essentially free. To regain this status is to gain the highest value *mokṣa.* It is in this sense only that we can characterise Indian philosophy as spiritual.

We are not yet out of the woods of confusion. If the whole value of Indian philosophy rests on the acceptance of consciousness conceived as a spiritual factor, then we have to examine and find out what exactly we mean by consciousness. I would like to analyse the feasibility of the concept itself in view of its importance in world philosophy today.

To say that man is a conscious being involves many things. The most important of them shows how man is not only a goal-seeking animal, but in this activity he plans, deliberates, adapts and achieves his goals. Man is unique in possessing this capacity. This is closely associated with his capacity to understand the world around him. The sphere of man's activities ranges over areas far beyond his immediate needs and satisfactions and enters into the field of enquiry where sheer acquiring of knowledge for the sake of knowledge provides adequate satisfaction. Breath-taking advances in scientific discoveries have confirmed man's faith in the power of his reason to control and transcend the world of nature of which he himself forms a part.

In this sense he has already gone beyond the mere empirical; he has already transcended his own limitations. Such self-transcendence is the basic essence of consciousness according to Indian philosophy. While the scientist directs this capacity for transcendence towards the outside world, the philosopher in India has, in the past, directed this capacity to transcend his own bodily limitations and find out his own true nature. Thus the results he has arrived at have necessarily to be "transcendental". "Transcendental" here does not mean opposed to the empirical but including and sublating it.

The above argument requires for its viability the fact of the existence of consciousness. We may, for the sake of convenience, say that the authenticity of Indian philosophy as a spiritual philosophy depends upon the firmness with which it can establish the existence of consciousness.

How is this done? The question is "By knowing what is all this known?"[1] The question implies that there is something, a knowledge of which provides the answers to all questions. This knowledge does not provide an epistemological solution. It is an ontic solution. The answer given in the same Upaniṣad is that this first principle of existence is the imperishable, the *akṣara*, that is, the first principle of existence not only exists, but also is aware that it can never be destroyed. It is this awareness that makes it the eternal and the imperishable. It is this "awareness" that is the ineffable joy of the worshipper and the fullness of knowledge of the philosopher.

At this stage, it may be countered by asking if this is not merely hypothetical. The answer to this is both 'yes' and 'no'. If the ontic status of consciousness is that which is challenged then the reply would be that it is a hypothesis. But there are hypotheses and hypotheses. In empirical science a hypothesis is usually taken to be a proposal to explain either matters of fact or how best facts

1 *Mu. Up.*, 1. 3.

could be conceived so as to provide an explanation of them. We do not use the word in either of these senses here. In the first instance we are proposing something which may or may not be conceivably proved. In the second case there is a reluctance to give any factual explanation, but we are calling upon the pragmatic element to justify the hypothesis. Both these will not serve the purpose here to establish an ontic fact. What we are postulating here is a metaphysical hypothesis. A metaphysical hypothesis is a wide-ranging, systematic framework within which everything is sought to be explained, "world hypotheses" as Stephen Pepper calls them. The sources for such hypotheses are self-evident. These hypotheses are justified by the role they play in ordering and unifying known facts of experience. We may also classify such hypotheses as "transcendental hypotheses". The characteristics of a transcendental hypothesis is "that things and processes in terms of which it is formulated could not conceivably be perceived by the senses, and therefore, strictly speaking could not be imagined either".[1] Thus the ontic status of consciousness is a hypothesis, but a hypothesis that originated from self-evident facts. In the article cited, Prof. Kneal goes on to explain a transcendental hypothesis further. While something transcendental cannot be imagined *a priori*, it can be conceived as possessing a "logical structure". Taking an example from the physical sciences there is a logical structure for the transcendental postulates like electrons and protons and these, inspite of possessing such a logical structure cannot be translated into perceptible objects, though they are essential to explain the laws of such perceptible objects. I wish to apply this idea to the existence of consciousness. Consciousness as an ontic existence is not translatable in terms of activities, although activities of bodies require its postulation for their explanation. For example, consciousness is not translatable to the mechanical movements of the limbs. But when a sudden ceasing of such activities, without any apparent obstruction, takes place, then the postulation of a consciousness is necessary to explain such activities. This argument can be multiplied and modified to suit all the activities of the human being. Thus logically, the existence of consciouness can be postulated, although such consciousness cannot be completely transformed into empirical facts.

[1] From a review of Prof. Kneal's book *Probability and Induction* by C. D. Broad in *Mind*, Jan. 1950, p. 98.

Usually a theory is postulated or a hypothesis is put forth either to act as a directive for further investigation or to serve as an explanation for hitherto unexplained facts. There is still another fact of theorising which we should not forget. This is that the theory must not only direct and explain, it must also be true. The truth of such a theory is usually established when the theory subsumes under it all known and possible empirical facts and also by the theory being the only explanation without any alternatives. Those who oppose the theory of consciousness as an ontic reality do so on grounds that there are other theories which may well explain many factors supposed to be explained by the consicousness theory. But on an examination we will find that there are some, such as aesthetic experience, choice and decision–making, self-control, which can only be explained by the consciousness theory.

Now let us try and explain the existence of consciousness as an implied fact of the processes of acquiring knowledge. The Upaniṣads say that the conscious Self or *Ātman* is "that by which the eyes see, the ears hear". This "that", a demonstrative symbol, cannot hang in the air and must imply a location, a "there". For a "that" without a "there" is meaningless. But where is this "there"? The *Kena Upaniṣad* answers, "There the eye goes not, speech goes not, nor the mind." The implication of these statements from the Upaniṣads is that all knowledge is made possible by the existence of something which is not itself accessible to the activities of the sense-organs but whose existence is by implication essential for the working of and for the understanding of the workings of the sense-organs. In other words, the Ultimate Reality, consciousness, is not a reality which is either the observed or the observable but a transcendental, non-translatable existence and is essential for all knowledge. It is that by which the eye sees and the ear hears.

Even if all that we have said so far is acceptable to the discerning reader, we still cannot escape the question of how we know that *Ātman* or consciousness exists? One answer would be the very self-evident nature of *Ātman*. Nobody says "I am not", for no one could make this statement without getting involved in a contradiction. Apart from this self-evidence, can we cite any other way to know the existence of consciousness? Consciousness is not knowable as an object of sense-experience for all sense-experiences are made possible by consciousness. It is not also "unknown", for if it is completely unknown, we can never speak of the "I" and say "I exist". Such existence is not a predicate, for then it should be possible to separate the predicate from the subject. The statement "I exist" is almost a tautologous statement in which the "I" is the same as "existence". There can be no anteriority and posteriority for the notions of "I" and "existence". It is the very awareness of the "I" which calls for the statement "I exist". Thus we find that starting from the empirical fact, "the eye sees", we go on to the trans-empirical fact of that by which the eye sees which is the self-aware existent "I" which is consciousness. The sole spiritual factor in Indian philosophy is therefore this "consciousness".

It is the existence of this "consciousness" that is challenged by modern Western thought both philosophical and scientific. Weighty arguments are put forth by the positivistic and analytical schools against the acceptance of consciousness as an epistimic requirement in the process of acquiring knowledge. This is neither the place nor the time to go into the questions raised by these thinkers. However, one fact must be placed on record. While we argue for the existence of consciousness the evidence for it given by psycho-pathology and psychiatry on the one hand and psychical research on the other hand should not be ignored. As I have already hinted, a refutable hypothesis cannot be a metaphysical or transcendental hypothesis. The moment we grant refutability to a metaphysical hypothesis we agree to the illogicality of that hypothesis. A metaphysical hypothesis cannot be a conditioned hypothesis involving an "if-then" relation. On the other hand it is something which is arrived at after examination and analysis, as the only answer capable of explaining and entailing all known facts. It is my claim that consciousness is such a postulation.

In thus outlining the problem of the spirituality involved in Indian philosophy I have digressed much from the traditional philosopher who arrives at consciousness via intuitive and mystical channels. The dangers involved in any such philosophy is that it becomes authoritarian even though it is supported by reasoning. It is my contention that any philosophical truth that has been propagated by the ancient seers is not merely intuitive or mystical. Their words have to be interpreted to mean that which is the result of cogitation and not merely of revelation. If this interpretation is not acceptable, then the various systems of philosophy, the various *darśanas* would clash, and since each system would claim revelation as its exclusive property, there could be no answer to the problem of their spirituality.

The establishment of a spiritual self by an appeal to traditional authority does not make it any the more authentic. But an understanding of such authority as something that is based on a hyper-critical self-examination and analysis of the world presents it with an empirical authorisation and a transcendental authority. If today, the Indian philosopher feels that he cannot add anything to the philosophy given by these ancient intellectual giants,[1] it is not because he is compelled by its supposedly revelatory claims, but because he feels that it is a logically superb structure. The modern Indian philosopher can only cast light on this structure borrowing such light from scientific discoveries. The moment he succumbs to the temptation of avoiding to do this, Indian philosophy stands at the beginning of its end. The Indian philosopher of today has much to do and much ground to traverse to achieve his ambition.

1 Dr. T. M. P. Mahadevan, a renowned Indian philosopher has repeatedly vouched for this position in his writings and speeches.

BIBLIOGRAPHY

Saṁskrit Texts in Translation

1. *Ātmabōdha (Self-knowledge) of Saṁkara,* (tr.) Swami Nikhilananda.
2. *Bhagavad Gīta,* (tr. and commentary) S. Radhakrishnan.
3. *Brahma Sūtra Bhāṣya of Rāmānūja,* (tr.) Thibaut, Sacred Books of the East Series.
4. *Brahma Sūtra Bhāṣya of Śaṁkara,* Shri Vani Vilas Press.
5. *Bṛhadāranyaka Upaniṣad with Śaṁkara's Commentary,* (tr.) Swami Madhavananda.
6. *Buddhist Logic of Dinnaga and Dharmakirti* (2 Volumes), (tr.) Stcherbatsky.
7. *Hymns from the Ṛg Veda,* (tr.) A. A. Macdonell.
8. *Hymns of the Ṛg Veda, The,* (2 Volumes), (tr.) R. T. H. Griffiths.
9. *Karma Mīmāmsa, The,* (commentary) A. B. Keith.
10. *Nyāya Bhaṣya with Vārtika of Udyōtakara,* (tr.) Ganganatha Jha, Indian Thought Series.
11. *Nyāya Sūtras,* (tr.) Ganganatha Jha, Indian Thought Series.
12. *Padārthadharma Saṁgraha of Praśastapāda,* (tr.) Ganganatha Jha.
13. *Sāṁkhya Karika of Iśvarakrishna, The,* (tr. and commentary) S. S. Suryanarayana Sastri.
14. *Sāṁkhya Philosophy, The,* (tr.) Nandalal Sinha, The Sacred Books of the Hindus Series.
15. *Sāṁkhya Pravacana Bhāṣya of Vijñana Biksu with Aniruddha's Commentary,* Vol. II, (tr.) Garbe, Harvard Oriental Series.
16. *Sāṁkhya System, The,* (tr.) A. B. Keith.
17. *Sarvadarśana Saṁgraha of Sayana,* (commentary) Madhusudana Sarasvati.
18. *Śāstra Dipika: A Mimāmsa Treatise.*
19. *Tarkabhāṣa of Kesava Miśra,* (tr.) Ganganatha Jha.
20. *Tarkasamgraha of Annambhatta,* (tr.) Bodas and Athalye.
21. *Tattvādhigama Sūtra of Umāsvati.*
22. *Tattvakaumudi,* (tr.) Ganganatha Jha.
23. *Thirteen Principal Upaniṣads, The,* (tr.) R. E. Hume.
24. *Vaiśeṣika Sūtras,* (tr.) Faddegon.
25. *Vaiśeṣika Sūtras of Kaāda,* Vol. VI, (tr.) Nandalal Sinha, Sacred Books of the Hindus.
26. *Vedānta Paribhāṣa of Dharmarajadvārin,* (tr.) S. S. Suryanarayana Sastri.
27. *Vedānta Sāra of Sadānanda,* (tr.) M. Hiriyanna.
28. *Vedānta Sāra of Sadānanda,* (tr.) Swami Nikhilananda.
29. *Vedic Hymns,* (tr.) Oldenburg, Sacred Books of the East Series.
30. *Vedic Mythology,* (tr.) A. A. Macdonell.
31. *Vivekachudāmani of Śaṁkara,* (tr.) T. M. P. Mahadevan, Samkar Vihar Series.
32. *Yoga Darśana with the Bhāṣya of Vyāsa, The,* (tr.) Ganganatha Jha.
33. *Yogasārasaṁgraha of Vijñana Bhikṣu, The,* (tr.) Ganganatha Jha.
34. *Yoga Sūtras of Pātanjali,* (tr.) E. Woods, Harvard Oriental Series.

Books in English

1. ARISTOTLE, *The Works of Aristotle,* (tr.) W. D. Ross, Vol. I, Oxford University Press, 1955.
2. BANERJEE, N. V., *Concerning Human Understanding*, George Allen and Unwin Ltd., 1958.
3. BOSANQUET, B., *Morphology of Knowledge*, The Clarendon Press, 1888.
4. BRADLEY, *The Principles of Logic,* Oxford University Press, 1950.
5. CARNAP, RUDOLPH, *Philosophy and Logical Syntax*, Routledge, Kegan Paul, 1935.
6. CARRINGTON-WHEATLEY, *Telepathy*, Methuen, 1945.
7. DATTA, D. M., *Six Ways of Knowing*, George Allen and Unwin Ltd., 1932.
8. FERM, VIRGILIUS, *A History of Philosophical Systems,* Little Field Adams Co., 1958.
9. GHURYE, G. S., *Caste, Class and Occupation,* Popular Book Depot, Bombay, 1961.
10. HIRIYANNA, M., *Outlines of Indian Philosophy*, George Allen and Unwin Ltd., 1932.
11. INGALLS, H., *Materials for Navya Nyaya Logic*, Vol. 40, Harvard Oriental Series, Harvard University Press, 1951.
12. JONES, W. T., *A History of Western Philosophy,* Harcourt Brace & Co., 1952.
13. JOHNSON, *Logic.*
14. KEITH, A. B., *Indian Logic and Atomism*, The Clarendon Press, 1921.
15. MAHADEVAN, T. M. P., *Outlines of Hinduism*, Chetana Press, 1956.
16. MALKANI, G. R. *Vedantic Epistemology*, Indian Institute of Philosophy, Amalner, 1953.
17. HENRY MARGENAH, *The Nature of Physical Reality*, McGraw Hill Book Co., Inc., 1950.
18. MAX MUELLER (tr.) *Kant's Critique of Pure Reason.*
19. PERRY, R. B., *Present Philosophical Tendencies*, George Braziller, 1955.
20. RADHAKRISHNAN, S., *Indian Philosophy* (2 Vols.) George Allen & Unwin Ltd., 1929.
21. RADHAKRISHNAN, S., *Philosophy of the Upaniṣads*, George Allen and Unwin Ltd., 1924.
22. RADHAKRISHNAN, S., and MOORE, C. A., *Source Book in Indian Philosophy*, Princeton University Press, 1957.
23. RHYS-DAVIDS, C.A.F., *The Birth of Indian Psychology and its Development in Buddhism*, Luzac & Co., 1926.
24. RHYS-DAVIDS, T. W., *Buddhism: Its History and Literature*, Luzac & Co.
25. ROSS, W. D. (tr.) *The Works of Aristotle*, Vol. I, Oxford University Press, 1955.
26. RUSSELL, B., *Problems of Philosophy,* Galaxy Books, 1959.
27. TRUEBLOOD, D. E., *The Logic of Belief,* Harper Brothers, 1942.
28. VIDYABHUSAN, S. C., *A History of Indian Logic of Gangesōpādhyaya*, Calcutta University Press, 1921.
29. WATSON, JOHN B., *The Ways of Behaviourism,* Harper Brothers, 1928.
30. WOODBRIDGE, F.J.E. (ed.) *Hobbes Selections,* Charles Scribner Sons, 1958.

GLOSSARY OF SAṀSKRIT TERMS

abhāva	:	non-existence, non-cognition
abhyāsa	:	the continuous thinking of God
ācāra	:	custom
acit	:	matter
adṛṣṭa	:	invisible potency that accounts for the interaction between body and mind
ahaṁkāra	:	egoism
ahiṁsa	:	abstinence from doing injury to others
ajīvadravyas	:	non-soul substances
akhyāti	:	a theory of erroneous knowledge expounded by the Prābhākara Mīmāmsa school where error is explained simply as want of discrimination between perception and memory
ālaya vijñāna	:	stream of consciousness
anaikāntika	:	the fallacy that leads to many conclusions
ānandamaya kōśa	:	the sheath of bliss
anantam	:	all -inclusive and eternal, a characteristic of reality
anavasāda	:	cheerful hope
anirvacanīya	:	indeterminable
anirvacaniya khyāti	:	a theory of erroneous knowledge which says that error is due to indefinable apprehension or indefinable knowledge
annamaya kōśa	:	the sheath of food
anṛta	:	that which is opposed to *ṛta*, the moral order of the Vedas
antahkarana	:	internal sense-organ
antaḥkarana vṛtti	:	modification of internal sense-organ which is mind
antarindriya	:	internal sense-organ
antaryāmin	:	Iśvara, God, the Indweller, the Immortal who dwells in whatever there is, whether matter or soul
ārjavam	:	integrity
ārtha	:	object
	:	material or economic well-being
arthāpatti	:	postulation, etymologically, a combination of two words; *artha*, fact and *āpatti*, supposition or assumption
arūpa	:	the formless substances—space, time, movement and stability
asamvaya kārana	:	non-inherent cause
āsana	:	a posture of the body where breath is controlled to purify the mind and prepare it to enter a trance-like state
asat-kalpa	:	as if non-existent
asatkhyāti	:	a theory of erroneous perception which says that it is the apprehension of a subjective cognition
asiddha	:	the fallacy of the unproved
āśramadharma	:	the duties of stages in life
āsteya	:	non-stealing
ātmakhyāti	:	a theory of erroneous perception which says that it is an apprehension of a subjective cognition
ātmavidyā	:	a study of the nature of Ultimate Reality.
āum	:	the mystic symbol
avatāra	:	the descent of God into the world for some purpose
anu, paramānu	:	atomic particles ; things of the world thus deduced

anunkramani	:	explanatory contents
anumāna	:	the process of inference
anupalabdhi	:	non-cognition also referred to as *abhāva*
anvayavyatirekī	:	affirmative-negative presence of the hetu
anvikṣakī	:	the science of enquiry
anvaya	:	a canon recommended by the Advaitin to establish the soundness of *vyāpti*
anyatākhyāti	:	a theory of erroneous knowledge which says that it is due to wrong perception
aparōkṣa	:	knowledge that is not through direct perception
apara vidyā	:	lower knowledge comprising of all the sciences and arts
aparigraha	:	abstnence from avarice
apauruṣeya	:	non-personal
apavarga	:	escape
aprama	:	wrong knowledge
aprāpyakārī	:	the senses as categorised by the Buddhists
apṛthaksiddhi	:	the dependent and inseparable relation between *acit* and *cit* with *Iśvara*
āraṁbha vāda	:	the doctrine of new creation; also known as *asatkārya vāda*, the doctrine of non-existent effect
baddha	:	one who is bound, and is seeking release
bhādita	:	the vitiated reason
bhakta	:	the devotee
bhakti	:	devotion to God
bhakti yōga	:	the discipline of devotion to God
bhakti mārga	:	the path of devotion, one of the three important pathways to achieve *mōkṣa*
bhāva	:	attitude; the attitude of the devotee towards God
bhava	:	the idea of becoming
bhava cakra	:	the wheel of existence
bhōkta	:	one who experiences
bhūtādī	:	infinite and supersensible elements
bhūtās	:	elements, especially the five fundamental elements, earth, water, fire, air, and ether, that are present in the beginning of creation
brahmacāri	:	one who walks in the path of *Brahman* or reality
brahmacārya	:	continence in things of sense enjoyment; the capacity to walk in the ways of *Brahman* or truth
brahman	:	etymologically, prayer; it is derived from the root, *bṛḥ*, "to grow" or "burst forth"
buddhī	:	the intelligent agent
cit	:	soul
cittavṛtti	:	a mental mode
dama	:	restraint
dāna	:	charity
darśana	:	literally, "sight", it generally refers to the six systems of traditional Indian philosophy
dāsyabhāva	:	the servant-master attitude; one of the six categories of attitudes of the devotee to God
dayā	:	compassion
deva	:	the shining one
dharma	:	duty, righteousness
dharmabhūtajñāna	:	attributive knowledge
digambara	:	the "sky-clad" monks, one of the two important sects of the Jainas; disciples of this sect wear no clothes
dravya	:	substance
dvija	:	the twice-born castes; the people of higher castes, Vaisyas and upwards were called twice-born as they were eligible to get initiated

ekāgra	: one-pointed concentration
gati	: motion
gṛhasta	: a family man
guna	: what determines the nature and character of a thing; character in the caste system
hetu	: reason
hetvābhāsā	: fallacious reason or middle term
hetuvidyā	: the science of reason or cause in an inference
indriya	: organ of sense-perception
Īśvara	: God
Īśvara-pranidhāna	: devotion to God
jarā-marana	: old age and death
jiva	: the soul, the individual self, "to continue to breath"
jīva dravya	: soul substance
jīvanamukta	: an individual who has realised *mōkṣa* while living in a body
jñāna	: knowledge, the nature of thought
jñānalakṣana	: a characteristic of reality
sannikarṣa	: extraordinary relation between a universal quality and a particular object
jñānamārga	: the path of knowledge; one of the three important pathways to achieve *mōkṣa*
jñānayōga	: the discipline of knowledge
jñānendriyas	: the five sensory organs of knowledge
jñāpti	: to ascertain between truth and falsity
kaivalya	: *mōkṣa*, liberation
kalpa	: cycle of time
kalyāna	: wishing well to all
kāma	: desire, egoistic attachment
kāmyakarma	: optional rites, actions that are performed with specific desire
kānta bhāva	: the attitude that prevails between husband and wife: one of the six categories of attitudes of the devotee to God
karma	: belief in fate and reincarnation; motion as action
karma mārga	: the path of action, one of the three important pathways to achieve *moksa*
karma yōga	: the discipline of action
karmendriyas	: the five organs of action
kartā	: one who is the agent of all actions
kevalānvayī	: agreement in presence
kevalavyatirekī	: agreement in absence
kevalin	: one who has attained perfection, Buddha
khyātivāda	: theory that explains illusion
kōśa	: sheath
kriyā	: doing good to others
kṣanikavāda	: the doctrine of momentariness
kṣatriya	: the warrior caste
kṣipta	: restless, wandering
lakṣana	: differentia
liṅga	: a sign, perception of which will enable one to arrive at the knowledge of some unperceived factor
lilā	: the play of God
lōkasaṁgraha	: the welfare of the whole society
madhurā bhāva	: the attitude that prevails between the beloved and the lover; one of the six categories of attitudes of the devotee to God
manana	: to cogitate upon what has been learnt and find out if the teaching is satisfactory from all points of view

manas	:	mind; the part played by it in perceptual knowledge
manōmaya kōśa	:	the sheath of intellect
māyā	:	the principle of ignorance, illusion; that which measures neither real nor unreal
mōha	:	delusion
mokṣa	:	liberation
mūdha	:	infatuated; forgetful
mukta	:	one who is released
naimittika karma	:	obligatory actions of ritual worship
nairātmyavāda	:	the doctrine of no-soul
nāma-rūpa	:	name and form
nāstika	:	heretics, those who were anti-Vedic
nidāna	:	the various links of the causal chain that binds one to suffering
nidhidhyāsana	:	contemplation on the truth
nigamana	:	conclusion
nirguna	:	devoid of all characteristics
niruddha	:	restricted or restrained
nirvikalpaka	:	indeterminate
nirvikalpaka pratyakṣa	:	indeterminate perception
niṣkāmakarma	:	desireless action.
niṣprapañca-vāda	:	a cosmic idea of reality or of *Brahman*
nityakarmas	:	daily actions of worship
nityānityavastu viveka	:	the descrimination between that which is permanent and that which is ephemeral
nivṛtti	:	the attitude of withdrawal, renunciation from worldly pursuits
nivṛtti mārga	:	one of the two paths to realise *mōkṣa*, an individual is required to renounce all involvement and lead the life of a recluse
niyama	:	daily observances which have the purpose of clearing the body and mind of obstruction
padārtha	:	category, the sevenfold classification of the Nyāya school
pakṣa	:	the locus in which the sign (*liṅga*) is perceived; subject
Pāli	:	spoken dialect of Samskrit
paramānus	:	discrete particles, one of the forms in which elements exist
pāramārthika	:	the transcendental level
pāramārthika sattā	:	the real existence
para vidyā	:	the higher knowledge
paryāyas	:	modes, according to Jaina philosophy; modification of these modes cause creation and destruction of the substance
paśu	:	the souls
Patī	:	the Lord
pradhāna	:	another name of *Prakṛti*
prajña	:	third of the four states of experience as depicted in the Upaniṣads which refers to the condition of deep sleep
prakaranasama	:	the reason which is equivalent to the proposition.
Prakṛti	:	matter, one of the two fundamental categories of reality
pramā	:	valid knowledge
pramāna	:	the method of acquiring valid knowledge; source of authoritative valid knowledge, Veda
pramāta	:	the subject
prameya	:	the object
prānamaya kōśa	:	the sheath of life

prāṇāyama	:	control of breath in a particular posture (*āsana*) of body to purify the mind and prepare it to enter a trance-like state
prapatti	:	complete surrender of the individual to the will of God
prasāda	:	grace of God
prātibhāsika	:	the illusory level
prātibhāsika sattā	:	apparent existence
pratijñā	:	challenge
pratītya samutpāda	:	literally, arising in correlation with; the law of dependent origination
pravṛtti	:	active tendency; involvement in the affairs of the world
pravṛtti mārga	:	one of the two paths to realise *mōkṣa*
pudgala	:	substance with form or *rūpa*
Puruṣa	:	the material cause of this universe the spirit, one of the two fundamental categories of reality; pure consciousness
puruṣārthas	:	human values
Puruṣasūkta	:	a hymn from the *Ṛg Veda*
ṛta	:	Vedas, later superseded by the concept of *dharma*; the cosmic law as well as truth and moral order (of the Vedas)
śabda	:	sound
śabdapramāṇa	:	verbal testimony
śabda tanmātra	:	sound essence
śadagātma	:	the five senses and mind together with their objects,
sadasatkhyāti	:	a theory attributing erroneous knowledge to perception of the unreal in the real
sādhana catuṣṭaya	:	the four pre-requisites that are laid down by ancient Indian seers, as essential for the quest for perfection
sādhya	:	that which is to be established in an inference
sakhya bhāva	:	the attitude that prevails between friends, one of the six categories of attitudes of a devotee to God
sākṣin	:	witness, the *jīva* designated as witness
Śakti	:	potency; capacity of the sense organ
sādṛsya	:	similarity
sama	:	equanimity
samādhi	:	concentration; meditation
samānādhikaranyam	:	the co-existence in the same locus, identity.
sāmānya	:	generality
saṁkhyā	:	number
samavāya	:	inherent relation between cause and effect as explained by Nyāya-Vaiśeṣika philosophy; subsistence or *paratantratā*
samavāyi kārana	:	inherent cause
saṁsāra	:	the cycle of birth and death
saṁskāra	:	action; mental impressions
samvṛttisatya	:	provisional reality worked at the empirical level
śānta bhāva	:	attitude that is maintained between the child and the parent, one of the six categories of attitudes of the devotee to God; the reciprocal
santōṣa	:	contentment
sanyāsa	:	renunciation
saptabhangīnaya	:	the seven-fold statements or judgements
śarīra	:	the body
satkhyāti	:	illusory knowledge explained as the apprehension of the real object
satpratipakṣa	:	the counterbalanced subject
satva	:	one of the three elements of *Prakṛti*, potential consciousness and pure existence alone

satya : speaking and living in truth
satyam : certainty, a characteristic of reality
sauca : cleanliness
savikalpaka : the determinate
savikalpaka pratyakṣa : definite or determinate perception
Śiva : God
skandhas : changing things that come into being and perish
smṛti : the remembered work; a branch of brahmanical sacred literature dealing with civil and religious law; a source of law of the social order, consisting of sacred literature of less antiquity and sanctity than *śruti*, which are the epics, the *Purānas* and *Dharma Śāstras;* to preserve existing order
sparśa tanmātra : touch essence
sraddhā : faith; a desire to learn
śravana : to hear what is stated in the scriptures and learn it from a competent master
śruti : source of *dharma*; sacred knowledge orally transmitted by the priests from generation to generation; generally taken to include the four Vedas with their *Brāhmanas* and Upaniṣads, to preserve existing order
sūdra : the lowest of the four *varnās*
svabhāva-vādins : the naturalists
svadharma : one's own duty
svādhyāya : studying in company
svarga : heaven
svarūpa lakṣana : definition with reference to essence
svataḥ-prāmānya vāda : a theory holding that knowledge carries with it its own validity and is self-revealing
savyabhicāra : the inconclusive reason
svetambaras : one of the two sects of Jainas; disciples of this sect wear white robes
sūnya : without any discrete individuality either subjective or objective
suttas : aphorisms of Buddha
syādvāda : "may be" theory; the doctrine of "may be"
tādātmya : identity
tad ekam : "that one"
tadutpatti : causality
taijasa : second of the four states of experience depicted, in the Upaniṣads; it refers to the vital self
tapas : purificatory actions
tarkaśāstra : the science of argumentation
tarkavidyā : science of debating
tatasthalakṣana : definition with reference to accidentals
tatva traya : the three ultimate factors
tat tvam asi : "that thou art"
Tirthānkaras : the Jaina prophets
titikṣa : endurance
Trimūrti : the conception of three Gods: Brahma, Viṣnu, and Śiva—each of these Gods represent one aspect of the universe such as creation, sustenance, and destruction
tripitaka : the three baskets
trivarga : the three golden aims of life, i.e. pertaining to *dharma*, *artha*, and *kāma*
turīya : last of the four states of experience, depicted in the Upaniṣads, referring to the condition that includes the first three states of experience and also goes beyond them
udāharana : example

upādāna kāranu	:	material cause
upādhi	:	the limiting adjunct, i.e. body and mind
upamāna	:	comparison as one of the sources of knowledge
upanaya	:	application
uparati	:	renunciation of formalism
utpatti	:	originating conditions
vādavidyā	:	the science of argumentation
vairāgya	:	renunciation, the feeling of rejection created by the ephemeral nature of an object; detachment
viśeṣa	:	discussion
vaiśya	:	the third of the twice-born castes
vākya	:	syllogism
vānaprastha	:	the third *āsrama* in the life of man, where one devotes his time to meditation
varna	:	very often the word is used to mean a caste
varnāśramadharma	:	the duties of an individual arising from his caste and stage of life
vāsana	:	impressions of past experience
vātsalya bhāva	:	the attitude that prevails between the parent and the child, one of the six categories of attitudes of devotee to God
vijñāna	:	consciousness; the knowledge entity
vijñānamaya kōśa	:	the sheath of discriminative knowledge
vikalpa	:	imaginative and constructive activity of mind
vikṣipta	:	distracted
vinaya	:	ethical treatises
viparītakhyāti	:	erroneous knowledge due to distortion of the presented with the remembered
viparyaya	:	erroneous perception
viruddha	:	the contradictory reason
viśva	:	first of the states of experience, depicted in the Upaniṣads referring to the condition of wakefulness
Viśvedevaḥ	:	"All God"
vyāvahārika sattā	:	the empirical existence
vyāpti	:	pervasion; this points out the invariable concomitance between *sādhya* and *pakṣa*
yādṛccha vādins or animittavādins	:	those who support the theory of accidentalism
yama	:	restraint; one of the stages of *samādhi* in Yoga
yathārthānubhava	:	presentational knowledge
yogaja	:	that which is born of yogic practices; a type of extraordinary perception

INDEX

abhādhitaviṣayatva, 181
abhāva, 57, 64, 65
Abhidamma Kōśa, 30
Abhidamma Pitaka, 29, 30
acāra, 37, 201
adharma, 68
Adhvārindra, Dharmaraja, 48
Aditi, 8
adṛṣṭa, 61, 110, 111, 219, 220
Advaita, 41, 46, 47, 48, 50, 82, 85, 86, 87, 89, 92, 93, 115, 118, 122, 128, 134, 142, 145, 146, 150, 154, 155, 160, 161, 164, 165, 175, 184, 187, 226, 227, 236
Advaitin, 89, 90, 91, 116, 118, 119, 121, 122, 123, 128, 129, 130, 131, 142, 145, 149, 150, 155, 160, 161, 162, 174, 175, 177, 179, 180, 184, 185, 186, 188, 190, 192
Agni, 7, 8, 96
ahamkāra, 75, 87, 113
ahimsa, 205
Aitareya Brahmana, 214
Aitareya Upaniṣad, 12
Ājātaśatru, 14, 215
Ājitnatha, 34
ajiva, 67, 68
ajiva dravyas, 70
ākāmkṣa, 193
ākāra, 128
ākāśa, 58, 77, 83, 84, 86
akhyāti, 163
alaukika, 140
alaya vijñāna, 80, 107, 108
Ālvārs, 210
anaikāntika, 181
Analysis of Mind (Russell, Bertrand), 143
ānanda, 102, 103, 118
Ānandalahari (Samkarācārya), 48
ānandamaya kośa, 25, 117, 118
Anantam, 19
Anatta vāda, 31
annamaya kōša, 25, 116
Ānnambhatta, 42, 110
anirvacanīya, 94, 155
anirvacanīya-khyāti, 164
Anselm, Saint, 136
antaḥkarana, 148, 159
antaḥkarana vṛtti, 149
antarātman, 22
antarindriya, 159
antaryāmin, 228
anu, 42, 54, 59, 232
anubhava, 135
anugatadharma, 179
anumāna, 169, 170
anupalabdhi, 186, 187
anupasamhārin, 182
anvaya, 180
anvayavyatireki, 176
anuvyavasāya jñāna, 161
Ānvikṣaki, 38, 42
anyatākhyāti, 163
aparā vidya, 121, 122
aparigraha, 205
aparokṣa, 145
apauruṣeya, 4
apavarga, 110
apramā, 151
aprāpyakāri, 156
apṛthak siddhi, 227
ārambha-vāda, 125
āranyakas, 6, 7
Ariṣtanemi, 34
Aristotle, 41, 57, 65, 73, 79, 127, 177
Aristotelian syllogism, 173
artha, 145, 199, 201, 202, 203, 213, 225
arthakriyākāritva, 153
arthāpatti, 177, 186
Arthaśastra (Kautilya), 202
Āryans, 26
asamavāyi kārana, 127
asamprajñatā, 167
āsana, 205, 206
Asanga, 30
āsati, 193
asatkalpa, 144
asatkārya-vāda, 125
asatkhyāti, 164
asiddha, 183
āsteya, 205
āśramas (stages of life), 37
āśrama dharma, 224
āsrayāsiddha, 183
āstika darśana, 38
atīndriya, 144
ātmakhyāti, 164
Ātman, 13, 15, 16, 18, 19, 24, 27, 31, 39, 48, 52, 94, 97, 98, 99, 100, 102, 103, 104, 107, 110, 111, 116, 117, 236, 240
Ātman-Brahman identity, 20, 31
Atharva Veda, 5
Ātma Vidyā, 38
avasarpinī, 68
avatāra, 27
avidya, 33, 49, 115

Bādarayāna, 38, 46, 47, 226
Bādarayāna Sūtras, 129
Bai, Mīra, 210, 217
Bāna, 216
Bauddha, 134, 170, 191, 226
Berkeley, 79, 80, 90, 107, 129
Berkeleyan subjectivism, 130
bhādita, 183, 184
bhakta, 209, 210, 213
bhakti, 209, 210, 229, 230
bhakti cult, 28
bhakti mārga, 208, 209, 210
Bhakti yoga, 213
Bhāmati (Vācaspati), 48
Bhāṣāpariccheda (Viswanātha), 42
Bhaskara, 47
bhāṣyas, 39, 42
Bhatta, Jayanta, 41
Bhatta, Kumārila, 45, 111
Bhatta Mimāmsika, 65, 66, 161, 179, 184, 185, 187, 188, 189
bhāvas, 65, 210
bhāva cakra, 33
Bhikṣu, Vijnana 43, 47, 113
Bhṛgu, 101, 102
bhūtādi, 76, 77
Bosanquet, 101, 189
Bradley, 130, 175, 189, 192
Bṛhadāṛanyaka Upaniṣad, 12, 15, 22, 23, 51, 99
Brahmā, 2
brahmacāri, 37, 224
brahmacarya, 11, 205
Brahman, 11, 13, 14, 15, 16, 18, 19, 20, 21, 22, 23, 25, 27, 47, 48, 49, 51, 90, 91, 92, 93, 94, 102, 103, 104, 116, 117, 119, 120, 121, 122, 123, 129, 130, 131, 209, 213, 224, 227, 228, 229, 230
Brahman-Atman, 29, 91, 103
Brāhmanas, 6, 7, 9, 12, 13, 37, 45, 47, 196, 231
Brahma-Parināma, 129
Brāhma Sūtras, 47, 226
Brentano, 150
Bṛhaspati, 36
Bṛhati, 45
Buddha, 11, 28, 29, 30, 31, 32, 33, 50, 53, 106, 107, 123, 156
buddhi, 74, 76, 113, 114, 166, 167, 190
Buddhism, 28, 29, 30, 31, 32, 33, 35, 37, 40, 48, 52, 53, 54, 55, 79, 80, 82, 90, 105, 106, 107, 108, 123, 124, 128, 155, 157
Buddhists, 146, 147, 148, 155, 156, 157, 161, 164, 178, 225
Buddhist idealism, 84, 142
Buddhist philosophy, 29, 53, 55, 63, 82, 105, 155, 156, 157
Buddhistic thought, 106, 161

Candrakīrti, 30
Carnap, Rudolf, 136
Carrington, Wheatly, 168
Cartesian rationalism, 136
Cārvākas, 35, 36, 37, 45, 50, 52, 57, 66, 82, 104, 105, 134, 144, 165, 170, 177, 178, 191, 195, 220, 226, 236
caste system, 28, 37, 216, 218, 220
Chāndogya Upaniṣad, 12, 16, 19, 92, 99, 120
Christ, 26
Chyavana, 215
citta, 106, 168
citta vṛtti, 148, 149, 159, 168

dama, 207
Darśanas, 25, 38, 123, 234, 242
Dasaratha, 216
dāsya bhāva, 210
Datta, Professor D. M., 167, 173
Democritus, 59, 60
Descartes, 70, 71, 94, 110, 118, 136
Deva, 7, 22
Devarddhi, 35
Dewey, John, 153, 154
dharma, 68, 82, 198, 199, 200, 201, 202, 203, 204, 206, 212, 213, 217, 218, 225
dharmabhūta-jñāna, 229
Dharmakirti, 155
Dharmaraja, 203
Dharmottara, 144
Dharma Sāstras, 199, 200, 201, 217, 221
Dharma Sūtras, 37, 199
dhvani, 190
Digambaras, 34
Dignaga, 41
Dikṣita, Appaya, 48
Dinnaga, 185
Divakara, Siddhasena, 35
dravya, 57, 64, 68
Dunne, 167
Dvaita, 46, 47, 226, 231, 235

ekāgra, 166
epic age, 26, 27, 28

Farquhar, 195
Fitchte, J. G., 81, 108, 122
Fichtean egocentricism, 82

gandha-tanmātra, 77
gandharvas, 14
Gandhi, Mahatma, 201
Gangesōpādhyāya, 41
Gārgi, 14, 20, 51
Gārgya Bālākī, 14
Garutman, 8
Gaudapāda, 47, 91
Gautama, 29, 38, 40, 139
Gautama (law giver), 216

Gestalt school of psychology, 150, 191
Gita, Bhagavad, 28, 48, 201, 204, 209, 211, 215, 218, 222, 226
Gōśala, 35
Gotama, 3
Govinda, 47
Govinda, Gita, 210
grahastha, 37, 224
Grihya Sūtras, 37, 199
gunas, 61, 72, 73, 74, 75, 87, 112
Guru maṭa, 45

Haribhadra, 35
Harṣavardhana, 41
Hedonism, 36
Hegel, 78, 102
Heraclitus, 28
hetu, 171, 172, 173, 174, 175, 180, 181, 183
hetvābhāsa, 180, 181
Hīnayāna Buddhism, 29, 30, 53, 54, 79, 106
Hiranyagarbha, 9, 20, 103, 104
Hobbes, 52, 134
Holt, E. B., 138
Hume, 66, 94, 105
Hymn of Creation, 10, 51

Indra, 3, 8, 16, 17, 92, 97, 98
indriya, 145, 146
Iśa Upaniṣad, 12
Iśvara, 7, 20, 21, 96, 104, 112, 119, 121, 122, 123, 129, 130, 197, 227, 228, 229
Iśvarakriṣna, 43
Iśvara pranidhāna, 206

Jaimini, 38, 45
Jaimini Sūtras, 45
Jainas, 67, 68, 69, 144, 158, 191, 226, 236
Jainism, 33, 34, 37, 67, 68, 70, 157, 158
Jain teachings, 34, 35, 68, 69, 158, 159, 170
James, William, 154, 157
Janaka, 215
jarā-marana, 33
jāti, 33, 54, 191
jīva, 25, 67, 68, 70, 111, 113, 115, 116, 117, 118, 119, 122, 128, 227, 229
jīva dravyas, 70
Jivanamukta, 209
Jivātman, 110, 115
jñāna, 46, 48, 111, 150, 151, 229, 231
jñānam, 19
jñānendriyas, 75
jñānalakṣana sannikarṣa, 162
jñāna mārga, 208, 209, 210, 213
jñāna yoga, 213
jñāpti, 151
Johnson, 193
Jung, 107

Kaikeya, Asvapati, 215
kaivalya, 44, 113
kala, 68
Kālidāsa, 43
kalpa, 2, 197
Kalpa Sūtras, 36, 199
kāma, 199, 201, 202, 203, 213, 225
kāmya karma, 211, 221, 222
Kanāda, 38, 42
Kāndali (Sridhara), 42
Kannappar, 217
Kant, Immanuel, 55, 78, 85, 88, 120, 136, 143, 149, 157, 186, 191, 203
kānta bhāva, 210
Kantian philosophy, 101
Kapila, 38, 43
kārana, 189
kāranam, 126
karma, 1, 28, 46, 54, 57, 61, 62, 157, 199, 218, 219, 220, 221, 222, 223, 228, 229, 230
karma mārga, 204, 208, 211
karma phala, 222
karma yoga, 213
karmendriyas, 75
Katha Upaniṣad, 12, 25
Kautilya, 202
Keith, Bareidale, 60, 61
Kena Upaniṣad, 12, 18, 240
Kevalānvayi, 176
kevalavyatireki, 176
kevalin, 34
khyātivādas, 162
Kiranavāli (Udayana), 42
Kneal, 239
kṣanikavāda, 28, 31, 52, 54
kṣipta, 166
Kumaralabdha, 30
Kusumānjali (Udayana), 110

Lakśmi, 230
Lalitā Sahasranāma (Samkarācārya), 48
Lankāvatara, 30
laukika, 140
Leucippus, 59
linga, 171, 172, 173
linga darśana, 171
Lōkāyatas, 36, 105

madhura bhāva, 210
Madhva, 36, 47, 226, 230, 231
Mādhyamika (Sunya vāda), 30, 80, 82, 83, 84, 108, 125, 164
Mahābhārata, 26, 27, 199, 200, 203, 216, 218
mahat, 74, 75
Mahavira (see also Vardhamana), 34
Mahāyāna Buddhism, 30, 54
Maheśvara, Lord, 22, 92
Maitreyi, 207
Maitri Upaniṣad, 15

Māndūkya Upaniṣad, 17, 47, 98
manana, 208
manas, 139, 140, 149, 160
Māndūkya Kārika, 47
Manikkavasagar, 231
manōmaya kōśa, 25, 117
mantras, 5, 6, 45, 46, 200
Manu, 37, 199, 201, 215, 217, 221
Manudharma Śāstra (also see *Manavadharma Śāstra*), 37, 199
Matarisvan, 8, 96
Max Müller, 5
māyā, 1, 87, 88, 92, 93, 94, 115, 116, 119, 121, 122, 223, 227
Megasthenes, 35
Mill, John Stuart, 126, 165, 177, 178, 179, 180
Mīmāmsa, 43, 45, 46, 64, 65, 66, 111, 134, 139, 140, 147, 154, 165, 170, 171, 197, 236, 237
Mīmāmsikas, 46, 65, 66, 111, 146, 163, 174, 175, 186
Mīmāmsa Sūtras, 45
Miśra, Mandana, 47
Miśra, Pārthasarathi, 46
Miśra, Śālikanātha, 45
Miśra, Vācaspati, 41, 44, 48
Mitra, 8
mōha, 110
mōkṣa, 25, 28, 38, 39, 43, 44, 45, 110, 112, 113, 132, 167, 169, 195, 199, 201, 203, 204, 206, 207, 208, 209, 211, 212, 213, 218, 220 222, 225, 229, 230, 236, 237
Montague, 194
Moore, G. E., 138
mūdha, 166
Mula-Mādhyama Kārika 30
Mundaka Upaniṣad, 21, 104, 121
mṛta dravyas, 62

Nagārjuna, 30, 82, 83, 84, 125
Nahuṣa, 216
naimittika karma, 221
nairātmya vāda, 28
Naiyāyika, 109, 110, 120, 125, 126, 127, 128, 130, 135, 137, 138, 139, 140, 141, 142, 143, 144, 145, 147, 148, 149, 150, 152, 153, 154, 160, 161, 169, 174, 175, 176, 178, 179, 180, 184, 185, 186, 187, 191
Naiyāyika syllogism, 173, 176
Nāmdev, 217
ñānalakṣana, 166
Nārada, 15
nāstikas, 35
nāstika darsanas, 104
Navya Nyāya, 42, 82
New Realism, The (Holt, E. B.), 138
nidānas, 33
nidhidhyāsana 208
nigamana, 172, 174, 175
nimitta kārana, 127
nirguna, 91
Nirguna Brahman, 104, 119, 121
niruddha, 166
nirvikalpaka, 140, 142, 143
nirvikalpaka pratyakṣa 140, 142, 143
niskāma karma, 211
niṣprapanca vāda, 103
nitya karma, 211, 221
nivṛtti mārga, 204
niyamas, 205, 206
Nodhas, 3
Nyāya, 38, 40, 41, 42, 45, 88, 126, 127, 134, 135, 137, 139, 140, 142, 145, 153, 160, 162, 163, 165, 166, 169, 170, 171, 174, 175, 179, 180, 183, 184, 185, 190, 194, 197, 236, 237
Nyāya Bhāsya, 41
Nyāya Bindu, 54, 140
Nyāyaratnākara (Miśra, Pārthasarathi), 46
Nyāya Sūtras, 41, 111
Nyāya theory of perception, 147
Nyāya-Vaiśesika, 39, 42, 56, 57, 58, 61, 62, 63, 64, 65, 66, 70, 109, 110, 111, 126, 127, 130, 146, 162, 166
Nyāyāvatara (Divakara, Siddhasena), 35
Nyāya Vārtika (Uddyōtakara), 41

Pancadasi (Vidyaranya), 48
pancamahābhūtas, 58
Pancapādika, 48
padārthas, 56, 57, 61
Padārthadharma Samgraha, 61
Padmapāda, 48
pakṣa, 171, 172, 174, 175, 181, 183
pakṣadharmatā, 181, 183
pāpa, 222
paramānus, 42, 58, 59, 60, 77
pāramārthika, 131
pāramārthika sattā, 90
Paramātman, 110, 111
parināma vāda, 130
parārthānumāna, 171
paratantratā, 66
parā vidya, 121, 122
Parimala (Dīkśita, Appaya), 48
Pārśvanātha, 34
Patanjali, 38, 43, 44
Pepper, Stephen, 239
Pierce, C.S., 154
Plato, 119
Prābhākara, 45, 46
Prābhākara Mīmāmsa, 66, 163
Prābhākara Mīmāmsikas, 187
pradhāna, 128
Prajāpati, 8, 9, 16, 17, 96, 97, 98
Prajna, 18, 20

Prajnavān, 23
Prakarana Pancika (Misra, Salikanātha), 45
prakaranasama, 182, 184
Pranāsātman, 48
Prakṛti, 43, 70, 71, 72, 73, 74, 76, 77, 78, 79, 86, 87, 92, 112, 113, 114, 128, 229, 230, 231, 232
pramā, 135, 137, 151, 189
pramāna, 39, 137, 183, 184, 185, 186, 187, 188, 189
pramāna mīmāmsa, 42
pramāta, 137
pramēya, 137
prāna, 116
prānāyama, 205, 206
prānamaya kōsa, 25, 117
prapanca, 122
prapatti, 209, 230
prārabdha karma, 220
prasāda, 230
Praśastapāda, 42
prābtihāsika, 131
prātibhāsika sattā, 90
pratijnā, 172, 174, 175
Prātitya samutpāda, 32, 124
pratyakṣa, 144
pravṛtti mārga, 204
pudgala, 67
pudgala parināma, 67
punya, 222
Purānas, 12, 27, 34, 104, 218
Puranic age, 36
Puruṣa, 4, 9, 10, 21, 43, 70, 71, 73, 74, 75, 78, 79, 99, 102, 112, 113, 114
puruṣārthas, 204
Purva-Mīmāmsa, 38, 40, 44, 45
Puruṣasūkta, 9, 10, 13, 102, 214

Radhakrishnan, Dr. Sarvepalli, 11, 26, 27, 88, 107
rājasa guna, 75, 86, 87
Rama, Lord Sri, 203, 216
Rāmānanda, 217
Rāmānujāchārya, 47, 144, 163, 209, 217, 226, 227, 228, 229, 230, 231
Rāmāyana, 26, 27, 203
rasa-tanmātra, 77
Reid, Thomas, 143
Rhine, J.B., 168
Rhys-Davids, 31, 32
Ṛg Veda, 3, 5, 9, 12, 20, 21, 22, 51, 96, 196, 200, 215, 217, 219, 221
Ṛsabha, 34
ṛta, 196, 198, 219
ṛtajāta, 196
ṛtajñā, 196
ṛtapa, 196
ṛtasyagōpa, 196
Rudra-Siva, 22, 24, 231
rūpa-tanmātra, 77
Russell, Bertrand, 133, 143

Śabara Svāmin, 45
sābda, 189, 194
śabda pramāna, 167, 185, 189, 194
sadāsatkhyāti, 164
śabda-tanmātra, 76, 77
ṣadagātmā, 33
Sadananda, 48, 93
sadasadvilakṣana, 94
Ṣaddarśanasamuccaya (Haribhadra), 35
sādhana catuṣtaya, 207
sādhya, 172, 173, 180, 181, 182, 183
Saguna Brahman, 104, 119, 120, 121
sahakārisakti, 128
Śaiva Āgamas, 226, 231
Śaiva Siddhānta, 226, 231
Śaivism, 226, 231, 232, 235
sakhya bhāva, 210
sākṣin, 118
Śakti, 147, 231, 232
śama, 207
samādhi, 44, 114, 167, 207
samānādhikaranyam, 178
sāmānya, 57, 62, 63, 66, 179
samānyalakṣana sannikarṣa, 165
samavāya, 57, 63, 66, 130, 160
samavāyi karanama, 127
Sāma Veda, 5, 12
samvṛttisatya, 125
Sambhandar, Tirujnāna, 217, 231
Samkarācārya, 43, 47, 48, 49, 85, 87, 88, 89, 90, 91, 92, 93, 115, 117, 118, 120, 128, 129, 165, 190, 226, 227, 230
——— on creation, 87
Sāmkhya, 38, 40, 43, 46, 67, 70, 71, 72, 73, 74, 75, 76, 77, 86, 87, 88, 112, 113, 114, 123, 128, 129, 135, 139, 140, 143, 147, 148, 149, 154, 164, 170, 184, 187, 236
——— and theory of evolution, 78, 79
Sāmkhya-Kārika (Isvarakriṣna), 43, 70, 72, 114
Sāmkhya Pravacana Bhāṣya, 43, 113
Sāmkhya Pravacana Sūtra, 43
Sāmkhya Sūtras, 76
samprajnatā, 167
samsāra, 218, 220, 231
samskāra, 33, 105, 167
samyoga, 160
Sanatkumāra, 15
sancita karma, 220
Sanjaya, 35
sānta bhāva, 210
Santanu, 216
santoṣa, 206
sanyāsa, 1, 34, 37, 224
sanyāsin, 47, 204
sapakṣasattva, 181
saptabhangī naya, 69
Saptapadārthi (Śivāditya), 42

Sāriraika Sūtra, 47
Sarvadarśana Samgraha (Madhavārya), 36
Śāstra Dīpika (Miśra, Pārthasarathi), 46
Śatapatha Brāhmana, 2
sat-khyāti, 163
satpratipakṣa, 183
sattva guna, 74, 75, 78, 86, 87
satya, 19, 205, 206
Satyavati, 216
sauca, 206
savikalpaka, 140
savikalpaka pratyakṣa, 141, 142, 144
savyābhicāra, 181, 182, 183
savyābhicāra, asādhārana, 182
Siddhārtha, 29
Śiva, Lord, 23, 27, 28, 232
Śivāditya, 42
Śivānanda-lahari (Samkaracārya), 48
skandhas, 68, 70
Slōkavārtika, 45
smṛti, 2, 37, 135, 201
smṛti satya, 83
Soundarya-lahari (Samkaracārya), 48
Sountrantika, 30, 53, 54, 55, 56, 80, 106, 157
sparśa-tanmātra, 76, 77
Spinoza, 64, 120
sraddhā, 11, 207
śravana, 207
Sridhara, 42
Śrouta Sutras, 37, 199
Śruti, 2, 37, 39, 199
sukṣma-bhutas, 86
Sundarar, 231
Sureśvara, 47
suṣupti, 99
sutras, 38, 39, 41
Sutra Bhāsya (Samkarācārya), 43, 85, 87
svabhāva vāda, 45
svabhāva vādins (naturalists), 26, 36
svadharma, 211, 212
svādhyāyā, 206
svalakṣana, 54, 55, 143
svārthānumāna, 171
svarupa lakṣana, 121
svataḥ-pramānya vāda, 161
Śvetaketu, 19
Śvetāmbaras, 34
Svetāśvatara Upaniṣad, 21, 22, 24, 27, 43, 92, 231
syādvāda, 68, 69, 157

tadātmya, 178
tadutpatti, 178
Taijāsa, 18, 20
Taittiriya Upaniṣad, 12, 23, 24, 25, 101, 116
tamasa guna (tamas), 75, 86, 87
tanmātras, 76, 77, 86
Tantrāvartika, 45
tapas, 206
Tarka-Samgraha (Annambhatta), 42
tarka śāstra, 42, 234
tarka vidyā (science of debating), 41
taṭasthalakṣana, 121, 129
Tātparyatīka (Miśra, Vācaspati), 41
tattvas, 74
Tattvacintāmani (Gangeśōpādhyāya), 41
Tattvārthādhigama Sutra (Umāsvati), 35
Tattvavaiśāradi (Miśra, Vacāspati) 44
Tīrthāmkaras, 34
Tiruvalluvar, 217
titikṣa, 207
Trimūrti, 27
Tri-pitaka, 29
tṛṣna, 33
Tukāram, 217
Tuptika, 45
Turīya, 17, 18, 20, 118

udāharana, 172, 173, 174, 175
Udayana, 41, 42, 110, 111
Uddalaka, 19
Uddyōtakara, 41, 109
Umāsvati, 35, 67, 158
upadāna kārana, 127
Upadeśa Sahasri (Samkarācārya), 48
upādhis, 115, 116
upalabdhiṛ, 106
upamāna, 184, 185, 186
upanaya, 172, 174, 175
Upaniṣads, 2, 6, 7, 10, 11, 12, 13, 14, 16, 18, 20, 21, 22, 24, 25, 27, 29, 30, 36, 38, 40, 45, 47, 48, 49, 51, 52, 59, 69, 91, 92, 94, 97, 98, 99, 104, 107, 115, 199, 207, 215, 226, 227, 229, 238, 240
uparati, 207
Uṣas, 8
utpatti, 151
Uttara Mīmāmsa, 38, 40, 44, 46
utsarpini, 68

vāda vidyā, 41
Vaibhāṣika, 30, 53, 54, 55, 80, 106, 157
vairāgya, 114, 207
Vaiśeṣika, 38, 40, 41, 42, 58, 59, 60, 61, 62, 63, 65, 127, 170, 194, 236, 237
Vaiśeṣika Sutras, 42
Vaiṣnavism, 229, 231, 232
vākya, 172, 193
Vallabhācārya, 47
vānaprastha, 224
Vardhamana (see also Mahavira), 34
varna, 190, 214, 215
varnāśrama dharma, 215

Varuna, 8
vāsanas, 80
Vasubandhu, 30
vātsalya bhāva, 210
Vatsyāyana, 41
Vedānta, 11, 139, 144, 147, 148, 149, 170, 185, 197
Vedanta-paribhāsa (Ādhvarindra, Dharmarāja), 48
Vedānta-sāra (Sadananda,), 48
Vedānta Sutras (Bādarayāna), 46, 47
Vedāntin, 180, 185
Vedas, 2, 3, 4, 5, 6, 7, 10, 11, 12, 15, 16, 22, 27, 28, 33, 34, 35, 38, 39, 44, 45, 46, 67, 94, 97, 102, 123, 165, 196, 197, 199, 200, 201, 217, 226, 230
Vedic age, 5, 52
Vedic cosmology, 14
Vedic gods, 2, 7, 8, 27, 92, 95, 96, 97
Vedic Indian 6, 7, 8, 9, 10, 94, 95, 96, 100, 103
Vedic mythology, 8
Vedic religion, 35
Vedic sacrifices, 218
Vidyāranya, 48
vijnāna, 33, 83, 101, 106, 107, 108, 156
vijnānamaya kōśa, 25, 117
vijnānavāda, 30, 82, 90, 107, 108
Vijnānavādin, 80, 81, 83, 84, 107, 108 157, 164
vikalpa, 144
vipakṣasattva, 181
viparītakhyāti, 163
viparyaya, 151
Virāt, 104
Viroçana, 97
viruddha, 182
viśeṣa 57, 63
viseṣa gunas, 58, 60
viśeṣanata, 187
Visiśtādvaita, 46, 47, 70, 144, 163, 226, 231, 235
Viṣnu, Lord, 27, 28, 229, 230, 231
Viśva, 18
Viśvakarma, 8, 9, 96
Viśwanātha, 42
Vivarana-Prāmeya Samgrāha (Vidyaranya), 48
vivarta vāda, 128, 131
Vivekacūdāmani (Samkarācārya), 48, 117
Vṛhadukta, 3
vyakti, 191
vyāpti, 172, 173, 175, 176, 177, 178, 179, 180, 181, 183
vyāpyatvāsiddha, 183
Vyāsa, 44
vyāvahārika satta, 90

Watson, John B., 134
Ways of Knowing (Montague), 194

Yādavaprākāsa, 47
Yādṛccha vadins, 36
Yājnavalkya, 14, 51, 207
Yajur Veda, 4, 12
Yama, 8, 96
yamas, 205, 206
yathārthānubhava, 137
Yoga, 25, 38, 40, 43, 44, 45, 114, 115, 166, 168, 169, 212
Yoga Bhāṣya, 168
Yogacāra, 30, 80, 81, 107, 164
yogaja, 166
Yoga Sutra (Patanjali), 44
yogin, 166, 167, 168, 169
yogyatā, 193
Yudhiṣtira, 200, 216
yuga, 200
yuga dharma, 200

Zeno, 83